8th Workshop on Language Technology for Cultural Heritage, Social Sciences, and Humanities

(LaTeCH 2014)

Held at the 14th Conference of the European Chapter of the Association for Computational Linguistics

Gothenburg, Sweden
26 April 2014

ISBN: 978-1-63266-401-3

Printed from e-media with permission by:

Curran Associates, Inc.
57 Morehouse Lane
Red Hook, NY 12571

Some format issues inherent in the e-media version may also appear in this print version.

Printed by Curran Associates, Inc. (2014)

For permission requests, please contact the Association for Computational Linguistics at the address below.

Association for Computational Linguistics
209 N. Eighth Street
Stroudsburg, Pennsylvania 18360

Phone: 1-570-476-8006
Fax: 1-570-476-0860

acl@aclweb.org

Additional copies of this publication are available from:

Curran Associates, Inc.
57 Morehouse Lane
Red Hook, NY 12571 USA
Phone: 845-758-0400
Fax: 845-758-2634
Email: curran@proceedings.com
Web: www.proceedings.com

Preface

The LaTeCH workshop series, which started in 2007, was initially motivated by the growing interest in language technology research and applications to the cultural heritage domain. The scope quickly broadened to also include the humanities and the social sciences. LaTeCH is currently the annual venue of the ACL Special Interest Group on Language Technologies for the Socio-Economic Sciences and Humanities (SIGHUM).

In the current, eighth edition of the LaTeCH workshop, we have received a record number of submissions, a subset of which has been selected based on a thorough peer-review process. The submissions were substantial not only in terms of quantity, but also in terms of quality and variety, underlining the interest of NLP and CL researchers in this exciting and expanding research area.

For this edition of LaTeCH, we attempted to focus on *Linked data in the Humanities*, an issue also addressed by our invited speaker, Gerhard Heyer in his talk about the Canonical Text Services protocol implementations in the digital humanities. Linked data has fairly recently regained a particular research interest in our field, as also indicated by the respective contributions to LaTeCH-2014. Apart for the recurring themes of linguistic variability in historical text, OCR error correction and annotation tools and resource development, we were delighted in this edition of our workshop to receive contributions about applications in social sciences and resource development for non-European languages and cultural heritage, such as the work on the Tagalog Linguistic Inquiry Dictionary, a dictionary for disaster terms in the Tagalog language of Philippines, and the work on the development of a wayang ontology, an ontology about the Indonesian shadow puppet mythology. The acceptance rate for LaTeCH-2014 was 68%.

We would like to thank all authors for the hard work that went into their submissions. We are also grateful to the members of the programme committee for their thorough reviews, and to the EACL 2014 organisers, especially the Workshop Co-chairs, Anja Belz and Reut Tsarfaty for their help with administrative matters.

Kalliopi Zervanou and Cristina Vertan

Organizers:

Kalliopi Zervanou (Co-Chair), Radboud University Nijmegen (The Netherlands)
Cristina Vertan (Co-Chair), University of Hamburg (Germany)
Antal van den Bosch, Radboud University Nijmegen (The Netherlands)
Caroline Sporleder, Trier University (Germany)

Program Committee:

Laura Alonso Alemany, Universidad Nacional de Cordoba (Argentina)
Ion Androutsopoulos, Athens University of Economics and Business (Greece)
Andrei Beliankou, Trier University (Germany)
Kristín Bjarnadóttir, Àrni Magnússon Institute for Icelandic Studies (Iceland)
Toine Bogers, Aalborg University, Copenhagen (Denmark)
Paul Buitelaar, DERI Galway (Ireland)
Mariona Coll Ardanuy, Trier University (Germany)
Thierry Declerck, DFKI (Germany)
Stefanie Dipper, Ruhr-Universität Bochum (Germany)
Milena Dobreva, University of Malta (Malta)
Mick O'Donnell, Universidad Autonoma de Madrid (Spain)
Ben Hachey, Macquarie University (Australia)
Iris Hendrickx, Radboud University Nijmegen (The Netherlands)
Elias Iosif, Technical University of Crete (Greece)
Jaap Kamps, University of Amsterdam (The Netherlands)
Vangelis Karkaletsis, NCSR Demokritos (Greece)
Mike Kestemont, University of Antwerp & Research Foundation Flanders (Belgium)
Dimitrios Kokkinakis, University of Gothenburg (Sweden)
Stasinos Konstantopoulos, NCSR Demokritos (Greece)
Piroska Lendvai, cliqz (Germany)
Barbara McGillivray, Oxford University Press
Joakim Nivre, Uppsala University (Sweden)
Nelleke Oostdijk, Radboud University Nijmegen (The Netherlands)
Csaba Oravecz Research Institute for Linguistics (HASRIL) (Hungary)
Petya Osenova, Bulgarian Academy of Sciences (Bulgaria)
Katerina Pastra, Cognitive Systems Research Institute (CSRI) (Greece)
Michael Piotrowski, Leibniz Institute of European History in Mainz (Germany)
Georg Rehm, DFKI (Germany)
Martin Reynaert, Tilburg University (The Netherlands)
Eric Sanders, Radboud University Nijmegen (The Netherlands)
Eszter Simon, Research Institute for Linguistics (HASRIL) (Hungary)
Herman Stehouwer, Max Planck for Plasmaphysics (Germany)
Mark Stevenson, University of Sheffield (UK)
Mariët Theune, University of Twente (The Netherlands)
Suzan Verberne, Radboud University Nijmegen (The Netherlands)
Manolis Wallace, University of Peloponnese (Greece)
Menno van Zaanen, Tilburg University (The Netherlands)
Svitlana Zinger, TU Eindhoven (The Netherlands)

Table of Contents

Workshop Program

Saturday, April 26, 2014

8:45–8:50	Welcome
8:50–9:30	Invited Talk by Gerhard Heyer: *A New Implementation for Canonical Text Services* Jochen Tiepmar, Christoph Teichmann, Gerhard Heyer, Monica Berti and Gregory Crane
	Session I: Linked data in the Humanities
9:30–9:45	*How to semantically relate dialectal Dictionaries in the Linked Data Framework* Thierry Declerck and Eveline Wandl-Vogt
9:45–10:05	*Bootstrapping a historical commodities lexicon with SKOS and DBpedia* Ewan Klein, Beatrice Alex and Jim Clifford
10:05–10:25	*New Technologies for Old Germanic. Resources and Research on Parallel Bibles in Older Continental Western Germanic* Christian Chiarcos, Maria Sukhareva, Roland Mittmann, Timothy Price, Gaye Detmold and Jan Chobotsky
10:25–11:00	Coffee break
	Session II: Spelling normalisation & sense disambiguation
11:00–11:20	*A Multilingual Evaluation of Three Spelling Normalisation Methods for Historical Text* Eva Pettersson, Beáta Megyesi and Joakim Nivre
11:20–11:40	*Enhancing the possibilities of corpus-based investigations: Word sense disambiguation on query results of large text corpora* Christian Poelitz and Thomas Bartz
11:40–12:00	*A Hybrid Disambiguation Measure for Inaccurate Cultural Heritage Data* Julia Efremova, Bijan Ranjbar-Sahraei and Toon Calders
12:00–12:15	*Automated Error Detection in Digitized Cultural Heritage Documents* Kata Gábor and Benoît Sagot
12:15–13:45	Lunch break

Saturday, April 26, 2014 (continued)

Session III: Social Science applications

13:45–14:05 *Mining the Twentieth Century's History from the Time Magazine Corpus*
Mike Kestemont, Folgert Karsdorp and Marten Düring

14:05–14:25 *Social and Semantic Diversity:*
Socio-semantic Representation of a Scientific Corpus
Thierry Poibeau, Elisa Omodei, Jean-Philippe Cointet and Yufan Guo

Poster Booster Session

14:25–14:35 *A Tool for a High-Carat Gold-Standard Word Alignment*
Drayton Benner

14:35–14:45 *CorA: A web-based annotation tool for historical and other non-standard language data*
Marcel Bollmann, Florian Petran, Stefanie Dipper and Julia Krasselt

14:45–14:55 *Developing a Tagalog Linguistic Inquiry and Word Count (LIWC) 'Disaster' Dictionary for Understanding Mixed Language Social Media: A Work-in-Progress Paper*
Amanda Andrei, Alison Dingwall, Theresa Dillon and Jennifer Mathieu

14:55–15:05 *Text Analysis of Aberdeen Burgh Records 1530-1531*
Adam Wyner, Jackson Armstrong, Andrew Mackillop and Philip Astley

15:05–15:15 *From Syntax to Semantics. First Steps Towards Tectogrammatical Annotation of Latin*
Marco Passarotti

15:15–15:25 *On the syllabic structures of Aromanian*
Sergiu Nisioi

15:25–16:00 Coffee break & Poster Session

Session IV: Knowledge resources acquisition

16:00–16:20 *A Gazetteer and Georeferencing for Historical English Documents*
Claire Grover and Richard Tobin

16:20–16:40 *Automatic Wayang Ontology Construction using Relation Extraction from Free Text*
Hadaiq Sanabila and Ruli Manurung

16:40–17:30 SIGHUM annual business meeting

A New Implementation for Canonical Text Services

Jochen Tiepmar
Christoph Teichmann
Gerhard Heyer
Computer Science Department
Leipzig University
billion-words@e-humanities.net

Monica Berti
Gregory Crane
Humboldt Chair of Digital Humanities
Leipzig University
monica.berti@uni-leipzig.de
crane@informatik.uni-leipzig.de

Abstract

This paper introduces a new implementation of the Canonical Text Services (CTS) protocol intended to be capable of handling thousands of editions. CTS was introduced for the Digital Humanities and is based on a hierarchical structuring of texts down to the level of individual words mirroring traditional practices of citing. The paper gives an overview of CTS for those that are unfamiliar and establishes its place in the Digital Humanities research. Some existing CTS implementations are discussed and it is explained why there is a need for one that is able to scale to much larger text collections. Evaluations are given that can be used to illustrate the performance of the new implementation.

1 Introduction

Canonical Text Services (CTS) (Smith, 2009)[1] is a standard that resulted from research in the Digital Humanities community on citation in a digital context. It consists of two parts: an URN scheme that is used to express citations and a protocol for the interaction of a client and a server to identify text passages and retrieve them.

CTS is an attempt to formalize citation practices which allow for a persistent identification of text passages and citations which express an ontology of texts as well as links between texts (Smith and Blackwell, 2012). The same citation scheme can be used across different versions of a text, even across language borders.

All these properties make CTS attractive as an approach to the presentation of large, structured collections of texts. The framework will have little impact however as long as there is no implementation that can scale to the amount of texts currently available for Digital Humanities research and still perform at a level that makes automatic processing of texts attractive. Therefore the implementation of the scheme presented here allows for large repositories without becoming infeasibly slow.

2 Overview of Canonical Text Services

For readers unfamiliar with Canonical Text Services this section provides a short introduction to the CTS protocol and explains its role in the wider context of the CITE architecture. In order to make the explanations given in this section a little more concrete they are followed by example applications of CTS. Before we go into the technical details of the CTS format, a general review of the motivations and approaches behind CTS will be helpful.

CTS incorporates the idea that citations provide an inherent ontology of text passages. A citation of the first word of the first sentence of section 1 in this paper, when made in exactly that way, implies part-whole relationships between the word and the sentence, the sentence and the section and finally the section and the whole article. Canonical Text Services derive their name from the assumption that each text which is included in a CTS repository is associated with a *canonical* way of cit-

[1] `http://www.homermultitext.org/hmt-doc/index.html`

ing it which has been established by a community of researchers working with the text or texts similar to it. Where no such schemes exist they may be defined when a work first enters a repository. These canonical citation schemes are especially common in Classics research from which much of the work on CTS originated. Such schemes often abstract away from any concrete manifestation of a text[2] in favour of schemes that can be applied across different incarnations. Returning to the example task of citing portions of this article, one could cite the same word by referencing a specific line. The latter approach is problematic, since simply printing the article with a different font size could completely change the lines in which words appear. For this reason canonical citations generally rely on logical properties of the text.

Using logical properties of the text implies that citations can be carried over from one specific incarnation to another. It may even be possible to apply the same citation scheme to versions that are written in different languages. This means that different versions of a text can form another element of a hierarchy. Here the part-whole relations are repeated, with different versions of a text belonging to larger groups as explained in section 2.1. When such citations are coupled with a service that resolves the citations and is capable of giving an inventory of all the citations it can resolve, then this can be a powerful tool in Digital Humanities research.

2.1 The CTS URN scheme

We give a short review of the structure of a CTS URN used to identify a text passage[3]. Any canonical reference must start with the prefix:

`urn:cts`

which simply identifies the string as an URN for a canonical citation. This is followed by three parts that contain the main information for every citation. The first of these parts identifies a name space in which the following elements of the citation are meaningful. This part allows for different authorities to define their own schemes for citing works. This section is followed by an identifier of the work that is cited. Finally the URN is completed by a string identifying a text node or passage in the work that is cited, which could correspond to a specific word, a section or even the complete work. To summarize the format of a CTS URN is:

`urn:cts:name_space:work_identifier:passage_identifier`

where the final part can be dropped in order to identify the complete text of a work. The ontology for the work level is given by the URN scheme itself which requires that the work identifier has the structure:

`text_group.work.version.exemplar`

here only the text group part is mandatory. Every other section can be dropped if every following section is also dropped. The text group can be used for any collection of texts that the manager of a CTS service would like to group together such as all the works of an author, all the works from a certain area or all the works created at a certain time. The work portion identifies a specific text within that group. The version part refers to a specific edition or translation of the work and finally the exemplar identifier selects a specific example of a version of a text. The latter three parts of a work identifier correspond to levels of the hierarchy posited by the Functional Requirements for Bibliographic Records (FRBR).

CTS URNs end with a passage identifier. This identifier can further be divided into the parts:

`Citable_Node@Subsection`

where the citable node must correspond to some XML element within the text that is cited. The hierarchy that is used in these nodes is up to the person managing the citations. The hierarchy can be expressed by separating different levels with the delimiter "." and every level can be omitted as long as all following levels are also omitted. A subsection can be used to select a smaller part of a citable node by identifying words to select. There are some additional options that can be used in a CTS URN, among them the option to combine passages into new subsections by using a range operator, and the interested reader is encouraged to consult the official documentation for

[2] For example a specific printing.

[3] For a more extensive discussion see `http://www.homermultitext.org/hmt-docs/specifications/ctsurn/`

the standard.

CTS URNs can be used to identify and connect text passages. A natural task in connection with citations is the retrieval of collections of citations and the text sections associated with them. This task is addressed in the next section.

2.2 The CTS Protocol

This section summarizes the CTS protocol for the retrieval of text sections and citations[4].

The first main request that the protocol defines is:

`GetPassage`

which can be used to retrieve a passage of a text associated to an URN in order to fulfil the actual purpose of a citation. This request also shows one of the main uses of the ontology that is implied in the way works and passages are cited. When a work identifier is "incomplete" then the service is allowed to pick an instance of the work to deliver. When a passage identifier is "incomplete" then the passage delivered includes all passages with identifiers that could complete it.

The second main request is:

`GetValidReff`

which is used to obtain all the citations at a certain level that the current repository can support. Here it is possible to state how many levels should be present in the answer.

The final request that will be discussed in this section is:

`GetCapabilities`

which is used to obtain the different texts known to a server and the way that they can be cited i.e. the structure of their passage identifiers.

With the given requests it is possible to fulfil the main tasks of a citation software: find citations and/or resolve them. Other systems can then build on top of these requests. One example for an architecture that includes CTS capabilities in a wider framework is CITE which is explained in the next section.

[4]More information can be found at `http://www.homermultitext.org/hmt-docs/specifications/cts/`

2.3 CTS in the Context of the CITE Architecture

The Collections, Indexes and Texts (CITE) architecture is a large framework for reference to the objects of study in Digital Humanities[5]. The general design philosophy is to use URNs as a modern way of encoding citations.

Besides providing a general framework for referencing objects and texts, with the latter task being implemented by CTS, CITE also defines a standard for encoding relations between references. An example would be to link a section of a text about geometry to a drawing which it uses as an example. The CITE architecture also includes protocols for resolving and obtaining the references that can be defined within it. Since CTS takes care of citations concerning texts and the tasks associated with them, an implementation of the CTS protocol is an important first step towards a complete implementation of the CITE architecture.

2.4 Example Applications

In this section we review two example applications for the CTS/CITE infrastructure: the generation of digital editions for the Classics and creating editions of so called fragmentary texts.

2.4.1 New Features of Digital Editions

Several features of a true digital edition have already begun to emerge: they have been implemented and they offer demonstrable benefits that justify such added labour as they demand. Each of the following features requires the ability to identify precise words and phrases in particular versions of a work. The CTS/CITE architecture provides a mechanism to support core new functions within the emerging form of born-digital editions:

1. Translators must work with the realization that they are to be aligned to the original and that they will, in fact, help make the original source text itself intellectually accessible to readers with no knowledge of the source language. Every reader should use the Greek and the

[5]More information on CITE can be found at `http://www.homermultitext.org/hmt-doc/cite/index.html`

Latin. Ideally, translators should align their own translations to the source text and provide notes explaining where and why the source text and translation cannot be aligned.

2. We need multi-texts, i.e., editions that can encapsulate the entire textual history of a work so that readers can see not only variants from the manuscript tradition but also variations across editions over time. No reader should ultimately ever have to wonder how a new edition varies from its predecessors. Encapsulating the full textual tradition of every work will take a very long time but we can begin by representing not only textual variants but also providing more than one digitized edition. Again, scholars need the functionality of the CTS/CITE architecture to represent the relationships among different versions of a work.

3. Editors of Greek and Latin texts must encode, at the very least, their interpretations of the morpho-syntactic functions of every word in every text. This should, in fact, impose little extra cost if editors are agonizing, as they should, over every word. Where the editor thinks that there are multiple interpretations that should be considered, then these should be provided along with an explanation of each. The morpho-syntactic analyses are fundamental to modern linguistic analysis and also provide a wholly new form of reading support.

4. All proper names must be aligned to authority lists such as the Pleiades Gazetteer or the Perseus Smith Dictionary of Greek and Roman Biography. We also need conventions for encoding our textual evidence for the relationship between different named entities (e.g., X is the son of Y). Such annotations enable new methods of analysing and visualising our sources with methods from geographic information systems and social network analysis.

5. All instances of textual reuse need to be annotated, including cases where we have reason to believe particular words and phrases are either quoted or paraphrased.

2.4.2 Fragmentary Texts

Among various example applications (Smith, 2009; Smith and Blackwell, 2012; Almas and Beaulieu, 2013), the CTS/CITE Architecture is being implemented by the Perseus Project for representing fragmentary texts of Classical lost authors. By fragmentary texts we mean texts preserved only through quotations and reuses by later authors, such as verbatim quotations, paraphrases, allusions, translations, and so on (Berti et al., 2009; Almas and Berti, 2013).

The first need for representing such texts is to visualize them inside their embedding context and this means to select the string of words that belong to the portion of text which is classifiable as reuse. The CTS/CITE Architecture provides us with a standard identifier syntax for texts, passages, and related objects and with APIs for services which can retrieve objects identified via these protocols (Smith and Blackwell, 2012).

For example, the following set of identifiers might be used to represent a reuse of a lost text of the Greek author Istros, which has been preserved by Athenaeus of Naucratis in the Deipnosophists, (Book 3, Chapter 6)[6] (Almas and Berti, 2013):

`urn:cts:greekLit:tlg0008.tlg001.perseus-grc1:3.6@`Ἴστρος[1]-συκοφάνται[1]

is a CTS URN for a subset of passage 3.6 in the perseus-grc1 edition of the work identified by tlg001 in the group of texts associated with Athenaeus, identified by tlg0008. The URN further specifies a string of text in that passage starting at the first instance of the word "Ἴστρος" and ending at the first instance of the word "συκοφάνται".

`urn:cite:perseus:lci.2`

is a CITE URN identifier for the instance of lost text being reused. This URN identifies an object from the Perseus Collection of Lost Content Items (lci) in which every item points to a specific text reuse of a lost author as it is represented in a modern edition.

[6]For a prototype interface see `http://perseids.org/sites/berti_demo/` (source code at `https://github.com/PerseusDL/lci-demo`)

These URNs represent distinct technology-independent identifiers for the two cited objects, and by prefixing them with the `http://data.perseus.org` URI prefix (representing the web address at which they can be resolved) we create stable URI identifiers for them, making them compatible with linked data best practices [7]:

`http://data.perseus.org/citations/urn:cts:greekLit:tlg0008.tlg001.perseus-grc1:3.6@`Ἴστρος[1]-συκοφάνται[1][8]

`http://data.perseus.org/collections/urn:cite:perseus:lci.2`

The CITE Objects URNs may be organized into various types of collections of data, such as representations of text reuses in traditional print editions, all text reuses attributed to a specific author, all text reuses quoted by a specific author, all text reuses dealing with a specific topic, all text reuses attributed to a specific time period, etc. CITE collections are used to define and retrieve distinct digital representations of discrete objects, including associated meta data about those objects. Example CITE collections used to support the encoding of text reuses for this project include the abstract lost text entities themselves, digital images of manuscripts of the extant source texts that quote those lost texts, commentaries on instances of text reuse and linguistic annotations of the quoted text (Almas et al., 2014).

3 Existing Implementations

There are two general purpose implementations of the CTS protocol that the authors of this paper are aware of. The first is an implementation based on a XML database. This implementation is part of the Alpheios project[9]. Using a XML database seems natural considering the fact that the CTS architecture requires data to take the form of XML files. It would be interesting to compare the performance of this implementation with that of the one that will be presented here, but since the Alpheios tool is not yet complete and has only been tested with a few hundred texts as input[10] any comparison would seem unfair.

The second project to implement the CTS protocol that we are aware of is based on a SparQL endpoint[11]. Similar to the XML based approach the use of SparQL for CTS is intuitive. The part-of relations that are implied by the structure of URNs could easily be modelled with triple expressions. The implementation has not yet been optimized to work with large numbers of input texts and is therefore not suited to a comparison with the tool presented in this paper. While the use of triples to encode the logical relations seems natural, it is necessary to reconstruct all relations already implied by the structure of the URN Strings. This means that there is a potential for optimization that can be exploited by using the structure of these strings in order to store all information implicitly.

4 A New Implementation

So far this paper has argued that Canonical Text Services can provide an important infrastructure for Digital Humanities research. Recently it has also been highlighted (Crane et al., 2012) that repositories of texts such as the Internet Archive[12] have the potential to allow Digital Humanities researchers to work with text collections that encompass billions or even trillions of words. CTS is one tool in the attempt to handle this mass of data without being overwhelmed by it. Since existing implementations of the CTS protocol are not yet able to scale to the data quantities that the Digital Humanities community could provide, we found it necessary to create a new implementation. In order to find out whether our implementation can deal with such a large number of texts, it will be necessary to give an evaluation of performance. This section introduces the main ideas concerning this new implementation and shows that it is indeed capable of the required scaling.

[7] `http://sites.tufts.edu/perseusupdates/beta-features/perseus-stable-uris/`

[8] At the time of this writing, complete implementation of the CTS standard for resolution of passage subreferences at the data.perseus.org address is still pending.

[9] `http://alpheios.net/`

[10] Personal communication with Bridget Almas, the main developer of the Alpheios CTS implementation.

[11] The implementation can be found at `https://github.com/neelsmith/sparqlcts`.

[12] `https://archive.org/index.php`

4.1 Using the Tree Structure of the Data

The main technical problem that needs to be solved in order to generate an efficient implementation of the Canonical Text Services protocol is the efficient mapping of URNs to texts, sections in these texts and the required meta data. Both tasks require the fast mapping of possible prefixes of valid identifiers. There are two obvious solutions to this problem.

The first is the use of a prefix tree or trie in order to be able to deal with underspecified data. This would make it possible to read in the portion of the URN that is specified and then either have a copy of the text or text section associated with this prefix associated with the tree node or construct the necessary information by visiting all daughter nodes. The former choice would be more efficient in terms of nodes visited, but the latter choice would require less memory.

The second option is the use of the lexicographic ordering of the URNs. Consider the set of strings $S = \{a.a.a, a.b.a, a.b.b, a.b.c, a.c.a, \ldots\}$. If all the strings are moved into a data structure that respects the lexicographic ordering of the strings, then all the strings matching $a.b\_*$[13] can be found by locating the position of the largest string that is lexicographically smaller than or equal to $a.b$ [14] and then visiting all following entries in the data structure until one lexicographically equal to or greater than $a.c$[15] is found. Since MySQL[16] already implements the B-Tree (Bayer and McCreight, 1972) data structure to manage its table indexes we chose this second approach for our implementation. It is used for the work identifiers to select a text that matches a prefix. In the case of passage identifiers all nodes that match a certain prefix are visited and the required text is constructed. The first approach of using prefix trees was also tested but did not lead to a significant decrease in the time or memory requirements since it was not native to the database used.

[13]Here $\_*$ denotes an arbitrary sequence of characters.

[14]In this case $a.a.a$.

[15]In this case $a.c.a$.

[16]See `www.mysql.com`.

4.2 Putting Everything into a Relational Database

With the problem of handling the URNs solved by tree structures, all that remains is to manage the data that can be found by using the URNs and keeping an index of the URNs. Because the CTS standard requires that the URNs of a work are ordered, this also means that this ordering needs to be preserved. This is achieved by simply keeping a column that stores a numbering. It is ensured that this numbering is sequential without gaps. This means that it is possible to retrieve a certain number of neighbours by simply incrementing and retrieving passages according to this counter. As a result the efficient retrieval of passages that span a range of URNs is possible with only 3 requests, implemented by retrieving the number of the first and last URNs in the range and then merging all text chunks in this range into one passage.

As mentioned earlier, the text of a retrieved section is built up from smaller parts when a node higher in the hierarchy is retrieved. We thereby reduce the amount of memory required since only segments of the data need to be stored. This is unlikely to be a bottleneck, since we assume that the length of a text is not a variable that can grow arbitrarily.

Meta data on the edition level is stored as a simple data entry. For each individual URN we store the language and type of its associated content.

4.3 Evaluation

Here we want to show that our implementation is able to scale to the large amounts of data potentially available to Digital Humanities researchers today and that it can handle the large amounts of data potentially generated by cooperative editing. In order to do this we designed tests that can be used to access the performance of our Canonical Text Services implementation. The following Tests were used:

1. retrieve a list of all editions, then get all the valid URNs and the full passage for each edition

2. collect the first 1000 editions, then obtain the first URN at the lowest level within

each edition and its second neighbour, retrieve the first full word for both[17], finally get the subsection between both words.

Test 1 measures the speed with which the data store can be explored even with a large number of editions and how quickly a passage spanning the whole edition can be constructed. It can be assumed that the time needed to execute will increase with the amount of editions that are added to a repository and with the length of the individual texts.

Test 2 checks how quickly the implementation can find subsections and is not expected to take substantially longer for our implementation as the number of editions increases. It is mainly intended to show that behaviour on single texts is not impacted by the number of editions managed and that the construction of larger passages from elementary chunks is handled efficiently.

Both tests were run by using a small seed of data[18] that was copied repeatedly in order to arrive at the number of necessary editions. The data will be made available. Our implementation ran on a server with a 2.4 GHz CPU and 1GB of RAM. The requests necessary for our tests ran on a different machine in order to factor in the problem of communication. In future tests it would be possible to distribute the requests between different clients to focus more on this point.

Figure 1 contains the results for Test 1. The amount of time taken is linear in the number of editions since every new text was generated once. While the construction of all the texts took several hours for the larger collections, the list of all editions was retrieved within a second or less. There is a surprising spike that could be due to factors external to our program which could have a strong impact on such comparatively short time measurements.

Figure 2 gives the results for Test 2. As expected the behaviour is not greatly impacted by the number of editions in the collection. The variation between the different numbers of editions is within a second for the complete task and the average time needed per retrieval task varies by only ten milliseconds.

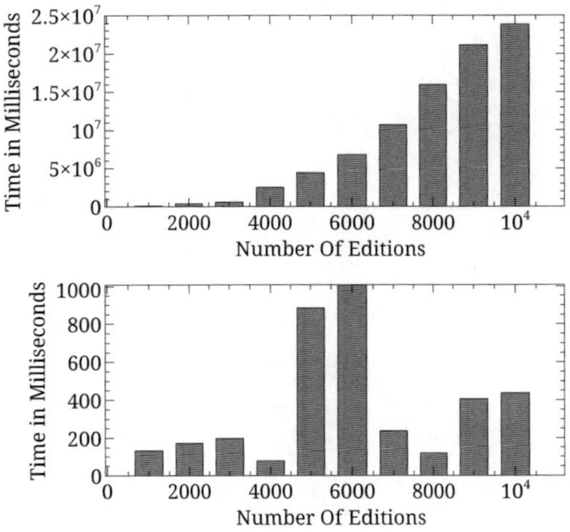

Figure 1: Evaluation results for test 1. The upper graph shows the overall amount of time taken to complete the test for different numbers of editions. The second graph shows the time it took to just retrieve the list of all the editions in the collection.

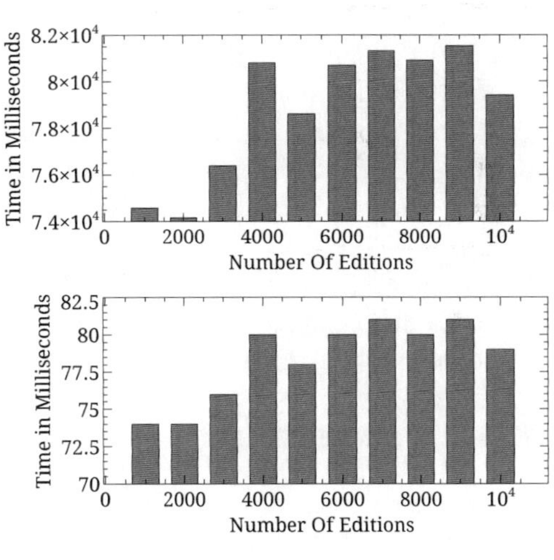

Figure 2: Evaluation results for test 2. The upper graph gives the amount of overall time elapsed in the retrieval of the subsections. The lower graph gives the amount of time needed on average per subsection retrieved. The average was rounded down.

[17] A word not containing special characters and longer than 2 characters.

[18] 1000 editions.

Both measures show a slight increase as the number of editions goes over 3000 but then stabilise.

Overall the experiments show that handling thousands of text is indeed feasible with our implementation on a relatively modest server even for the hardest possible task of reconstructing all the texts in the collection from their smallest parts. Subtasks that do not require retrieving all the texts show little impact from increasing the number of editions.

5 Conclusion

This paper gave a short introduction into the use of the Canonical Text Services Protocol for Digital Humanities research. It also presented a new implementation of the CTS protocol that can handle large amounts of data. The tools that we presented will be made available at:

`http://ctstest.informatik.uni-leipzig.de/`

This address is also used to house the data presented in the evaluation as well as some additional statistics that were generated.

At the time of this writing a new version of the CTS standard was close to completion. As soon as it is published we plan to make our implementation fully compliant. Currently there are still some details in which our implementation diverges from this newest version of the standard. Once this process is complete the next step will be the creation of a permanent CTS capable repository that will be integrated with the CLARIN research infrastructure (Boehlke et al., 2013).

Acknowledgements

Parts of the work presented in this paper are the result of the project "Die Bibliothek der Milliarden Wörter". This project is funded by the European Social Fund. "Die Bibliothek der Milliarden Wörter" is a cooperation project between the Leipzig University Library, the Natural Language Processing Group at the Institute of Computer Science at Leipzig University, and the Image and Signal Processing Group at the Institute of Computer Science at Leipzig University.

References

Bridget Almas and Marie-Claire Beaulieu. 2013. Developing a new integrated editing platform for source documents in classics. *Literary and Linguistic Computing*, 28(4):493–503.

Bridget Almas and Monica Berti. 2013. Perseids collaborative platform for annotating text reuses of fragmentary authors. In *DH-Case 2013. Collaborative Annotations in Shared Environments: metadata, vocabularies and techniques in the Digital Humanities.*

Bridget Almas, Monica Berti, Dave Dubin, Greta Franzini, and Simona Stoyanova. 2014. The linked fragment: TEI and the encoding of text reuses of lost authors. paper submitted to the Journal of the Text Encoding Initiative - Issue 8 - Selected Papers from the 2013 TEI Conference.

Rudolf Bayer and Edward Meyers McCreight. 1972. Organization and maintenance of large ordered indexes. *Acta Informatica*, 1(3):173–189.

Monica Berti, Matteo Romanello, Alison Babeu, and Gregory Crane. 2009. Collecting fragmentary authors in a digital library. In *Proceedings of the 9th ACM/IEEE-CS joint conference on Digital Libraries*, pages 259–262.

Volker Boehlke, Gerhard Heyer, and Peter Wittenburg. 2013. IT-based research infrastructures for the humanities and social sciences — developments, examples, standards, and technology. *it - Information Technology*, 55(1):26–33.

Gregory Crane, Bridget Almas, Alison Babeu, Lisa Cerrato, Matthew Harrington, David Bamman, and Harry Diakoff. 2012. Student researchers, citizen scholars and the trillion word library. In *Proceedings of the 12th ACM/IEEE-CS Joint Conference on Digital Libraries*, pages 213–222.

D. Neel Smith and Christopher W. Blackwell. 2012. Four URLs, limitless apps: Separation of concerns in the Homer Multitext architecture. In *Donum natalicium digitaliter confectum Gregorio Nagy septuagenario a discipulis collegis familiaribus oblatum: A Virtual Birthday Gift Presented to Gregory Nagy on Turning Seventy by His Students, Colleagues, and Friends.* The Center of Hellenic Studies of Harvard University.

D. Neel Smith. 2009. Citation in classical studies. *Digital Humanities Quarterly*, 3(1).

How to semantically relate dialectal Dictionaries in the Linked Data Framework

Thierry Declerck
University of Saarland
Computer Linguistics Department
Postach 15 11 50
D-66041
declerck@dfki.de

Eveline Wandl-Vogt
Institute for Corpus Linguistics and Text Technology, Austrian Academy of Sciences.
Sonnenfelsgasse 19/8, A-1010 Vienna
Eveline.Wandl-Vog@ oeaw.ac.at

Abstract

We describe on-going work towards publishing language resources included in dialectal dictionaries in the Linked Open Data (LOD) cloud, and so to support wider access to the diverse cultural data associated with such dictionary entries, like the various historical and geographical variations of the use of such words. Beyond this, our approach allows the cross-linking of entries of dialectal dictionaries on the basis of the semantic representation of their senses, and also to link the entries of the dialectal dictionaries to lexical senses available in the LOD framework. This paper focuses on the description of the steps leading to a SKOS-XL and *lemon* encoding of the entries of two Austrian dialectal dictionaries, and how this work supports their cross-linking and linking to other language data in the LOD.

1 Introduction

The starting point for our work is given by two Austrian dialectal dictionaries: The Dictionary of Bavarian dialects of Austria (*Wörterbuch der bairischen Mundarten in Österreich*, WBÖ)[1] and the Dictionary of the Viennese dialect (*Wörterbuch der Wiener Mundart*, WWM)[2]. Both dictionaries have been made available to us in an electronic version: WBÖ in a proprietary XML schema and WWM in Microsoft Word. We used the TEI "OxGarage"[3] service to convert the WWM Word document into a TEI compliant XML representation. Table 1 below shows partially an example of an entry in the printed version of WBÖ.

Table 1: An example for an entry in the WBÖ

Puss, Puss(e)lein
M. (jedoch meist neutr.Dem.), Kuß („Busserl"), Gebäck, PflN s-,mbair. m. SI, Egerl. nur als → (*Zwick*[*er*])-, Simmersdf. Igl.; Schallw., vgl. KLUGE[20] 114; frühnhd. *buß* M. Kuß GÖTZE Frühnhd.Gl. 44; s.a. KRANZMAYER Kennw. 10; entl. ins Magy. als *puszi* Kuß u. *puszedli* Gebäck KOBILAROV-GÖTZE 355f., ins Slow. als *pûšek* Kuß PLETERŠNIK 2,366 u. ins Kä.Slow. als *pushei* Kuß GUTSMANN Dt.-Wind.Wb. 261. — Bayer.Wb. 1,295, Schwäb. Wb. 1,1558.

In a previous work we ported elements of WBÖ onto SKOS[4] in order to be able to publish entries

---

[1] http://verlag.oeaw.ac.at/Woerterbuch-der-bairischen-Mundarten-in-Oesterreich-38.-Lieferung-WBOe

[2] See (Hornung & Grüner, 2002).

[3] See http://oxgarage.oucs.ox.ac.uk:8080/ege-webclient/

[4] "SKOS - Simple Knowledge Organization System - provides a model for expressing the basic structure and content of concept schemes such as thesauri, classification schemes, subject heading lists, taxonomies, folksonomies, and other similar types of controlled vocabulary. As an application of the Resource Description Framework (RDF), SKOS allows concepts to be composed and published on the World Wide Web, linked with data on the Web and integrated into other concept schemes."

of this dictionary in the Linked Data[5] cloud (Wandl-Vogt & Declerck, 2013). We used recently a similar approach for porting the TEI Version of the WWM dictionary into SKOS, leading to few modifications in our previous model.

A motivation for this additional step was to investigate if our SKOS-based model can support the (automatised) cross-linking of the dialectal dictionary data[6]. In this particular case, we can take advantage of a property of dialectal dictionaries concerning the expression of meanings of entries: Although conceived as monolingual reference works, dialectal dictionaries share with bilingual dictionaries the fact that they express the meanings of their entries in a different language. The meta-language for expressing the meanings of entries in both WBÖ and WWM is Standard German, sometimes accompanied by Austrian German. This is exemplified in the WBÖ entry "Puss" in Table 1 above, which is using both the Standard German "Kuß" and the Austrian German "Busserl" for expressing one meaning of the word "Puss" (this meaning being "kiss"). Other meanings are "Gebäck" and "PflN"[7]. Additional lines for the entry "Puss" in WBÖ, not displayed in this submission due to lack of space, are giving more details on those meanings, précising that in the "Gebäck" case we deal with a small sweet pastry ("Kl. süßes Gebäck") and in the "PflN" case with a "bellis perennis" flower.[8]

The related entry in WWM dictionary is "Bussal", which is displayed in Table 2.

Table 2: The related entry in the WWM dictionary

Bussal, Bussi, Bussl, das, 1) Kuss (Syn.: *Schm$tss*); 2) kleines Süßgebäck; Pl. *Bussaln;* viele Komp. wie *Nussbussal* usw. –

We can see that this entry carries two meanings, which are the same as the two first meanings of the WBÖ entry "Puss". Linking entries in distinct dialectal dictionaries can thus be implemented on the basis of meanings that are shared across the dictionaries. But, while for the second meaning the readers familiar with the German language will immediately recognize that both strings "Kl. süßes Gebäck" (WBÖ) and "kleines Süßgebäck" (WWM) have the same meaning, this is not evident for other readers and for computer program that should cross-link the dictionary data from those two sources.

In order to automatically cross-link entries from both dictionaries, we wrote first a program for extracting the strings expressing the meanings for each entry and applied an algorithm for comparing the extracted strings. For this latter task, it is necessary to first linguistically analyse the strings, since pure string matching cannot provide accurate comparisons: lemma reduction and PoS tagging are giving additional indicators for matching strings expressing meanings. To mark linguistically analysed meanings as related, use also semantic representation languages developed in the context of W3C standardization, more specifically SKOS-XL[9] and *lemon*[10]

2 Extraction and Linguistic Analysis of Strings marking Meanings

We wrote for the extraction of strings marking the meanings of entries task specific Perl scripts, adapted to the XML schemas of WBÖ and WWM (in its converted TEI format). Second, we provided an automatic linguistic analysis of those extracted meanings, using lexical and syntactic analysis grammars written with the NooJ finite

(http://www.w3.org/TR/skos-primer/)

[5] For more details see http://linkeddata.org/.

[6] The topic of "cross-linking" is in fact very relevant to lexicographers, as can be seen in (Wandl-Vogt, 2005).

[7] The word "Gebäck" (*pastry*) is Standard German and the string "PflN" is an abbreviation for the German name "Pflanzenname" (*name of a plant*)

[8] More details are given in (Author2 & Author1, 2013). We concentrate in this submission on the sense "small sweet pastry" to exemplify our approach.

[9] http://www.w3.org/TR/skos-reference/skos-xl.html

[10] http://lemon-model.net/ and (McCrae et al., 2012).

state platform [11]. This included tokenization, lemmatisation, Part-of-Speech (POS) tagging and constituency as well as dependency analysis.

The strings marking in both dictionaries the "sweet pastry" meaning are enriched with the following linguistic features:

WBÖ: (NP süßes (ADJ, lemma = süß, MOD) Gebäck (N, lemma = Gebäck, HEAD))

WWM: (NP (kleines (ADJ, lemma = klein, MOD) Süßgebäck (N, compound: süß (ADJ, lemma = süß, MOD) + Gebäck (N, lemma = Gebäck, HEAD)), HEAD))

In those examples (*sweet pastry* and *small sweet pastry*), we can see the distinct serializations of similar meanings in German. The second example uses a compound noun ("Süßgebäck"), which has the same meaning as the simple nominal phrase in the first example ("süßes Gebäck"). In order to automatically establish this similarity, it is necessary to perform a morphological decomposition of the head noun in the second example. It is also necessary to have the lemma of the adjective in the first example, in order to compare it with the first element of the compound noun in the second example.

The fact, that both linguistically analysed meanings (strings) share the same lemmas for adjectival modifiers and head nouns is the basis for cross-linking the entries. This cross-linking has to be expressed in Semantic Web standards (e.g. compatible to RDF) in order to be published in the Linked Data cloud.

3 Porting the Dictionary Data into the Linked Open Data framework

3.1 Porting the dictionaries into SKOS

Analogue to the described SKOSification of WBÖ (see Wandl-Vogt & Declerck, 2013), the WWM was ported into SKOS. Departing from the former experiment, we decided to not encode anymore the whole dictionary as a SKOS concept scheme. Rather we introduce the listing of entries (each encoded as a skos:Concept) as being member of a skos:Collection. Complementary to this, extracted senses (see former section) are each encoded as skos:Concept being included in a skos:ConceptScheme. This decision is due to the fact that the senses can be organized along the line of (SKOS) semantic relations, whereas the strings marking the entries are in fact just member of a list, which is building the dictionary. The headword (string) of the dictionary entries is encoded as a value of the SKOS-XL prefLabel property. Alternative strings (like "Bussi" in the WWM example in Table 2) are encoded with the SKOS-XL altLabel property. The use of SKOS-XL allows us to "reify" the value of the range of the label properties, and thus to have there not only a literal but further information, like PoS. Since senses are also represented in the dictionaries by strings, we apply the same procedure: a sense has skos-xl labels in which we can encode the lemma of the components of the strings, the corresponding PoS but also related senses, within the local concept scheme or in the LOD, like for example with objects in the DBpedia instantiation of Wiktionary[12].

3.2 Representing the meanings in lemon

The linguistically analysed meanings cannot be (straightforwardly) represented in SKOS, and for this we opted for the *lemon* model, which has been developed specifically for the purpose of representing linguistic information of lexical entries related to knowledge organization systems. The *lemon* encoding of the meanings is incorporated as the value of the SKOS-XL "Label" property. Taking as an example the one meaning of "Puss" in WBÖ that consists of two words ("süßes Gebäck", *sweet pastry*), we can see that it is for necessary to tokenize the string representing the meaning of the entry "Puss": the first token can then be lemmatized to "süß" (*sweet*), while for the second token the lemma is identical to the written form used. We represent the

[11] See http://www.nooj4nlp.net/pages/nooj.html

[12] So for example the sense „Kuss" for both the entries „Puss" and „Bussal" is declared as being a skos:exactMatch with the URL: http://wiktionary.dbpedia.org/page/Kuss-German-Noun-1de. From there we can get then all multilingual equivalents listed in this resource.

tokenization information using the *lemon* property "decomposition".

4 Cross referencing of dictionary entries through similar meanings

The establishment of a relation between "Puss" in WBÖ and "Bussal" in WWM is made possible on the base of the successful mapping of both the adjectival modifier "süß" and the head noun "Gebäck", which are present in both the definitions in WBÖ and WWM. This similarity is encoded using the "related" property of SKOS. Interesting is also the fact that a user searching the electronic version of the dictionaries could give the High German form "Gebäck" and would get from both dictionaries all the entries which have this word in their definition. The same for the High German adjectival form "süß".

Instead of the meanings we extracted from the dictionaries, we can use the DBpedia instantiation of Wiktionary as a reference for the senses of the entries of the dictionary, pointing directly to linguistic and knowledge objects that are already in the LOD. Using the "decomposition" and "subSenses" properties of *lemon*, we link to URLs in DBpedia/Wiktionary representing the sense for each token.

5 Conclusion

We described the actual state of RDF/SKOS/lemon modeling of (senses of) entries of dialectal dictionaries, so that those entries can be cross-linked via their similar senses. We have shown that NL processing of the strings for marking the meanings of the entries is necessary in order to make them comparable. We further have shown that our encoding of the entries of the dictionaries is also supporting the linking to already existing lexical senses and other language data in the LOD. The model have been implemented in the TopBraider composer[13] and all the entries of the dictionaries, as instances of the defined classes and properties, are automatically mapped onto the corresponding Turtle syntax[14] and will be made available very soon as deferentiable URLs, making thus less-resourced language data available in the LOD. Future work will consist in applying a similar approach to historical and geographical contexts given in the entries of the dialectal dictionaries.

Acknowledgments

The work by University of Saarland described in this paper is partially supported by the PHEME project, funded by the European Commission under number 611233.

References

Wandl-Vogt, E. and Declerck, T. (2013) Mapping a Traditional Dialectal Dictionary with Linked Open Data. In Proc. of eLex 2013, Tallin, Estonia.

Hornung, M., Grüner, S. (2002) Wörterbuch der Wiener Mundart; Neubearbeitung. öbvhpt, Wien.

McCrae, J., Aguado-de-Cea, G., Buitelaar P., Cimiano P., Declerck, T., Gómez-Pérez, A., Gracia, J., Hollink, L., Montiel-Ponsoda, E., Spohr, D., Wunner, T. (2012) Interchanging lexical resources on the Semantic Web. In: Language Resources and Evaluation. Vol. 46, Issue 4, Springer:701-719.

Miles, A., Matthews, B., Wilson, M. D., Brickley, D. (2005) SKOS Core: Simple Knowledge Organisation for the Web. In Proc. International Conference on Dublin Core and Metadata Applications, Madrid, Spain,

Moulin, C. (2010) Dialect dictionaries - traditional and modern. In: Auer, P., Schmidt, J.E. (2010) (eds) Language and Space. An International Handbook of Linguistic Variation. Volume 1: Theories and Methods. Berlin / New York. pp: 592-612.

Romary, L. (2009) Questions & Answers for TEI Newcomers. Jahrbuch für Computerphilologie 10. Mentis Verlag,

Schreibman, S. (2009) The Text Encoding Initiative: An Interchange Format Once Again. Jahrbuch für Computerphilologie 10. Mentis Verlag.

Wandl-Vogt, E. (2005) From paper slips to the electronic archive. Cross-linking potential in 90 years of lexicographic work at the Wörterbuch der bairischen Mundarten in Österreich (WBÖ). In: Complex 2005. Papers in computational lexicography. Budapest: 243-254.

Wörterbuch der bairischen Mundarten in Österreich (WBÖ) (1963-). Wien. Accessed at http://hw.oeaw.ac.at/wboe/31205.xml?frames=yes (25.5.2)

---

[13] http://www.topquadrant.com/tools/IDE-topbraid-composer-maestro-edition/

[14] http://www.w3.org/TeamSubmission/turtle/

Bootstrapping a historical commodities lexicon with SKOS and DBpedia

Ewan Klein
ILCC, School of Informatics
University of Edinburgh
EH8 9AB, Edinburgh, UK
ewan@inf.ed.ac.uk

Beatrice Alex
ILCC, School of Informatics
University of Edinburgh
EH8 9AB, Edinburgh, UK
balex@inf.ed.ac.uk

Jim Clifford
Department of History
University of Saskatchewan
Saskatoon, SK S7N 5A5, Canada
jim.clifford@usask.ca

Abstract

Named entity recognition for novel domains can be challenging in the absence of suitable training materials for machine-learning or lexicons and gazetteers for term look-up. We describe an approach that starts from a small, manually created word list of commodities traded in the nineteenth century, and then uses semantic web techniques to augment the list by an order of magnitude, drawing on data stored in DBpedia. This work was conducted during the *Trading Consequences* project on text mining and visualisation of historical documents for the study of global trading in the British empire.

1 Introduction

The *Trading Consequences* project[1] aims to assist environmental historians in understanding the economic and environmental consequences of commodity trading during the nineteenth century. We are applying text mining to large quantities of historical text in order to convert unstructured textual information into structured data that can be queried and visualised. While prior historical research into commodity flows (Cronon, 1991; Cushman, 2013; Innis and Drache, 1995; McCook, 2006; Tully, 2009) has focused on a small number of widely traded natural resources, the large corpora of digitised documents processed by *Trading Consequences* is giving historians data about a much broader range of commodities. A detailed appraisal of trade in these resources will yield a significantly more accurate picture of globalisation and its environmental consequences.

In this paper we focus on our approach to building a lexicon to support the recognition of commodity terms in text. We provide some background to this work in Section 2. In Section 3, we describe the process of creating the lexicon; this starts from a manually collected seed set of commodity terms which is then expanded semi-automatically using DBpedia.[2] An evaluation of the quality of the commodity lexicon is provided in Section 4.

[1] http://tradingconsequences.blogs.edina.ac.uk/

[2] http://www.dbpedia.org

2 Background

Figure 1 shows an overview of the architecture of the *Trading Consequences* system. Input documents are processed by the text mining pipeline, which is based on the LT-XML2[3] and LT-TTT2[4] toolkits (Grover et al., 2008). After initial format conversion, the text undergoes language identification and OCR post-correction and normalisation.[5] It is then processed further by shallow linguistic analysis, lexicon and gazetteer lookup, named entity recognition and grounding, and relation extraction (see Figure 2).

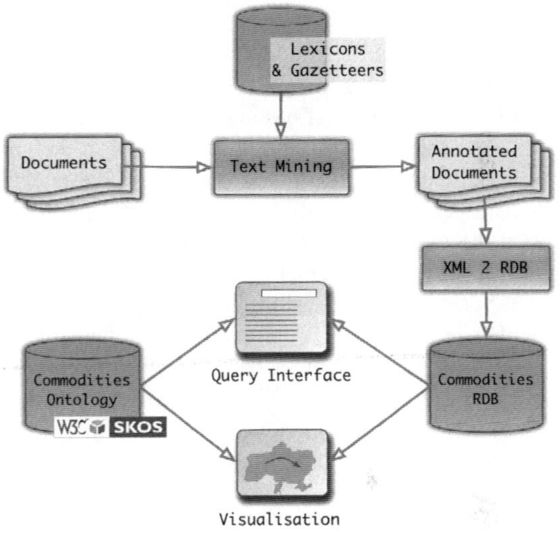

Figure 1: Architecture of the *Trading Consequences* prototype.

In *Trading Consequences*, we determine which commodities were mentioned when and in relation to which

[3] LT-XML2 includes APIs for parsing XML documents (both as event streams and as trees), creating them, serialising them and navigating them with XPath queries; see http://www.ltg.ed.ac.uk/software/ltxml2.

[4] LT-TTT2 is built around the LT-XML2 programs and provides NLP components for a variety of text processing tasks such as tokenisation and sentence-splitting, chunking and rule-based named entity recognition. It includes a third party part-of-speech tagger and lemmatiser; see http://www.ltg.ed.ac.uk/software/lt-ttt2.

[5] For more details on dealing with OCR errors, see (Lopresti, 2008; Alex et al., 2012).

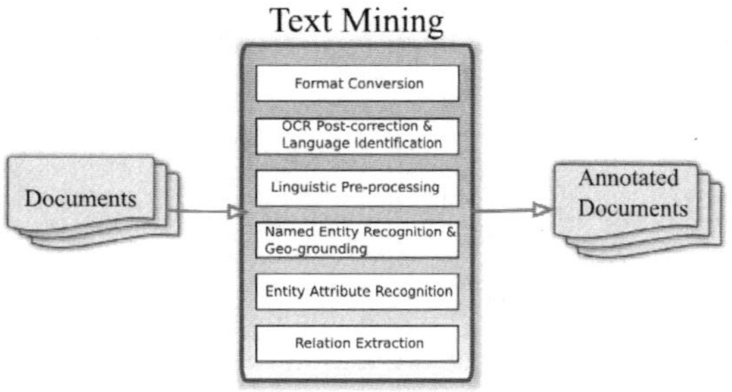

Figure 2: Architecture of the text mining component

locations. We also determine whether locations are mentioned as points of origin, transit or destination and whether vocabulary relating to diseases and disasters appears in the text. All mined information is added back into the XML documents as different layers of stand-off annotation.

The annotations are subsequently used to populate a relational database. This stores not just metadata about the individual document, but also detailed information that results from the text mining, such as named entities, relations, and how these are expressed in the relevant document in context. Visualisations and a query interface access the database so that users can either search the mined information directly through textual queries or browse the data in a more exploratory manner. A temporal dimension for the visualisation is provided by correlating commodity mentions in documents with the publication date of those documents. All information mined from the collections is linked back to the original documents of the data providers.

We analyse textual data from a variety of sources, including the House of Commons Parliamentary Papers (HCPP)[6] from ProQuest;[7] the Early Canadiana Online data archive (ECO) from Canadian.org;[8] the Directors' Correspondence Collection from the Archives at Kew Gardens available at Jstor Global Plants (LETTERS);[9] Adam Matthew's Confidential Print collections (CPRINT);[10] and a subpart of the Foreign and Commonwealth Office Collection (FCOC) from Jstor.[11] Together these sources amount to over 10 million pages of text and over 7 billion word tokens. Table 1 provides an overview of the number of documents and OCR scan images per collection or sub-collection available to the *Trading Consequences* consortium.

We used a variety of techniques for carrying out named entity recognition, covering not only commodities, but also places, dates and amounts. Figure 3 shows some of the entities which we extract from the text,

Collection	# of docs	# of images
HCPP	118,526	6,448,739
ECO	83,016	3,938,758
LETTERS	14,340	n/a
CPRINT	1,315	140,010
FCOC	1,000	41,611

Table 1: Number of documents and images per collection. One image usually corresponds to one document page, except in the case of CPRINT, where it mostly corresponds to two document pages. The LETTERS collection does not contain OCRed text but summaries of hand-written letters.

e.g. the places *Padang* and *America*, the year *1871*, the commodity *cassia bark* and the quantity and unit *6,127 piculs*. We are also able to identify that *Padang* is an origin location and *America* is a destination location and to ground both locations to geographical coordinates. The commodity-place relations *LOC(cassia bark, Padang)* and *LOC(cassia bark, America)*, visualised by the red arrows in Figure 3, are also identified. In this paper, our focus is on commodity mentions, and we will discuss these in more detail in the next section.

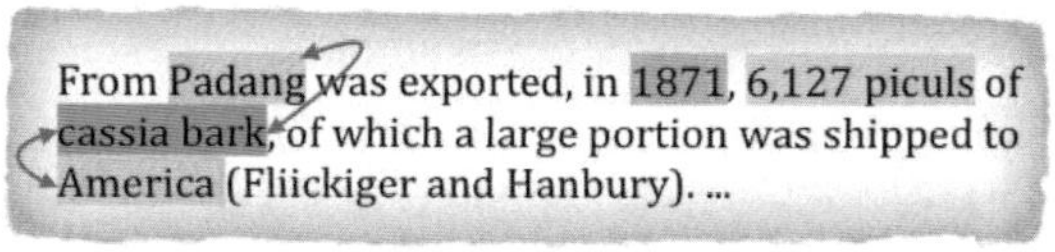

Figure 3: Excerpt from *Spices* (Ridley, 1912). Extracted entities are highlighted in colour and relations are visualised using arrows.

3 Lexicon Construction

In recent years, the dominant paradigm for NER has been supervised machine learning (Tjong Kim Sang and De Meulder, 2003). However, to be effective, this requires a considerable investment of effort in manually preparing suitable training data. Since we lacked the resources to create such data, we decided instead to provide the system with a look-up list of commodity terms. While there is substantial continuity over time in the materials that are globally traded as commodities, it is difficult to work with a modern list of commodity terms as they include many things that did not exist, or were not widely traded, in the nineteenth century. There are also a relatively large number of commodities traded in the nineteenth century that are no longer used, including a range of materials for dyes and some nineteenth century drugs. As a result, we set out to develop a new lexicon of commodities traded in the nineteenth century.

Before discussing in detail the methods that we used, it is useful to consider some of our requirements. First

[6] http://parlipapers.chadwyck.co.uk/home.do
[7] http://www.proquest.co.uk
[8] http://eco.canadiana.ca
[9] http://plants.jstor.org/
[10] http://www.amdigital.co.uk
[11] http://www.jstor.org/

we wanted to be able to capture the fact that there can be multiple names for the same commodity; for example, rubber might be referred to in several ways, including not just *rubber* but also *India rubber*, *caoutchouc* and *caouchouc*. Second, we wanted to include a limited amount of hierarchical structure in order to support querying, both in the database interface and also in the visualisation process. For example, it ought be possible to group together *limes*, *apples* and *oranges* within a common category (or hypernym) such as `Fruit`. Third, we wanted the freedom to add arbitrary attributes to terms, such as noting that both nuts and whales are a source of oil.

These considerations argued in favour of a framework that had more structure than a simple list of terms, but was more like a thesaurus than a dictionary or linguistically-organised lexicon.[12] This made SKOS (Simple Knowledge Organization System—Miles and Bechhofer (2009)) an obvious choice for organising the thesaurus. SKOS assumes that the 'hierarchical backbone' of the thesaurus is organised around *concepts*. These are semantic rather than linguistic entities, and serve as the hooks to which lexical labels are attached. SKOS employs the Resource Description Framework (RDF)[13] as a representation language; in particular, SKOS concepts are identified by URIs. Every concept has a unique 'preferred' (or canonical) lexical label (expressed by the property `skos:prefLabel`), plus any number of alternative lexical labels (expressed by the property `skos:altLabel`). Both of these RDF properties take string literals (with an optional language tag) as values.

The graph in Figure 4 illustrates how SKOS allows preferred and alternative lexical labels to be attached to a concept such as `dbp:Natural_Rubber`. Figure 4 illustrates a standard shortening for URIs,

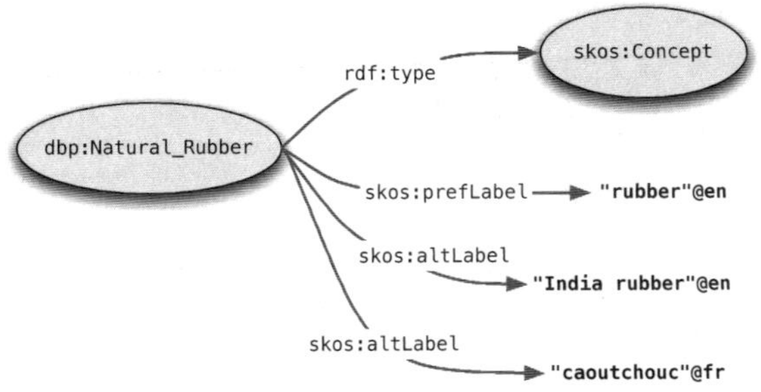

Figure 4: Preferred and alternative lexical labels in SKOS.

where a prefix such as `dbp:` is an alias for the namespace `http://dbpedia.org/resource/`. Consequently `dbp:Natural\_Rubber` is an abbreviation that expands to the full URI `http://dbpedia.org/resource/Natural\_Rubber`. In an analogous way, `skos:` and `rdf:` are prefixes that represent namespaces for the SKOS and RDF vocabularies respectively.

While a SKOS thesaurus provides a rich organisational structure for representing knowledge about our domain, it is not in itself directly usable by our text mining tools; a further step is required to place the `prefLabel` and `altLabel` values from the thesaurus into the XML-based lexicon structure required by the LT-XML2 toolkit during named entity recognition. We will discuss this in more detail in Section 3.2.

In the remainder of this section, we first describe how we created a seed set of commodity terms manually and then explain how we used it to bootstrap a much larger commodity lexicon.

3.1 Manual Curation from Archival Sources

We took as our starting point the records of the *Boards of Customs, Excise, and Customs and Excise, and HM Revenue and Customs* held at the National Archives.[14] They include a collation of annual ledger books listing all of the major goods, ranging from live animals to works of art, imported into Great Britain during any given year during the nineteenth century. These contain a wealth of material, including a list of the quantity and value of the commodities broken down by country. For the purpose of developing a list of commodities, we focused on the headings at the top of each page, drawing on the four books of the 1866 ledgers, which were the most detailed year available.[15] All together, the 1866 ledgers listed 760 different import categories. This data was manually transferred to a spreadsheet in a manner which closely reflected the original, and a portion is illustrated in Figure 5. In *Trading Consequences* we restricted our analysis to raw materials or lightly processed commodities and thereby discarded all commodities which did not fit this definition.

The two major steps in converting the Customs Ledger records into a SKOS format were (i) selecting a string to serve as the SKOS `prefLabel`, and (ii) associating the `prefLabel` with an appropriate semantic concept. Both these steps were carried out manually.[16]

For obvious reasons, we wanted as far as possible to use an existing ontology as a source of concepts. We initially experimented with UMBEL,[17] an extensive upper ontology in SKOS format based on OpenCyc (Matuszek et al., 2006). However UMBEL's coverage of relevant plants and botanical substances was poor, lacking

[12] The Lemon lexicon model (McCrae et al., 2010) is based on SKOS, but its richer structure, while linguistically well motivated, is more complex than we require for our application.

[13] `http://www.w3.org/RDF/`

[14] `http://discovery.nationalarchives.gov.uk/SearchUI/details?Uri=C67`

[15] The customs ledgers used for creation of the seed set of commodities is stored at The National Archives (collection CUST 5).

[16] Assem et al. (2006) present a methodology for converting thesauri to SKOS format, but the resources that their case studies take as a starting point are considerably more extensive and richly structured than the data we discuss here.

[17] `http://umbel.org`

Animals Living - Asses
Animals Living - Goats
Animals Living - Kids
Animals Living - Oxen and Bulls
Animals Living - Cows
Animals Living - Calves
Animals Living - Horses, Mares, Geldings, Colts and Foals
Animals Living - Mules
Animals Living - Sheep
Animals Living - Lambs
Animals Living - Swine and Hogs
Animals Living - Pigs (sucking)
Animals Living - Unenmumerated
Annatto - Roll
Annatto - Flag
Antimony - Ore of
Antimony - Crude
Antimony - Regulus
Apples - Raw
Apples - Dried
Aqua Fortis - Nitric Acid

Figure 5: Sample spreadsheet entries derived from 1866 Customs Ledger.

for instance entries for *alizarin*, *bergamot* and *Dammar gum*, amongst many others. We eventually decided instead to base the ontology component of the lexicon on DBpedia (Bizer et al., 2009; Mendes et al., 2012), a structured knowledge base whose core concepts correspond to Wikipedia pages, augmented by Wikipedia categories, page links and infobox fields, all of which are extracted as RDF triples.

Figure 6 illustrates a portion of the converted spreadsheet, with columns corresponding to the DBpedia concept (using `dbp:` as the URI prefix), the `prefLabel`, and a list of `altLabels`. Note that *asses* has been normalised to a singular form and that it occurs as an `altLabel` for the concept `dbp:Donkey`. This data

Concept	prefLabel	altLabel
dbp:Cork_(material)	cork	
dbp:Cornmeal	cornmeal	indian corn meal, corn meal
dbp:Cotton	cotton	cotton fiber
dbp:Cotton_seed	cotton seed	
dbp:Cowry	cowry	cowrie
dbp:Coypu	coypu	nutria, river rat
dbp:Cranberry	cranberry	
dbp:Croton_cascarilla	croton cascarilla	cascarilla
dbp:Croton_oil	croton oil	
dbp:Cubeb	cubeb	cubib, Java pepper
dbp:Culm	culm	
dbp:Dammar_gum	dammar gum	gum dammar
dbp:Deer	deer	
dbp:Dipsacus	dipsacus	teasel
dbp:Domestic_sheep	domestic sheep	
dbp:Donkey	donkey	ass
dbp:Dracaena_cinnabari	dracaena cinnabari	sanguis draconis, gum dragon's blood

Figure 6: Customs Ledger data converted to SKOS data types.

(in the form of a CSV file)[18] provides enough information to build a rudimentary SKOS thesaurus whose root concept is `tc:Commodity`.[19] The following listing illustrates a portion of the thesaurus for *donkey*.[20]

```
dbp:Donkey
   a        skos:Concept ;
   skos:prefLabel "donkey"@en ;
   skos:altLabel "ass"@en ;
   skos:broader tc:Commodity ;
   prov:hadPrimarySource
          "customs records 1866" .
```

Translated into plain English, this says: `dbp:Donkey` is a `skos:Concept`, its preferred label is `"donkey"`, its alternative label is `"ass"`, it has a broader concept `tc:Commodity`, and the primary source of this information (i.e., its provenance) are the customs records of 1866. Once we have an RDF model of the thesaurus, it becomes straightforward to carry out most subsequent processing via query, construct and update operations in SPARQL (Prud'Hommeaux and Seaborne, 2008; Seaborne and Harris, 2013), the standard language for querying RDF data.

3.2 Bootstrapping the Lexicon

The process just described allows us to construct a small 'base' SKOS thesaurus containing 319 concepts. However it is obviously a very incomplete list of commodities, and by itself would give us poor recall in identifying commodity mentions. Many kinds of product in the Customs Ledgers included open ended subcategories (i.e., *Oil - Seed Unenumerated* or *Fruit - Unenumerated Dried*). Similarly, while the ledgers provided a comprehensive list of various gums, they only specified *anchovies*, *cod*, *eels*, *herrings*, *salmon* and *turtle* as types of fish, grouping all other species under the 'unenumerated' subcategory.

One approach to augmenting the thesaurus would be to integrate it with a more general purpose SKOS upper ontology. In principle, this should be feasible, since merging two RDF graphs is a standard operation. However, trying this approach with UMBEL threw up several practical problems. First, UMBEL includes features that go beyond the standard framework of SKOS and which made graph merging harder to control. Second, this technique made it extremely difficult to avoid adding a large amount of information that was irrelevant to the domain of nineteenth century commodities.

Our second approach also involved graph merging, but tried to minimise manual intervention in determining which subparts of the general ontology to merge into. We have already mentioned that one of our original motivations for adopting SKOS was the presence of a concept hierarchy; nevertheless, we had little need for a multi-layered hierarchy of the kind found in many

[18]Together with other resources from *Trading Consequences*, the word list is available as `base_lexicon.csv` from the Github repository `https://github.com/digtrade/digtrade`.

[19]The conversion from CSV to RDF was carried out with the help of the Python `rdflib` library (`https://rdflib.readthedocs.org`).

[20]The prefixes `tc:` and `prov:` are aliases for `http://vocab.inf.ed.ac.uk/tc/` and `http://www.w3.org/ns/prov\#` respectively.

upper ontologies. In addition to a class hierarchy of the usual kind, DBpedia contains a level of *category*, derived from the categories that are used to tag Wikipedia pages. Figure 7 illustrates categories, such as *Domesticated animals*, that occur on the page for *donkey*. We believe that such Wikipedia categories provide a useful and (for our purposes) sufficient level of abstraction for grouping together the 'leaf' concepts that correspond to lexical items in the SKOS thesaurus (e.g., a concept like `dbp:Donkey`). Within DBpedia, these categories are contained in the namespace `http://dbpedia.org/resource/Category:` (for which we use the alias `dbc:`) and are related to concepts via the property `dcterms:subject`. Given that the concepts in

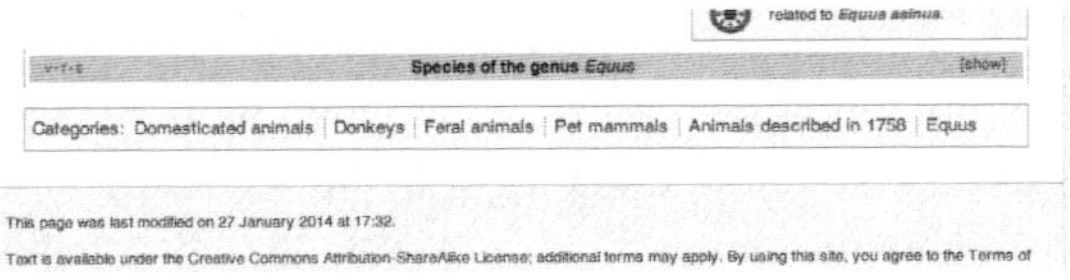

Figure 7: Wikipedia categories at the bottom of the page for `Donkey`.

our base SKOS thesaurus are drawn from DBpedia, it is simple to augment the initial SKOS thesaurus G in the following way: for each leaf concept L in G, augment G with a new triple of the form $\langle L$ `skos:broader` $C\rangle$ (i.e., L has broader concept C) whenever L belongs to category C in DBpedia. To illustrate, given our `Donkey` example above, we would supplement it with the following triple:

```
dbp:Donkey
    skos:broader dbc:Domesticated_animal
```

We can retrieve all of the categories associated with each leaf concept by sending a federated query that accesses both the DBpedia SPARQL endpoint and a local instance of the Jena Fuseki[21] server which hosts our SKOS thesaurus. Since some of the categories recovered in this way were clearly too broad or out of scope, we manually filtered the list down to a set of 355 categories before merging the new triples into the base thesaurus.

Our next step also involved querying DBpedia, this time to retrieve all new concepts C which belonged to the categories recovered in the first step; we call this *sibling acquisition*, since it allows us to find siblings of leaf concepts that are children of the Wikipedia categories already present in the thesaurus. The key steps in the procedure are illustrated in Figure 8 (where the top node is the root concept in the SKOS thesaurus, viz. `tc:Commodity`). To continue our earlier example, the presence of `dbc:Domesticated_animal` in the hierarchy triggers the addition of concepts for animals such as camel, llama and water buffalo. Given a base thesaurus with 319 concepts, sibling acquisition

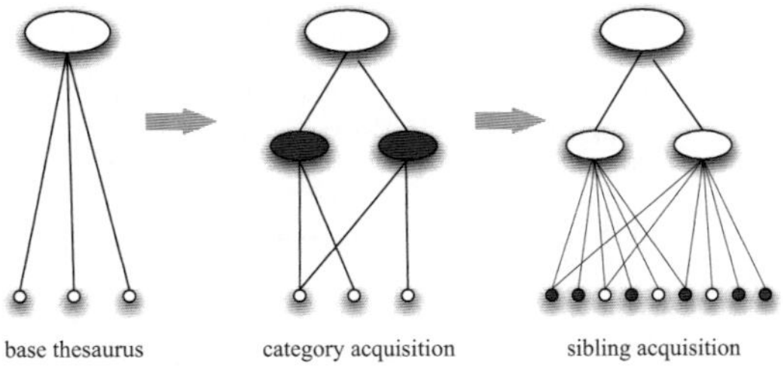

Figure 8: Sibling acquisition. A base thesaurus is augmented with new categories (indicated as black ovals), and these in turn lead to the addition of new leaf concepts (indicated as black circles) which they are broader than.

expands the thesaurus to a size of 17,387 concepts.[22] This query-based methodology contrasts with, though is potentially complementary to, a machine learning approach to bootstrapping named entity systems as described, for example, by Kozareva (2006).

We mentioned earlier that in order for LT-TTT2 to identify commodity mentions in text, it is necessary to convert our SKOS thesaurus into an XML-based lexicon structure. A fragment of such a lexicon is illustrated in Figure 9. The preferred and alternative lexical labels are represented via separate entries in the lexicon, with their value contained in the `word` attribute for each entry. The concept and category information is stored in corresponding attribute values; the pipe symbol (|) is used to separate multiple categories. We have already seen that alternative lexical labels will include synonyms and spelling variants (e.g., *chinchona* versus *cinchona*). The set of alternative labels associated with each concept was further augmented by a series of postprocessing steps such as pluralisation; hyphenation and dehyphenation (*cocoa nuts* versus *cocoa-nuts* versus *cocoanuts*; and the addition of selected head nouns to form compounds (*apple* > *apple tree*, *groundnut* > *groundnut oil*). Such variants are also stored in the lexicon as separate entries. The resulting lexicon contained 20,476 commodity terms.

During the recognition step, we perform case-insensitive matching against the lexicon in combination with context-dependent rules to decide whether or not a given string is a commodity; the longest match is preferred during lookup. Linguistic pre-processing is important in this step — for example, we exclude word tokens tagged as verb, preposition, particle or adverb in the part-of-speech tagging. As each lexicon entry is associated with a DBpedia concept and at least one category, both types of information are added to the extracted entity mentions for each successful match, thereby linking the text-mined commodities to the hierarchy present in the *Trading Consequences* commodity thesaurus.

[21] `http://jena.apache.org/documentation/serving_data/`

[22] We accessed DBpedia via the SPARQL endpoint on 16 Dec 2013, which corresponds to DBpedia version 3.9.

```
<lex>
  ...
  <lex category="Rubber|Nonwoven_fabrics" concept="Natural_rubber" word="caoutchouc"/>
  <lex category="Rubber|Nonwoven_fabrics" concept="Natural_rubber" word="indian rubber"/>
  <lex category="Rubber|Nonwoven_fabrics" concept="Natural_rubber" word="rubber"/>
  ...
</lex>
```

Figure 9: Lexicon entries for the example presented in Figure 4.

4 Evaluation

4.1 Methodology

The quality of text mining software is often evaluated intrinsically in terms of the precision, recall and balanced F-score of its output compared to a human annotated gold standard. We also use this methodology to gain a better understanding of the quality of the commodity lexicon. We therefore prepared a gold standard by randomly selecting 25 documents extracts from each of the five collections listed in Table 1. Since many of the documents were too long to annotate in their entirety, we split each file into sub-sections of equal size (5000 bytes) and randomly selected one subsection per document containing one or more commodities and commodity-location relations. This resulted in a set of 125 files which we divided into a pilot set of 25 documents (5 per collection) and a main annotation set of 100 documents (20 per collection).

Annotator 1 was provided with guidelines on marking up entities and relations, and was asked to annotate the 25 pilot documents using the BRAT annotation tool (Stenetorp et al., 2012).[23] After an opportunity to clarify any issues, Annotator 1 carried out the main annotation by correcting the system output and adding any information that was missed by the text mining component. We refer to the resulting human-annotated dataset as the *gold standard* and compare our system output against it. Table 2 shows that relative to our gold standard annotations, the text mining prototype, which uses the expanded commodity lexicon described in Section 3.2), identified commodity mentions with a precision (P) of 0.59, a recall (R) of 0.56 and an F-score of 0.57.

These scores are determined with a strict evaluation where each commodity mention identified by the system has to match the manually annotated mention exactly in terms of its boundaries and type to count as a true positive. As soon as one boundary differs — for example, if the annotator identified *palm* and the system identified *palm trees* —- the mis-match counts as both a false positive and a false negative. In order to understand how often the commodity extraction results in a boundary error, we also applied a lax evaluation where a true positive is counted if both boundaries match exactly; or if the left boundary differs and the right matches; or if the left boundary matches and the right differs. The improved scores for the lax evaluation listed in Table 2 show that boundary errors significantly impact on system performance, with an equally negative effect on recall and precision.

Table 2 also gives inter-annotator agreement (IAA) scores for 25% of the gold standard. IAA was calculated by comparing the markup of Annotator 1 with a second annotator (Annotator 2) for the same data. The strict and lax scores show that IAA is not particularly high (F=0.72 and F=0.80) for a task that we expected to be fairly easy and that boundary errors are also one of the reasons for the disagreement, albeit not to such a large extent as in the system evaluation. After having carried out some error analysis of the double-annotation, we realised that Annotator 2 had not completely understood our definition of commodity and had mistakenly included machinery and tools (e.g., *scissors*) as well as general terms related to commodities (e.g., *produce*). Annotator 2 also missed several relevant commodity mentions which Annotator 1 had correctly identified. For these reasons, Annotator 2's markup was ignored when evaluating the text mining output.

4.2 Analysis and Lexicon Modification

When examining the output of the text mining prototype, we found that it had identified a total of 31,169,104 commodity mentions (tokens) across all five collections. However, these corresponded to only 5,841 different commodity terms (types). Since the *Trading Consequences* thesaurus contains 20,476 commodity terms, only 28.5% of the content in the lexicon corresponds to identifiable commodity mentions in the text. The top 1,757 most frequent commodity terms occur at least 100 times in our data; they make up a total of 31,113,978 commodity mentions in the text and therefore amount to 99.8% of all commodity mentions found. Figure 10 presents the average frequency distribution of different commodity terms (separated into bins) across all text collections.

The difference between the strict and lax boundary evaluations described above provide evidence that some of the commodity mentions in text were substrings of commodity terms in the lexicon (e.g., *seal* vs. *sealskins*) and vice versa. A detailed error analysis showed that incorrect and missing entries in the lexicon further decrease precision and recall, respectively, and OCR errors occurring in the commodity terms in the

[23] The pilot data is not included in the gold standard that is used for the evaluation.

	Evaluation	TP	FP	FN	P	R	F-score
Text Mining Prototype	**Strict**	**616**	**431**	**491**	**0.59**	**0.56**	**0.57**
	Lax boundaries	791	256	316	0.76	0.71	0.73
IAA	**Strict**	**283**	**112**	**109**	**0.72**	**0.72**	**0.72**
	Lax boundaries	314	81	80	0.78	0.80	0.80

Table 2: Precision (P), recall (R) and F-score figures for evaluating the performance of the commodity recognition prototype, as well as numbers of true positive (TP), false positive (FP) and false negative (FN) mentions. These figures are compared against equivalent inter-annotator agreement (IAA) scores in 25% of the gold standard documents. We provide evaluation scores for strict and lax boundary matching of entity mentions.

	Evaluation	TP	FP	FN	P	R	F-score
Text Mining Prototype	**Strict**	**616**	**431**	**491**	**0.59**	**0.56**	**0.57**
	Lax	791	256	316	0.76	0.71	0.73
(i) Removal of lexicon errors	Strict	603	331	504	0.65	0.54	0.59
	Lax	765	169	342	0.82	0.69	0.75
(ii) Context Rules	Strict	664	483	443	0.58	0.60	0.59
	Lax	777	370	330	0.68	0.70	0.69
(iii) Bigram-based additions	Strict	673	441	434	0.60	0.61	0.61
	Lax	855	259	252	0.77	0.77	0.77
Modified Lexicon: combination of (i)–(iii)	**Strict**	**652**	**353**	**455**	**0.65**	**0.59**	**0.62**
	Lax	792	213	315	0.79	0.72	0.75

Table 3: Precision (P), recall (R) and F-score figures for evaluating the performance of the commodity recognition prototype compared to the same scores for two optimisation steps. We provide evaluation scores for strict and lax boundary matching of entity mentions.

text also considerably reduce recall (Alex and Burns, to appear). In our gold standard, 9.1% (101 of 1,107) of all manually annotated commodity mentions contain one or more OCR errors. In order to improve the accuracy of the lexicon, we carried out three modifications, which are described below.

Step (i): Removal of errors from lexicon All commodity terms below that of rank 1,757 (in bin 1,701–1,800 and subsequent bins) have a frequency of less than 100. In *Trading Consequences* we are particularly interested in frequently occurring commodities as we aim to identify trends in trade. Consequently one of the authors of this paper (an environmental historian) manually checked the correctness of the top 1,757 commodity terms. 84 of them (4.8%) were considered to be errors (either real errors, OCR errors, commodities outside our scope, or overly-ambiguous terms) and were therefore deleted from the lexicon.

We then tested the effect this change had on the performance for against the gold standard. The scores in Table 3 show that step (i), deleting incorrect entries from the lexicon, has an expected positive effect on precision, which increased by 0.06 (to P=0.65). It also resulted in a small decrease in recall since Annotator 1 had marked several instances of the word *bread* as commodity mentions, which is arguably at the boundary of our definition of 'natural resources or lightly processed commodities'. He had also annotated *paper* and *linen* as commodity mentions, which are not within our definition. Eliminating incorrect terms from lexicon does not reduce the number of boundary errors made by the prototype, and consequently the lax boundary evaluation still results in an increase of 0.16 in F-score compared to the strict evaluation (F=0.59 versus F=0.75), the same as is the case for the prototype.

Step (ii): Context rules Having examined the boundary errors made by the prototype, we also applied rules to extend commodity mentions to the left or right in certain contexts. We shift a boundary to the left if a recognised commodity mention is preceded by a noun or proper noun starting with an uppercase letter or if it is preceded by another commodity mention. This boundary shift is carried out to capture noun phrases in which the recognised commodity mention is a head noun which is then specified further by its immediate left context (e.g., *coffee* is extended to *Liberica coffee* or *oil* is combined with *coconut* to yield *coconut oil*). We shift a boundary to the right in the case where a recognised commodity is followed by the word *tree* or *trees* (e.g., *palm trees*). We tested the effect of applying these context rules to the prototype (see step (ii) in Table 3). While this post-processing step decreases precision very slightly, recall increases by 0.4.

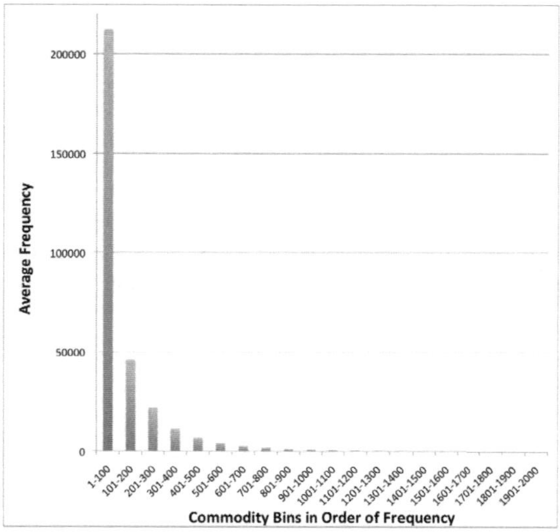

Figure 10: Average frequency distribution of different commodity terms split into bins of size 100. The *Trading Consequences* data contains a total of 5,841 different commodity terms. The graph is capped at the most frequent 2,000 terms as it would otherwise show a long invisible tail of very low average frequencies.

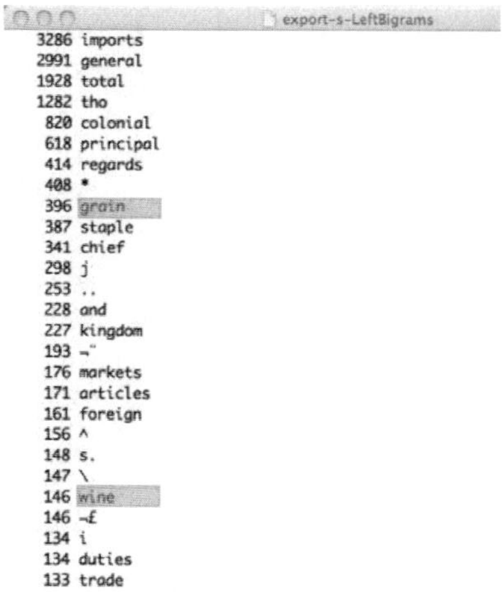

Figure 11: Most frequent tokens followed by the word *export* or *exports* found in the text-mined output of the HCPP data. This list excludes all occurrences where the left context is already recognised as a commodity. The commodities *grain* and *wine* have been marked by an expert historian as commodities that are missing from the lexicon.

Step (iii): Bigram-based additions Finally, we conducted a frequency-based bigram analysis for a set of trade-related terms like *import*, *export*, *farm*, *plantation* of the text-mined collections (see an example in Figure 11). We manually examined frequently occurring left and right contexts of such words with the aim of identifying a list of terms for commodities of importance in the nineteenth century but which were not already contained in the lexicon and were therefore missed by the text mining. We identified a list of 294 commodity terms (including plural forms and spelling variants) which we added to the lexicon. Step (iii) in Table 3 shows that this change increases recall by 0.05 and precision by 0.01. When combining steps (i)–(iii), we obtain the highest overall F-score of 0.62 with the strict evaluation.

5 Conclusion

In many named entity recognition tasks, there is reasonable agreement in advance about the ontological scope of a given class. For example, when identifying mentions of people, locations, companies or dates in a corpus, we are not in doubt as to what constitutes these classes. By contrast, in the *Trading Consequences* project, our goal was precisely to gain a better understanding of what counted as a traded commodity during the nineteenth century. In other words, we were not only bootstrapping a lexicon, but were also trying to bootstrap the ontological class 'commodity' that was true for a specific time period. Given a small number of clear cases extracted from customs records, we used the categorial similarity of other entities to our seed set as means of extrapolating to a much larger set of candidate commodities. However, it is only when these candidates can be found as mentions in our corpus that we gain confidence in the belief that we really have identified new commodities. From the perspective of historical inquiry, progressing from around a dozen or so well-studied commodities in nineteenth century trade to around 2,000 is a significant step forward.

The process of sibling acquisition via SPARQL query to DBpedia is a novel contribution, as far as we are aware, and we have argued that it can help to generate a lexicon which can be used as part of standard techniques in natural language processing. Although computational linguists are still relatively unfamiliar with RDF as a data model, we believe that its flexibility make it well suited to capturing the combination of lexical and encyclopaedic knowledge that is central to the digital history research described here. In addition, by basing our concepts on DBpedia, the 'linking' aspect of Linked Data (Heath and Bizer, 2011) gives us the potential to connect our commodity thesaurus to a wealth of other sources of knowledge about commodities.

Acknowledgments

The *Trading Consequences* project is a Digging Into Data II project (CIINN01) funded by Jisc, AHRC and SSHRC. It is a collaboration between the School of Informatics at the University of Edinburgh, EDINA, SACHI at the University of St. Andrews, together with York University and the University of Saskatchewan in Canada. We are grateful to Kate Byrne and to the three reviewers for their insightful comments on the paper.

References

Beatrice Alex and John Burns. to appear. Estimating and rating the quality of optically character recognised text. In *Proceedings of DATeCH 2014*.

Bea Alex, Claire Grover, Ewan Klein, and Richard Tobin. 2012. Digitised historical text: Does it have to be mediOCRe? In *Proceedings of the LThist 2012 workshop at KONVENS 2012*, pages 401–409.

Mark Assem, Véronique Malaisé, Alistair Miles, and Guus Schreiber. 2006. A method to convert thesauri to SKOS. In York Sure and John Domingue, editors, *The Semantic Web: Research and Applications*, volume 4011 of *Lecture Notes in Computer Science*, pages 95–109. Springer Berlin Heidelberg.

Christian Bizer, Jens Lehmann, Georgi Kobilarov, Sören Auer, Christian Becker, Richard Cyganiak, and Sebastian Hellmann. 2009. Dbpedia — a crystallization point for the web of data. *Web Semantics*, 7(3):154–165, September.

William Cronon. 1991. *Natures Metropolis: Chicago and the Great West*. W. W. Norton, New York.

Gregory T Cushman. 2013. *Guano and the Opening of the Pacific World: A Global Ecological History*. Cambridge University Press, Cambridge.

Claire Grover, Sharon Givon, Richard Tobin, and Julian Ball. 2008. Named entity recognition for digitised historical texts. In *Proceedings of the Sixth International Conference on Language Resources and Evaluation (LREC'08)*, pages 1343–1346, Marrakech, Morocco.

Tom Heath and Christian Bizer. 2011. *Linked Data: Evolving the Web into a Global Data Space*. Synthesis Lectures on the Semantic Web: Theory and Technology. Morgan & Claypool.

Harold Innis and Daniel Drache. 1995. *Staples, Markets, and Cultural Change Selected Essay*. McGill-Queens University Press, Montreal.

Zornitsa Kozareva. 2006. Bootstrapping named entity recognition with automatically generated gazetteer lists. In *Proceedings of the Eleventh Conference of the European Chapter of the Association for Computational Linguistics: Student Research Workshop*, EACL '06, pages 15–21, Stroudsburg, PA, USA.

Daniel Lopresti. 2008. Optical character recognition errors and their effects on natural language processing. In *Proceedings of the second workshop on Analytics for Noisy Unstructured Text Data*, pages 9–16.

Cynthia Matuszek, John Cabral, Michael J Witbrock, and John DeOliveira. 2006. An introduction to the syntax and content of Cyc. In *AAAI Spring Symposium: Formalizing and Compiling Background Knowledge and Its Applications to Knowledge Representation and Question Answering*, pages 44–49.

Stuart McCook. 2006. Global rust belt: *Hemileia Vastatrix* and the ecological integration of world coffee production since 1850. *Journal of Global History*, 1(2):177–195.

John McCrae, Guadalupe Aguado de Cea, Paul Buitelaar, Philipp Cimiano, Thierry Declerck, Asunción Gómez Pérez, Jorge Gracia, Laura Hollink, Elena Montiel-Ponsoda, Dennis Spohr, and Tobias Wunner, 2010. *The Lemon Cookbook*. The Monnet Project. `http://lemon-model.net/lemon-cookbook.pdf`.

P.N. Mendes, M. Jakob, and C. Bizer. 2012. DBpedia: A multilingual cross-domain knowledge base. In *Proceedings of the International Conference on Language Resources and Evaluation (LREC 2012)*.

Alistair Miles and Sean Bechhofer. 2009. SKOS simple knowledge organization system reference. W3C recommendation, W3C, August. `http://www.w3.org/TR/2009/REC-skos-reference-20090818/`.

E. Prud'Hommeaux and A. Seaborne. 2008. Sparql query language for rdf. *W3C working draft*, 4(January).

Henry Nicholas Ridley. 1912. *Spices*. London, Macmillan and co. Ltd.

Andy Seaborne and Steven Harris. 2013. SPARQL 1.1 query language. W3C recommendation, W3C, March. `http://www.w3.org/TR/2013/REC-sparql11-query-20130321/`.

Pontus Stenetorp, Sampo Pyysalo, Goran Topić, Tomoko Ohta, Sophia Ananiadou, and Jun'ichi Tsujii. 2012. BRAT: A web-based tool for NLP-assisted text annotation. In *Proceedings of the Demonstrations at the 13th Conference of the European Chapter of the Association for Computational Linguistics*, EACL '12, pages 102–107, Stroudsburg, PA, USA. Association for Computational Linguistics.

Erik F. Tjong Kim Sang and Fien De Meulder. 2003. Introduction to the CoNLL-2003 shared task: Language-independent named entity recognition. In *Proceedings of the Seventh Conference on Natural Language Learning*, CONLL '03, pages 142–147, Stroudsburg, PA, USA.

John Tully. 2009. A victorian ecological disaster: Imperialism, the telegraph, and gutta-percha. *Journal of World History*, 20(4):559–579.

New Technologies for Old Germanic. Resources and Research on Parallel Bibles in Older Continental Western Germanic

Christian Chiarcos, Maria Sukhareva, Roland Mittmann, Timothy Price, Jens Chobotsky, and **Gaye Detmold**
Goethe University Frankfurt, Germany
{lastname}@em.uni-frankfurt.de

Abstract

We provide an overview of on-going efforts to facilitate the study of older Germanic languages currently pursued at the Goethe-University Frankfurt, Germany.

We describe created resources, such as a parallel corpus of Germanic Bibles and a morphosyntactically annotated corpus of Old High German (OHG) and Old Saxon, a lexicon of OHG in XML and a multilingual etymological database. We discuss NLP algorithms operating on this data, and their relevance for research in the Humanities.

RDF and Linked Data represent new and promising aspects in our research, currently applied to establish cross-references between etymological dictionaries, infer new information from their symmetric closure and to formalize linguistic annotations in a corpus and grammatical categories in a lexicon in an interoperable way.

1 Background

We describe on-going efforts at the Goethe University Frankfurt on the study of older Continental Western Germanic languages, in particular, Old High German (OHG, ancestor of German), Old Saxon (OS, ancestor of Low German) and (to a lesser extent) Old Low Franconian (OLF, ancestor of Dutch) and their relation to Old English (OE), Gothic, German and other Germanic languages as well as the relation of OHG and OS religious texts to their Latin sources. This line of research is conducted in the context of two larger efforts, the Old German Reference Corpus and the LOEWE cluster "Digital Humanities", in collaboration with the Applied Computational Linguistics group at the Goethe-Universitt Frankfurt.

The Old German Reference Corpus is a DFG-funded project that emerged from the Deutsch Diachron Digital (DDD) initiative, conducted in cooperation between HU Berlin, U Frankfurt and U Jena, and aims to provide a morphosyntactically annotated, exhaustive reference corpus of Old High German and Old Saxon. The LOEWE cluster "Digital Humanities",[1] funded through a programm of the State of Hessen, is a collaboration between U Frankfurt, TU Darmstadt and Freies Deutsches Hochstift Frankfurt aiming to develop methodologies and infrastructures to facilitate information-technological support of research in the humanities.

The collaboration between the humanities and NLP described here is guided by different, though converging interests: For the **humanities**, the language resources, annotations, alignment and tools created in collaboration with NLP researchers represent novel instruments complementing traditional philological approaches, e.g., to investigate emergence and decay of syntactic patterns.

From an **NLP perspective**, the Germanic languages provide a test-bed to develop strategies for novel algorithms for alignment and annotation projection. In particular, the abundance of parallel (Bible) texts for all major language stages of most Germanic languages, the excellent NLP support for modern Germanic languages, and the availability of a considerable body of annotated historical texts allow us to study the impact of the factor of *diachronic relatedness* when building resources for low-resource languages.

2 Corpus Data

Along with annotated corpora provided by third parties (Tab. 1), two important data sets have been constructed in the course of our research. These include a massive, verse-aligned Bibles corpus

[1] http://www.digital-humanities-hessen.de

covering all Germanic languages, and the Old German Reference Corpus. In additional, a thematical alignment of quasi-parallel text within and across biblical texts was extrapolated from the literature.

2.1 Germanic parallel Bible corpus

Bible data represents the majority of parallel data available for historical Germanic languages, and for the case of OS and OHG, gospel harmonies represent even the majority of data currently known. Hence, we began compiling a corpus of Bible texts, excerpts and fragments for all Germanic languages marked up with IDs for verses (if possible), chapters and books. For data representation, we employed an XML version of the CES-scheme developed by (Resnik et al., 1997). Having outgrown the scale of Resnik's earlier project by far, we are currently in transition to TEI P5 XML format. At the moment, 271 texts with about 38.4M tokens have already been processed (Tab. 2). Copyright prevents redistributing most of this data under a free or an academic license, but we plan to share the extraction and conversion scripts we used. . Except for automatically parsed Bibles in modern English, German and Swedish, the texts in this collection are not annotated. Where annotations are available from other corpora (Tab. 1), however, these were aligned with our Bibles.

2.2 Old German Reference Corpus

The Old German Reference Corpus (*Referenzkorpus Altdeutsch*) (Mittmann, 2013) is a joint project in cooperation between HU Berlin, U Frankfurt and U Jena, conducted in the wider context of the Deutsch Diachron Digital (DDD) initiative. The DDD initiative aims to provide deeply-annotated reference corpora of different historical stages of German. The Old German Reference Corpus comprises all preserved texts from the oldest stages of continental Western Germanic (OHG and OS) dating from ca. 750 to 1050 CE, 650,000 tokens in total. Among the largest coherent subcorpora are Tatian (OHG), Otfrid of Weissenburg (OHG) and the Heliand (OS). From these, only Tatian can be verse-aligned with the gospels (and is included in Tab. 1 and 2), while the Heliand and Otfrid are free renderings of the gospels. For these, the literature provides a section-level alignment only.

The DDD builds on the earlier efforts of the TITUS project (Thesaurus of Indo-European Text and Language Materials, *Thesaurus Indogermanischer Text- und Sprachmaterialien*) that provided digitized editions of texts in old Germanic languages as well as other Indo-European and selected non-Indo-European languages (Gippert, 2011).[2]

The annotations are mostly derived from the literature and existing glossaries that provide grammatical information for all known OHG and OS words, together with their exact source. These have been digitized, automatically applied to the text, manually refined using the annotation software ELAN,[3] augmented with metadata, and finally published via the ANNIS database (Linde and Mittmann, 2013).

The annotated corpus is published under a CC-BY-SA license over `http://www.laudatio.org`, where ELAN and relANNIS files are provided. So far, the OHG Tatian is available, further data sets are currently in preparation.

2.3 Thematical alignment within and across biblical texts

Translations of religious texts are well-suited for language comparison as well as NLP experiments exploiting parallel data as they are not only faithfully translated, but also, they come with a verse-level alignment which can serve as a basis for statistical word-level alignment, using, e.g., GIZA++ (Och and Ney, 2003). Where such a verse-level is not explicitly given, it can be automatically identified for actual translations. However, for independent compositions such as gospel harmonies, alignment is harder to identify and can only be established at the level of sections. In addition, similar links also exist *between* different parts of the Bible, e.g., parallel passages in different gospels.

For these, an index providing a coarse-grained thematical alignment at the level of sections was extrapolated from the literature. This index can be exploited to increase the coverage of the alignment: where no exact translation is available (historical language data is often fragmentary), a thematically matching section is retrieved. Furthermore, consulting the verse under consideration together with renderings of quasiparallel parts of the same text allows historical linguists to grasp the degree of grammatical variability for the phenomena they are interested in. Language comparison can thus be particularly well accomodated if mul-

[2] `http://titus.uni-frankfurt.de/texte/texte2.htm#ahd` and `#asachs`

[3] `http://www.lat-mpi.eu/tools/elan`

language	period		syntax	tok.	corpus
	Modern	19th	CS	21K	(Kroch et al., 2010)
	British	18th	CS	32K	(Kroch et al., 2010)
	Early	17th	CS	22K	(Kroch et al., 2004)
English	Modern	16th	CS	21K	(Kroch et al., 2004)
	Middle	14th	CS	66K	(Kroch and Taylor, 2000)
	Old	10th	CS	78K	(Taylor et al., 2003b)
			DS	7K	(Haug and Jøhndal, 2008)
Icelandic	Middle	16th	CS	40K	(Rögnvaldsson et al., 2012)
High	Early Mod.	16th	CS	27K	(Light, 2013)
German	Old	9th	CH	41K	Sect. 2.2
Gothic		4th	DS	56K	(Haug and Jøhndal, 2008)

Table 1: Verse-aligned older Germanic Bible texts from various corpora with manual annotations for morphosyntax and syntax (CH chunks, CS constituents, DS dependencies)

	after 1900	1800-1900	1600-1800	1400-1600	1100-1400	before 1100
				Insular West Germanic		
English	2	2	2	6	3 (+2)	1
Pidgin/Creol	2					
Scots	(6)			(1)		
				Continental West Germanic		
Frisian	2 (+8)	(12)				
Dutch	4		1	5		(1)
L. Franconian	(47)	21				
Afrikaans	3					
German	3	1	(19)	1 (+4)	1 (+1)	1
dialects	3 (+2)					
Yiddish	1					
Low German	3 (+18)	(66)		(2)		1
Plautdietsch	2					
				North & East Germanic		
Danish	1					
Swedish	3			(3)	(1)	
Bokmål	2					
Nynorsk	2					
Icelandic		1		1		
Faroese	1					
Norn			(2)			
Gothic						1
tokens	21.8M	3.2M	2.7M	9.2M	1.2M	0.2M

Table 2: Verse-aligned texts in the Germanic parallel Bible corpus (parentheses indicate marginal fragments with less than 50,000 tokens)

tiple versions of the same passage in the same language can be provided.

To exploit redundancy and to enlarge the number of parallel and quasi-parallel passages for a given phenomenon searched in the corpus, cross-references within the Bible and between the Bible and derived texts have been identified. For example, coarse-grained thematical alignment between different gospels is provided by the Eusebian Canon Tables and their subordinate Ammonian sections and are extendable to the Latin Tatian. For OS Heliand, a free adaptation of gospels, we have only a section-level thematical alignment with Tatian provided by Sievers (1872).

Information on these cross-references has been digitized and employed to create an interlinked index of thematically similar sections in the gospels and the OS and OHG gospel harmonies. Our Bible data is thus accompanied with an index that links disparate texts from different time periods and in distinctive styles and variant languages on the basis of thematical similarity as identified in the literature. For gospels and gospel harmonies, we identified 4560 inter-text groups made up of the related chunks between all the originals and languages involved that represents the basis for a more fine-grained level of alignment (Price, 2012).

	West Germanic					other		reconstr.	
lexicon	OE	OHG	OS	OLF	OFr	ON	Got	PGmc	PIE
entries (XML, in K)									
	25	24	9	2	13	12	5	9	7
triples (RDF, in M)									
	1.2	1.6	.6	.2	.6	.7	.4	.2	.2
lemon:Words & links (in K)									
OE	25					1			
OHG	2	26	7	2	3	1			
OS	1	4	9	1	2	1			
ON	1				1	14			
Got	1	1			1	1	6		
PGmc	5	3	3	1	2	4	2	8	
PIE	2	1	1	1	1	1	1		8
German	16	23	8	4	10	12	7	6	3
English		10	4	2	5		9		2
symmetric closure of etym. links (triples *per lang.* in K)									
	+11	+14	+11	+5	+9	+8	+5	+21	+9
links to (L)LOD data sets (triples *per data set* in K)									
OLiA	24	22	8	2	12	11	5	8	7
lexvo	132	186	82	21	68	82	49	14	15
Glottolog	15	11	8	3	7	11	6	9	13

Table 3: Statistics on the etymological dictionaries, including Old Low Franconian (OLF), Old Frisian (OFr), Old Norse (ON), Gothic (Got), Proto-Germanic (PGmc) and Proto-Indo-European (PIE)

3 Linked Lexicon Data

A large lexical database of etymologically linked dictionaries of old Germanic languages (OS, OHG, OE, Gothic, Old Norse, Old Frisian, Old Low Franconian, Proto-Germanic; also Proto-Indo-European) has been developed in the context of the LOEWE cluster 'Digital Humanities' at the U Frankfurt. Building on the etymological and translational dictionaries of Old Germanic languages by Gerhard Köbler,[4] the project 'Historical Linguistic Database' developed user-friendly means of comparing etymologically related forms between historical dialects and their daughter languages (Price, 2012). The original PDF data were converted into an XML representation, cross-references have been resolved and the results are

[4]`http://www.koeblergerhard.de/ahdwbhin.html`

imported into an XML database. A web interface has been developed, that transforms user queries into XQuery and visualizes the results in a convenient way using XSLT.

To provide a machine-readable representation of the etymological dictionaries, an **RDF version** has been compiled. Applying the Linked Data paradigm (Bizer et al., 2009) to etymological lexicons is particularly promising as they are characterized by a heavy linkage across different languages, so that etymological lexicons for different languages are very likely to complement each other. RDF provides the means to represent the cross-language linking using a uniform formalism, and subsequently, to facilitate information aggregation over multiple etymological lexicons as well as language-specific lexical resources.

We converted the Köbler lexicons to RDF in conformance to the Lemon model (McCrae et al., 2011), an LMF-based vocabulary to represent machine-readable lexicons by using Semantic Web standards. This conversion followed the three main objectives:

(i) linkability: XML-based query languages such as XQuery and XPath, used to create the user interface to the lexicons, limit our lexicon to a tree-structure representation. However, as our lexicons complement each other, it would be desirable to provide explicit cross-references between these entries, and to allow them to be queried jointly. Within the RDF data model, the relations within and beyond a single lexicon can be represented and queried with equal ease, surmounting constraint imposed by XML.

(ii) interoperability: Instead of resource-specific abbreviations for languages and grammatical categories, we represent linguistic information and meta data by reference to community-maintained vocabularies publicly available as part of the (Linguistic) Linked Open Data cloud, namely lexvo (de Melo, to appear, ISO 639-3 language codes), Glottolog (Nordhoff and Hammarström, 2011, language families) and OLiA (Chiarcos, 2008, linguistic categories). Reusing vocabularies shared among many parties over the Web of Data has the advantage that resources dealing with related phenomena in the same language can be easily identified and their information integrated without additional conversion steps.

(iii) inference: The original lexicons were distributed in individual PDF files, and the XML representation was created as a faithful representation of their content, augmented with markup for relevant linguistic features. These files, however, provided complementary information, so that, say, a lexicon entry in the OS dictionary provided a reference to an etymological corresponding OHG entry, but this reference was not found in the OHG dictionary. Such gaps can be easily detected (and filled) through symmetric closure in the RDF data model.

The results of this conversion are summarized in Tab. 3. In the original XML (first row), every entry corresponds to a lemma of the language under consideration, with different etymologies (and/or senses) being associated with it. In RDF (second row), each of these homographs (together with its definition number) is defined as a `lemon:Word` with a homography relation with the homograph set (represented by a `lemon:Word` *without* definition number). The number of `lemon:Words` is thus slightly higher than the number of entries in the original dictionaries. Differently from the XML, however, information from different data sets can be easily aggregated, and triples originating from one document can be complemented with triples from another, shown here for the symmetric closure of etymological relations (third row) that can be easily generated using a simple SPARQL pattern like `CONSTRUCT { ?o ?p ?s } WHERE {?s ?p ?o}`. The last row shows links to other data sets from the (Linguistic) Linked Open Data cloud. Most original entries were complemented with grammatical information using different (and not fully consistent) abbreviations. For the most frequent abbreviations used, a link to the corresponding OLiA concept was generated. These definitions are thus *interoperable* beyond these lexicons and can be compared, e.g., with those of lexical-semantic resources for Modern German and English as compiled in (Eckle-Kohler et al., to appear). Similarly, language abbreviations were mapped to ISO 639-3 codes (in lexvo), or, where these were not available, to Glottolog. Even though the number of data in historical languages is constantly increasing and there is a demand for fine-grained language codes for them, neither of the aforementioned resources provide such codes. So we had to use a link to the corresponding language family instead.

language	period	scheme	corpus reference
English	Modern	PTB	(Taylor et al., 2003a; Kroch et al., 2010)
	Early Mod.	PPCEME	(Kroch et al., 2004)
	Middle	PPME2	(Kroch and Taylor, 2000)
	Old	YCOE	(Taylor et al., 2003b)
		PROIEL	(Taylor et al., 2003b)
High German	Modern	STTS	(Schiller et al., 1999)
	Early Mod.	PCENHG	(Light, 2013)
	Old	Sect. 2.2	
		T-CODEX	(Petrova et al., 2009)
Dutch	Modern	Alpino	(Bouma et al., 2001)
Old Norse		Menota	(Haugen et al., 2008)
Danish	Modern	EAGLES	(Leech and Wilson, 1996)
Swedish	Modern	Mamba	(Nivre et al., 2006)
Icelandic		IcePaHC	(Rögnvaldsson et al., 2012)
Gothic		PROIEL	(Haug and Jøhndal, 2008)

(a) Morphosyntactic annotations

language	period	scheme	corpus reference
English	Modern	PTB	(Taylor et al., 2003a; Kroch et al., 2010)
		Stanford deps	(De Marneffe and Manning, 2008)
		Penn2Malt deps	(Johansson and Nugues, 2007)
	Early Mod.	PPCEME	(Kroch et al., 2004)
	Middle	PPME2	(Kroch and Taylor, 2000)
	Old	YCOE	(Taylor et al., 2003b)
		PROIEL	(Taylor et al., 2003b)
High German	Modern	TIGER	(Brants et al., 2004)
		Tüba-D/Z	(Telljohann et al., 2003)
		NEGRA	(Skut et al., 1997)
	Early Mod.	PCENHG	(Light, 2013)
Dutch	Modern	Alpino	(Bouma et al., 2001)
Swedish	Modern	Mamba	(Nivre et al., 2006)
Icelandic		IcePaHC	(Rögnvaldsson et al., 2012)
Gothic		PROIEL	(Haug and Jøhndal, 2008)

(b) Syntactic annotations

Table 4: List of annotation schemes represented as OWL2/DL ontologies and relevant Germanic corpora

4 NLP methods applied

We sketch selected NLP applications developed on the data described before, the automated phrase-level alignment of quasi-parallel text, and two experiments on annotation projection on parallel text. All of these experiments are still in a relatively early stage.

4.1 Automated phrase-level alignment of quasi-parallel text

The needs of historical lingustics demand a more fine-grained alignment than the currently available thematical alignment of Heliand with Tatian and the gospels. We thus investigate parallel phrase detection between Heliand (OS) and Tatian (OHG), resp., Heliand and the West Saxon gospels (OE).

To identify cognate phrases, we explore 6 types of similarity metrics $\delta(w_{OS}, w_{OHG})$ for every OS word w_{OS} and its potential OHG cognate w_{OHG}.

1. geometry δ_g = difference between the relative positions of w_{OS} and w_{OHG}.

2. identity $\delta_i(w_{OS}, w_{OHG}) = 1$ iff $w_{OHG} = w_{OS}$ (0 otherwise)

3. lexicon $\delta_{lex}(w_{OS}, w_{OHG}) = 1$ iff $w_{OHG} \in W$ (0 otherwise) where W is a set of possible OHG translations for w_{OS} suggested by a lexicon, i.e., either

direct etymological link in (the symmetric closure of) the etymological dictionaries, or

indirect shared German gloss in the etymological dictionaries

4. orthography similarity measure based on character replacement likelihood:

relative Levenshtein similarity $\delta_{lev}(w_{OS}, w_{OHG}) = 1 - \frac{ld}{|w_{OS}|+|w_{OHG}|}$ where ld is the standard Levenstein distance and $|w_{OS}|$ and $|w_{OHG}|$ are the number of characters in each word.

statistical character replacement probability as approximated by a character-based statistical machine translation system (Neubig et al., 2012)

5. normalization $\delta_{norm}(w_{OS}, w_{OHG}) = \delta_i(w'_{OS}, w_{OHG})$, with w'_{OS} being the OHG 'normalization' of the original w_{OS}. Here, normalization uses a weighted Levenshtein distance and a fixed list of OHG target words (Bollmann et al., 2011).

6. cooccurrences $\delta_p(w_{OS}, w_{OHG}) = P(w_{OS}|w_{OHG})P(w_{OHG}|w_{OS})$, calculated on thematically aligned sections from both texts.

For any two thematically aligned OS and OHG word vectors, we thus span up a similarity matrix between both word vectors on the basis of these metrics. On the matrices, different operations can be applied to calculate similarity derived metrics, including point-wise multiplication or addition, thresholds and a smoothing operator, that aligns words due to the similarity of its neighbors. The resulting matrix is then decoded by a greedy algorithm that aligns the words with the highest score, and then iterates for the remaining words.

At the moment, we provide a graphical interface over a webpage that allows a philologist to dynamically define an alignment function and that provides a graphical visualization of the result. During a partial qualitative evaluation a historical linguist was asked to compare the results of alignment based on various metrics applied to a small text passage. He took into consideration the overall match of the topic of the aligned passages as well as the number of parallel passages that the metrics failed to align. Eventually, it was indicated that the best results can be achieved by combining multiple metrics. A combination of either direct lexicon-based or normalization-based alignment and geometrical alignment appears to be particularly promising. Yet, systematic experiments to automatically explore this feature space are still being prepared and depend on the availability of a gold alignment for selected verses.

4.2 Projecting dependency relations

As shown in Tab. 1, we only possess shallow syntactic annotations of OHG (and OS) text. We are thus particularly interested in establishing richer syntactic annotations. A challenging aspect in this respect is the limited availability of parallel training data for historical language stages. However, due to diachronic relatedness, we may expect that syntactic patterns of Old Germanic languages are preserved in their modern descendants. Such an approach requires a consistent hyperlemmatization, e.g., against a modern language

We tested this idea on Bible texts from four corpora with closely related annotation schemes for syntax (Tab. 1, corpora with CS-syntax): Icelandic (IS), Early Modern High German (DE), Middle English (ME) and Old English (OE). These schemes originate in the Penn Treebank scheme (Taylor et al., 2003a), and we thus parsed a modern English Bible with a parser trained on the Penn Treebank. As older Germanic languages are characterized by a higher degree of word order flexibility than Modern English, we converted historical and modern annotations to dependency relations using standard tools for this task (Johansson and Nugues, 2007). Word-alignment was obtained with GIZA++ and 1:1 alignment was enforced using the translation table. Then, we projected dependency relations and the English words as hyperlemmas for the historical texts. The historical texts had comparable POS annotation that was only slightly normalized across the corpora as it preserved more morphological information than Modern English POS tags.

On these projections, a fragment-aware parser was trained using the English (hyper)lemmas and the original POS tags (Spreyer and Kuhn, 2009). We limited the amount of parallel data available to a training set of 437 sentences per language and a test set of 174 per language. Our hypothesis was that in this setting, (projected) training data from related languages can be used *in place of* training data for the language under consideration, *if* the amount of data is sufficient *and* the languages are sufficiently closely related. Furthermore, we assumed that with an increasing number of languages considered (and thus training set size), the quality of the projected annotations would continuously improve *as long as* the languages are sufficiently closely related.

For evaluation, we employed the unlabeled attachment score (UAS) (Collins et al., 1999) on the test data and compared with the (dependency version of) the original annotation in these corpora. Tab. 5 compares the performance of a parser trained on target language data with parsers trained on (hyperlemmatized) related languages. The scores in the second column are the baseline UAS where the parser was applied to the same language as it was trained on. The third column shows the difference with the parser applied to a language but trained on projections into another language. The fourth and the fifth column provides the results of the parser trained on one or two additional related languages respectively.

The results showed that, among the West Germanic languages (but not IS), a parser trained on two or more related languages can reach the same performance or even outperforms a parser trained on the target language. Furthermore, a parser trained on (projected) annotations from two or more related languages is likely to outperform a parser trained on a single related language. Accordingly, in absence of parallel texts for the target language, the parser can be successfully trained on annotation projections from two or more related languages. It should be noted, however, that the overall performance of the parser was relatively poor. This may be, however, an artifact of the great grammatical divergency between Modern English (and, to a limited degree, ME: reduced morphology, strict word order) and older Germanic languages (rich morphology, flexible word order).

Subsequent experiments will thus address the

inclusion of richer morphological features, projections from other languages and evaluation against another set of dependency (DS) annotations for Gothic and Old English (Tab. 1), for which related annotation schemes for Latin, Greek and Czech are available – all of these languages are characterized by rich morphology and flexible syntax.

Tgt	on Tgt lang.	on related languages: Best monoling. model	ΔUAS	Best biling. model	ΔUAS	Triling. model	ΔUAS
DE	.41	IS	$+.02^{n.s.}$	+ME	$+.05^{*}$	+OE	$+.04^{**}$
IS	.32	ME	$-.06^{***}$	+DE	$-.03^{n.s.}$	+OE	$-.04^{*}$
ME	.60	IS	$-.04^{***}$	+OE	$-.01^{n.s.}$	+DE	$-.02^{n.s.}$
OE	.30	ME	$.00^{n.s.}$	+IS	$.00^{n.s.}$	+DE	$.00^{n.s.}$

Table 5: Performance of parsing models (UAS difference vs. 2nd col. with χ^2: $^{*}\ p < .05$, $^{**}\ p < .01$, $^{***}\ p < .005$)

4.3 Harmonization of grammatical features

Another line of studies addresses the projection of grammatical features as represented in POS tags and dependency labels. Unfortunately, modern and historical language stages are annotated according to a great variety of annotation schemes which can not be trivially mapped to a generalization without substantial loss of information (as, e.g., in the approach by Petrov et al., 2012). For processing of multilingual corpora the problem of heteroginity of linguistic annotations is very acute. Above, we described an experiment that used PTB style annotations only. This limitation was imposed by the annotation schema of the target corpora that had PTB style syntactic annotations.

We thus follow Chiarcos (2008) and represent the most relevant Germanic annotation schemes as OWL2/DL ontologies, and link these to an overarching Reference Model. Unlike a tagset, whose string-based annotations require disjoint categories at a fixed level of granularity, this ontology-based approach allows to decompose the semantics of annotations and consider all aspects independently. For example, a tagger may correctly identify plural agreement but incorrectly assume that it pertains a noun, as in the Penn Treebank tag `NNS`. In the original tagset, a corresponding tag for, say, adjectives, does not exist, but using the ontology, a plural adjective could nevertheless be represented in the form of different RDF triples. With lexicon data being available in RDF and linked to the OLiA Reference Model, as well (Sect. 3), the incorrect word class can be spotted, and corrected, but the agreement information could remain unaffected.

These annotations have also been successfully employed in ensemble combination architectures, where information from different sources (say, NLP tools) was integrated on the basis of the Reference Model and disambiguated using ontological axioms (Chiarcos, 2010; Pareja-Lora and Aguado de Cea, 2010). In an annotation projection scenario, these sources could be projections from different languages annotated according to different schemes, e.g., German, English, Swedish or Latin. These experiments are currently being conducted, but Annotation Models for several schemes are already available (Tab. 4).

5 Digital Humanities

Our ultimate goal is to facilitate studies of historical and empirical linguists and philologists.

One research question under consideration is whether the Heliand influenced Luther (Price, 2012), who, apparently, possessed one copy. Based on a thorough comparison of thematically aligned passages, evidence for or against this hypothesis may be gathered, and this investigation can be simplified by limiting the search to parallel phrases automatically identified (Sect. 4.1).

Another research question pertains to divergencies between, e.g., OHG texts and their Latin source. As most OHG material is translated in a literal fashion, and the word order was relatively flexible, the OHG syntax may have been adjusted to mirror the Latin original. Research of OHG syntax thus concentrates on passages where OHG syntax differs from the Latin source (Hinterhölzl and Petrova, 2009).

Different types of divergencies have been identified by qualitative research. Early translations unlike modern ones tend to be very literal, often not being only word by word translation but also preserving the syntax of the original. Nevertheless, due to strong grammatical differences between two languages, various divergencies on (morpho)syntactic and lexical levels were unavoidable. Such, the transition from the Latin synthetic to OHG analytic wordforms in case of the deponent verbs is systematically observed. Also the changes of the word position as well as missing a word in translation or adding a word that is not present in the Latin original can be frequently found. Such divergencies can be often explained by stylistic or pragmatic reasons as well as by personal preferences of the translator.

This line of research is currently supported through automated word-level alignment between the OHG and Latin versions of Tatian. We built a parallel corpus using GIZA++ and used the TreeAligner (Lundborg et al., 2007) for search and evaluation. On this basis, a philological comparison of OHG Tatian and its Latin source is being conducted. More helpful, however, would be a comparison of different syntactic patterns in OHG and Latin which motivates our experiments in annotation projection (Sect. 4.2).

Finally, our experiments in the ontology-based harmonization of different annotation schemes (Sect. 4.3) will facilitate subsequent typological and linguistic comparison across corpora with manual annotations for syntax and/or morphology according to different schemes.

6 Summary

We sketched major research directions on the development of resources, NLP tools and algorithms to facilitate the study Old Germanic languages currently pursued at the Goethe-University Frankfurt in the context of two related research initiatives, the LOEWE cluster 'Digital Humanities' and the project 'Old German Reference corpus'.

Our efforts resulted in the creation of the following resources:

- a massive **parallel corpus** of TEI-conformant Bibles including all contemporary Germanic languages as well as early stages of Germanic languages (Sect. 2.1).

- an exhaustive, **morphosyntactically annotated corpus of OHG and OS** with morphosyntactic annotations. Annotations were automatically derived from glossaries and manually refined (Sect. 2.2).

- an index providing a **thematical alignment** of the four gospels with each other as well as with OHG and OS gospel harmonies (Sect. 2.3). This high quality alignment provides a solid basis for further more fine-grained automatic alignment (Sect. 4.1).

- XML versions of **lexical resources**, including etymological dictionaries of Old Germanic languages (Sect. 3)

- an RDF-based **linked etymological database** of Old Germanic languages compiled from the latter (Sect. 3)

- a Linked Data representation of **annotation schemes** for corpora, NLP tools and grammatical features in the linked lexicon data (Sect. 3, 4.3)

The resources created provide an excellent testbed for various NLP algorithms, particularly for experiments on alignment and annotation projection techniques: We developed different metrics for **quasi-parallel alignment** applied to the corpus of gospel harmonies (Sect. 4.1). For subsequent analysis, evaluation and refinement by historical linguists, we provide a graphical visualization and user interface in a form of a webpage. This is an on-going project and further research will aim at refining metrics and their combination.

Our massive parallel corpus is a perfect prerequisite for **annotation projection** (Sect. 4.2). Our experiments on annotation projections and cross-lingual parser adaptation showed that it is possible to use (hyperlemmatized) training data from multiple closely related languages *in place of* training data for the language under consideration, and on small sets of parallel training data available, this did not lead to a significant loss of performance. The only exception in the experiment (IS) is also most remote from the other languages considered.

A severe limitation of this experiment was that it required operating on (variants of) the same annotation scheme. Another line of our research is focused on researching of ways to surmount such restrictions. We thus adopt a modular approach with annotation schemes linked to the OLiA Reference Model to harmonize annotations and grammatical features from lexicons (Sect. 4.3).

Finally, applications of these algorithms and resources in research questions in philology, historical linguistics and comparative linguistics were sketched in Sect. 5.

While most resources described in this paper have been developed for several years at the Goethe-University Frankfurt, the increased focus on NLP and Linked Data represent novel developments pursued by the newly established Applied Computational Linguistics Lab at the Goethe University Frankfurt. Different aspects of research sketched in this paper thus describe on-going activities at different degrees of completion.

Acknowledgements

The research of Christian Chiarcos, Maria Sukhareva, Tim Price, Gaye Detmold, and Jens Chobotsky described in this paper was supported by the research cluster 'Digital Humanities' at the Goethe-University Frankfurt, funded through the LOEWE programme of the federal state of Hessia. The research of Roland Mittmann was conducted in the project 'Old German Reference corpus', funded by the Deutsche Forschungsgemeinschaft (DFG).

References

Christian Bizer, Tom Heath, and Tim Berners-Lee. 2009. Linked Data – The story so far. *International Journal on Semantic Web and Information Systems (IJSWIS)*, 5(3):1–22.

Marcel Bollmann, Florian Petran, and Stefanie Dipper. 2011. Rule-based normalization of historical texts. In *Proceedings of the Workshop on Language Technologies for Digital Humanities and Cultural Heritage (LaTeCH-2011)*, pages 34–42, Hissar, Bulgaria, September.

Gosse Bouma, Gertjan Van Noord, and Robert Malouf. 2001. Alpino: Wide-coverage computational analysis of Dutch. *Language and Computers*, 37(1):45–59.

Sabine Brants, Stefanie Dipper, Peter Eisenberg, Silvia Hansen-Schirra, Esther König, Wolfgang Lezius, Christian Rohrer, George Smith, and Hans Uszkoreit. 2004. Tiger: Linguistic interpretation of a german corpus. *Research on Language and Computation*, 2(4):597–620.

Christian Chiarcos. 2008. An ontology of linguistic annotations. *LDV Forum*, 23(1):1–16.

Christian Chiarcos. 2010. Towards robust multi-tool tagging. An OWL/DL-based approach. In *Proc. of the 48th Annual Meeting of the Association for Computational Linguistics (ACL-2010)*, pages 659–670, Uppsala, Sweden.

Michael Collins, Lance Ramshaw, Jan Hajič, and Christoph Tillmann. 1999. A statistical parser for Czech. In *Proc. of the 37th Annual Meeting of the Association for Computational Linguistics (ACL-1999)*, pages 505–512, Maryland, June.

Marie-Catherine De Marneffe and Christopher D Manning. 2008. The Stanford typed dependencies representation. In *Proceedings of the COLING-2008 Workshop on Cross-Framework and Cross-Domain Parser Evaluation*, pages 1–8.

Gerard de Melo. to appear. Lexvo.org: Language-related information for the linguistic linked data cloud. *Semantic Web Journal*, pages 1–7.

Judith Eckle-Kohler, John McCrae, and Christian Chiarcos. to appear. lemonUby – A large, interlinked, syntactically-rich resource for ontologies. *Semantic Web Journal: Multilingual Linked Open Data*.

Jost Gippert. 2011. The TITUS Project. 25 years of corpus building in ancient languages. In *Perspektiven einer corpusbasierten historischen Linguistik und Philologie. Internationale Tagung des Akademienvorhabens "Altägyptisches Wörterbuch" an der Berlin-Brandenburgischen Akademie der Wissenschaften*, pages 169–192, Berlin, December.

Dag TT Haug and Marius Jøhndal. 2008. Creating a parallel treebank of the old Indo-European bible translations. In *Proceedings of the Language Technology for Cultural Heritage Data Workshop (LaTeCH 2008)*, pages 27–34, Marrakech, Morocco, June.

Odd Einar Haugen, Tone Merete Bruvik, Matthew Driscoll, Karl G Johansson, Rune Kyrkjebø, and Tarrin Wills. 2008. The Menota handbook: Guidelines for the electronic encoding of Medieval Nordic primary sources.

Roland Hinterhölzl and Svetlana Petrova. 2009. *Information Structure and Language Change: New Approaches to Word Order Variation in Germanic*. Mouton de Gruyter.

Richard Johansson and Pierre Nugues. 2007. Extended constituent-to-dependency conversion for English. In *Proceedings of the 16th Nordic Conference on Computational Linguistics (NoDaLiDa-2007)*, pages 105–112, Tartu, Estonia, May.

Anthony Kroch and Ann Taylor. 2000. The Penn-Helsinki Parsed Corpus of Middle English (PPCME2). Department of Linguistics, University of Pennsylvania. CD-ROM.

Anthony Kroch, Beatrice Santorini, and Lauren Delfs. 2004. The Penn-Helsinki Parsed Corpus of Early Modern English (PPCEME). Department of Linguistics, University of Pennsylvania. CD-ROM.

Anthony Kroch, Beatrice Santorini, and Ariel Diertani. 2010. The Penn-Helsinki Parsed Corpus of Modern British English (PPCMBE). Department of Linguistics, University of Pennsylvania. CD-ROM.

Geoffrey Leech and Andrew Wilson. 1996. EAGLES guidelines: Recommendations for the morphosyntactic annotation of corpora.

Caitlin Light. 2013. Parsed Corpus of Early New High German (PCENHG), v. 0.5. University of Pennsylvania, `http://enhgcorpus.wikispaces.com/`.

Sonja Linde and Roland Mittmann. 2013. Old German Reference Corpus. Digitizing the knowledge of the 19th century. In Paul Bennett, Martin Durrell, Silke

Scheible, and Richard J. Whitt, editors, *New Methods in Historical Corpus Linguistics = Korpuslinguistik und interdiziplinre Perspektiven auf Sprache – Corpus linguistics and Interdisciplinary perspectives on language (CLIP)*, volume 3 of *Korpuslinguistik und interdiziplinre Perspektiven auf Sprache – Corpus linguistics and Interdisciplinary perspectives on language (CLIP)*, Tübingen. Narr.

Joakim Lundborg, Torsten Marek, Maël Mettler, and Martin Volk. 2007. Using the Stockholm TreeAligner. In *Proceedings of the 6th Workshop on Treebanks and Linguistic Theories (TLT-2007)*, pages 73–78.

John McCrae, Dennis Spohr, and Philipp Cimiano. 2011. Linking lexical resources and ontologies on the semantic web with lemon. In *The Semantic Web: Research and Applications*, pages 245–259. Springer.

Roland Mittmann. 2013. Digitalisierung historischer Glossare zur automatisierten Vorannotation von Textkorpora am Beispiel des Altdeutschen. *Journal for Language Technology and Computational Linguistics (JLCL)*, 27(2):39–52.

Graham Neubig, Taro Watanabe, Shinsuke Mori, and Tatsuya Kawahara. 2012. Machine translation without words through substring alignment. In *Proc. of the 50th Annual Meeting of the Association for Computational Linguistics (ACL-2012)*, pages 165–174, Jeju Island, Korea, July.

Joakim Nivre, Jens Nilsson, and Johan Hall. 2006. Talbanken05: A Swedish treebank with phrase structure and dependency annotation. In *Proc. of the 5th International Conference on Language Resources and Evaluation (LREC-2006)*, pages 1392–1395.

Sebastian Nordhoff and Harald Hammarström. 2011. Glottolog/langdoc: Defining dialects, languages, and language families as collections of resources. In *Proceedings of the First International Workshop on Linked Science 2011 (LISC-2011)*.

Franz Josef Och and Hermann Ney. 2003. A systematic comparison of various statistical alignment models. *Computational Linguistics*, 29(1):19–51.

Antonio Pareja-Lora and Guadalupe Aguado de Cea. 2010. Ontology-based interoperation of linguistic tools for an improved lemma annotation in Spanish. In *Proc. of the 6th International Conference on Language Resources and Evaluation (LREC-2010)*, Valetta, Malta, May.

Slav Petrov, Dipanjan Das, and Ryan McDonald. 2012. A universal part-of-speech tagset. In *Proc. of the 8th International Conference on Language Resources and Evaluation (LREC-2012)*, pages 2089–2096, Istanbul, Turkey.

Svetlana Petrova, Michael Solf, Julia Ritz, Christian Chiarcos, and Amir Zeldes. 2009. Building and using a richly annotated interlinear diachronic corpus: The case of Old High German Tatian. *TAL*, 50(2):47–71.

Timothy Blaine Price. 2012. Multi-faceted alignment: Toward automatic detection of textual similarity in gospel-derived texts. In *Proceedings of Historical Corpora 2012*, Frankfurt, Germany.

Philip Resnik, Mari Broman Olsen, and Mona Diab. 1997. Creating a parallel corpus from the book of 2000 tongues. In *Proc. of the Text Encoding Initiative 10th Anniversary User Conference (TEI-10)*.

Eiríkur Rögnvaldsson, Anton Karl Ingason, Einar Freyr Sigurdsson, and Joel Wallenberg. 2012. The Icelandic Parsed Historical Corpus (IcePaHC). In *Proc. of the 8th International Conference on Language Resources and Evaluation (LREC-2012)*, Istanbul, Turkey, May.

Anne Schiller, Simone Teufel, Christine Stöckert, and Christine Thielen. 1999. Guidelines für das Tagging deutscher Textcorpora mit STTS. Technical report, Universitäten Stuttgart und Tübingen.

Wojciech Skut, Brigitte Krenn, Thorsten Brants, and Hans Uszkoreit. 1997. An annotation scheme for free word order languages. In *Proc. of the 5th Conference on Applied Natural Language Processing*, pages 88–95.

Kathrin Spreyer and Jonas Kuhn. 2009. Data-driven dependency parsing of new languages using incomplete and noisy training data. In *Proc. of the 13th Conference on Computational Natural Language Learning (CoNLL-2009)*, pages 12–20, Boulder, CO, June.

Ann Taylor, Mitchell Marcus, and Beatrice Santorini. 2003a. The Penn Treebank: An overview. In Anne Abeill, editor, *Treebanks*, pages 5–22. Springer, Dordrecht.

Ann Taylor, Anthony Warner, Susan Pintzuk, and Frank Beths. 2003b. The York-Toronto-Helsinki parsed corpus of Old English prose.

Heike Telljohann, Erhard W Hinrichs, Sandra Kübler, Heike Zinsmeister, and Kathrin Beck. 2003. Stylebook for the Tübingen treebank of written German (TüBa-D/Z). Technical report, Seminar für Sprachwissenschaft, Universität Tübingen, Germany.

A Multilingual Evaluation of Three Spelling Normalisation Methods for Historical Text

Eva Pettersson[1,2], **Beáta Megyesi**[1] **and Joakim Nivre**[1]
(1) Department of Linguistics and Philology
Uppsala University
(2) Swedish National Graduate School
of Language Technology
firstname.lastname@lingfil.uu.se

Abstract

We present a multilingual evaluation of approaches for spelling normalisation of historical text based on data from five languages: English, German, Hungarian, Icelandic, and Swedish. Three different normalisation methods are evaluated: a simplistic filtering model, a Levenshtein-based approach, and a character-based statistical machine translation approach. The evaluation shows that the machine translation approach often gives the best results, but also that all approaches improve over the baseline and that no single method works best for all languages.

1 Introduction

Language technology for historical text is a field of research imposing a variety of challenges. Nevertheless, there is an increasing need for natural language processing (NLP) tools adapted to historical texts, as an aid for researchers in the humanities field. For example, the historians in the Gender and Work project are studying what men and women did for a living in the Early Modern Swedish society (Ågren et al., 2011). In this project, researchers have found that the most important words in revealing this information are verbs such as *fishing*, *selling* etc. Instead of manually going through written sources from this time period, it is therefore assumed that an NLP tool that automatically searches through a number of historical documents and presents the contained verbs (and possibly their complements), would make the process of finding relevant text passages more effective.

A major challenge in developing language technology for historical text is that historical language often is under-resourced with regard to annotated data needed for training NLP tools. This problem is further aggravated by the fact that historical texts may refer to texts from a long period of time, during which language has changed. NLP tools trained on 13th century texts may thus not perform well on texts from the 18th century. Furthermore, historical language usually shows a substantial variation in spelling and grammar between different genres, different authors and even within the same text written by the same author, due to the lack of spelling conventions.

To deal with the limited resources and the high degree of spelling variation, one commonly applied approach is to automatically normalise the original spelling to a more modern spelling, before applying the NLP tools. This way, NLP tools available for the modern language may be used to analyse historical text. Even though there may be structural differences as well between historical and modern language, spelling is the most striking difference. Moreover, language technology tools such as taggers often to some degree rely on statistics on word form n-grams and token frequencies, implying that spelling modernisation is an important step for improving the performance of such tools when applied to historical text. This paper presents an evaluation of three approaches to spelling normalisation: 1) a filtering approach based on corpus data, 2) an approach based on Levenshtein edit distance, and 3) an approach implementing character-based statistical machine translation (SMT) techniques. These approaches have previously solely been evaluated in isolation, without comparison to each other, and for one or two languages only. We compare the results of the different methods in a multilingual evaluation including five languages, and we show that all three approaches have a positive impact on normalisation accuracy as compared to the baseline. There is no single method that yields the highest normalisation accuracy for all languages, but for four out of five languages within the scope of our study, the SMT-based approach gives the best results.

2 Related Work

Spelling normalisation of historical text has previously been approached using techniques such as dictionary lookup, edit distance calculations, and machine translation.

Rayson et al. (2005) tried an approach based on dictionary lookup, where a mapping scheme from historical to modern spelling for 16th to 19th century English texts was manually created, resulting in the VARD tool (VARiant Detector) comprising 45,805 entries. The performance of the normalisation tool was evaluated on a set of 17th century texts, and compared to the performance of modern spell checkers on the same text. The results showed that between a third and a half of all tokens (depending on which test text was used) were correctly normalised by both VARD and MS Word, whereas approximately one third of the tokens were correctly normalised only when using VARD. The percentage of tokens correctly normalised only by MS Word was substantially lower; approximately 6%. VARD was later further developed into VARD2, combining the original word list with data-driven techniques in the form of phonetic matching against a modern dictionary, and letter replacement rules based on common spelling variation patterns (Baron and Rayson, 2008).

Jurish (2008) argued that due to the lack of orthographic conventions, spelling generally reflects the phonetic form of the word to a higher degree in historical text. Furthermore, it is assumed that phonetic properties are less resistant to diachronic change than orthography. Accordingly, Jurish explored the idea of comparing the similarity between phonetic forms rather than orthographic forms. For grapheme-to-phoneme conversion, a module of the IMS German Festival text-to-speech system (Black and Taylor, 1997) was used, with a rule-set adapted to historical word forms. Evaluation was performed on a corpus of historical German verse quotations extracted from *Deutsches Wörterbuch*, containing 5,491,982 tokens (318,383 types). Without normalisation, approximately 84% of the tokens were recognised by a morphological analyser. After normalisation, 92% of the tokens were recognised. Adding lemma-based heuristics, coverage increased further to 94% of the tokens.

A Levenshtein similarity approach to normalisation was presented by Bollmann et al. (2011) for Early New High German, where Levenshtein-based normalisation rules were automatically derived from a word-aligned parallel corpus consisting of the Martin Luther Bible in its 1545 edition and its 1892 version, respectively. Using this normalisation technique, the proportion of words with a spelling identical to the modern spelling increased from 65% in the original text to 91% in the normalised text. This normalisation method was further evaluated by Bollmann (2013), comparing the performance of the RFTagger applied to historical text before and after normalisation. For every evaluation text, the tagger was trained on between 100 and 1,000 manually normalised tokens, and evaluated on the remaining tokens in the same text. For one manuscript from the 15th century, tagging accuracy was improved from approximately 29% to 78% using this method.

Another Levenshtein-based approach to normalisation was presented by Pettersson et al. (2013b), using context-sensitive, weighted edit distance calculations combined with compound splitting. This method requires no annotated historical training data, since normalisation candidates are extracted by Levenshtein comparisons between the original historical word form and present-day dictionary entries. However, if a corpus of manually normalised historical text is available, this can optionally be included for dictionary lookup and weighted Levenshtein calculations, improving precision. This technique was evaluated for Early Modern Swedish, and in the best setting, the proportion of words in the historical text with a spelling identical to the modern gold standard spelling increased from 64.6% to 86.9%.

Pettersson et al. (2013a) treated the normalisation task as a translation problem, using character-based SMT techniques in the spelling normalisation process. With the SMT-based approach, the proportion of tokens in the historical text with a spelling identical to the modern gold standard spelling increased from 64.6% to 92.3% for Early Modern Swedish, and from 64.8% to 83.9% for 15th century Icelandic. It was also shown that normalisation had a positive effect on subsequent tagging and parsing.

Language technology for historical text also has a lot in common with adaptation of NLP tools for handling present-day SMS messages and microblog text such as Twitter. In both genres there is a high degree of spelling variation, ad hoc abbreviations and ungrammatical structures imposing the problem of data sparseness. Similar methods for spelling normalisation may thus be used for both tasks. Han and Baldwin (2011) presented a method for normalising SMS and Twitter text based on morphophonemic similarity, combining lexical edit distance, phonemic edit distance, prefix substring, suffix substring, and the longest common subsequence. Context was taken into account by means of dependency structures generated by the Stanford Parser applied to a corpus of New York Times articles. In the best setting, a token-level F-score of 75.5% and 75.3% was reported for SMS messages and Twitter texts respectively.

3 Approaches

3.1 The Filtering Approach

The filtering approach presupposes access to a parallel training corpus of token pairs with historical word forms mapped to their modernised spelling. In the normalisation process, whenever a token is encountered that also occurred in the training data, the most frequent modern spelling associated with that token in the training corpus is chosen for normalisation. Other tokens are left unchanged.

3.2 The Levenshtein-based Approach

The Levenshtein-based approach was originally presented by Pettersson et al. (2013b). In its basic version, no historical training data is needed, which is an important aspect considering the common data sparseness issue, as discussed in Section 1. Instead, a modern language dictionary or corpus is required, from which normalisation candidates are extracted based on edit distance comparisons to the original historical word form. If there is parallel data available, i.e. the same text in its historical and its modernised spelling, this data can be used to make more reliable Levenshtein calculations by assigning weights lower than 1 to frequently occurring edits observed in the training data. The weights are then calculated by comparing the frequency of each edit occurring in the training corpus to the frequency with which the specific source characters are left unchanged, in accordance with the following formula:

$$\frac{\text{Frequency of Unchanged}}{\text{Frequency of Edit} + \text{Frequency of Unchanged}}$$

Context-sensitive weights are added to handle edits affecting more than one character. The context-sensitive weights are calculated by the same formula as the single-character weights, and include the following operations:

- double deletion: *person**ne**s* → *persons*
- double insertion: *strait* → *strai**gh**t*
- single-to-double substitution: *ju**g**e* → *ju**dg**e*
- double-to-single substitution: *m**oo**st* → *m**o**st*

For all historical word forms in the training corpus that are not identical in the modern spelling, all possible single-character edits as well as multi-character edits are counted for weighting. Hence, the historical word form *personnes*, mapped to the modern spelling *persons*, will yield weights for double-to-single deletion of *-ne*, as illustrated above, but also for single deletion of *-n* and single deletion of *-e*.

Finally, a tuning corpus is used to set a threshold for which maximum edit distance to allow between the original word form and its normalisation candidate(s). Based on the average edit distance between the historical word forms and their modern spelling in the tuning corpus, the threshold is calculated by the following formula (where 1.96 times the standard deviation is added to cover 95% of the cases):

$$\text{avg editdistance} + (1.96 * \text{standard deviation})$$

If several normalisation candidates have the same edit distance as compared to the source word, the most frequent candidate is chosen, based on modern corpus data. If none of the highest-ranked normalisation candidates are present in the corpus, or if there are several candidates with the same frequency distribution, a final candidate is randomly chosen.

3.3 The SMT-based Approach

In the SMT-based approach, originally presented by Pettersson et al. (2013a), spelling normalisation is treated as a translation task. To address changes in spelling rather than full translation of words and phrases, *character-based* translation (without lexical reordering) is performed, a well-known technique for transliteration and character-level translation between closely related languages (Matthews, 2007; Vilar et al., 2007; Nakov and Tiedemann, 2012). In character-level SMT, phrases are modeled as character sequences instead of word sequences, and translation models are trained on character-aligned parallel corpora whereas language models are trained on character N-grams.

Since the set of possible characters in a language is far more limited than the number of possible word forms, and the same corpus will present a larger quantity of character instances than token instances, only a rather small amount of parallel data is needed for training the translation models and the language models in character-based translation. Pettersson et al. (2013a) showed that with a training and tuning set of only 1,000 pairs of historical word forms mapped to modern spelling, a normalisation accuracy of 76.5% was achieved for Icelandic, as compared to 83.9% with a full-sized training corpus of 33,888 token pairs. Their full experiment on varying the size of the training data is illustrated in Figure 1.

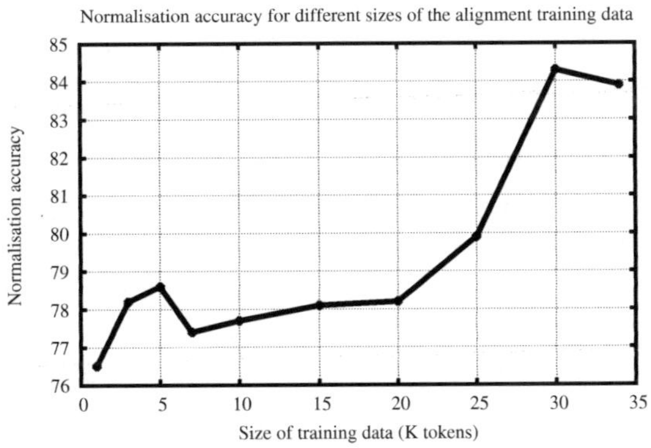

Figure 1: Normalisation accuracy when varying the size of the alignment training data.

We use the same set of training data for the SMT approach as for the filtering approach and for the assignment of weights in the Levenshtein-based approach, i.e. a set of token pairs mapping historical word forms to their manually modernised spelling. These corpora have the format of one token per line, with blank lines separating sentences. To fully adapt this format to the format needed for training the character-based translation models, the characters within each token are separated by space. The SMT system will now regard each character as a word, the full token as a sentence and the entire sentence as a section.

The SMT engine used is Moses with all its standard components. A phrase-based model is applied, where the feature weights are trained using MERT with BLEU over character-sequences as the objective function. The maximum size of a phrase (sequence of characters) is set to 10.

Two different character alignment techniques are tested: (i) the word alignment toolkit GIZA++ (Och and Ney, 2000), and (ii) a weighted finite state transducer implemented in the m2m-aligner (Jiampojamarn et al., 2007). GIZA is run with standard word alignment models for character unigrams and bigrams, whereas the m2m aligner implements transducer models based on context-independent single character and multi-character edit operations. The transducer is trained using EM on (unaligned) parallel training data, and the final model can then be used to produce a Viterbi alignment between given pairs of character strings.

An example is given in Figure 2, where the Icelandic word forms *meðr* $\rightarrow$ *meður* and *giallda* $\rightarrow$ *galda* have been aligned at a character-level using the m2m-aligner. In this example, the ϵ symbol represents empty alignments, meaning insertions or deletions. The ϵ symbol in the source word *meðr* denotes the insertion of *u* in the target word *meður*. Likewise, the ϵ symbol in the target word *galda* denotes the deletion of *i* as compared to the source word *giallda*. Furthermore, the alignment of *giallda* to *galda* illustrates the inclusion of multi-character edit operations, where the colon denotes a 2:1 alignment where both letters *l* and *d* in the source word correspond to the single letter *d* in the target word.

```
m|e|ð|ε|r|          m|e|ð|u|r|
g|i|a|l|l:d|a|      g|ε|a|l|d|a|
```

Figure 2: m2m character-level alignment.

4 Data

In the following, we will describe the data sets used for running the filtering approach, the Levenshtein edit distance approach, and the character-based SMT approach for historical spelling normalisation applied to five languages: English, German, Hungarian, Icelandic, and Swedish. For convenience, we use the notions of training, tuning and evaluation corpora, which are well-known concepts within SMT. These data sets have been created by extracting every 9th sentence from the total corpus to the tuning corpus, and every 10th sentence to the evaluation corpus, whereas the rest of the sentences have been extracted to a training corpus.[1]

In the filtering approach, there is in fact no distinction between training and tuning corpora, since both data sets are combined in the dictionary lookup process. As for the Levenshtein edit distance approach, the training corpus is used for extracting single-character and multi-character edits by comparing the historical word forms to their modern spelling. The edits extracted from the training corpus are then weighted based on their relative frequency in the tuning corpus.

The historical texts used for training and evaluation are required to be available both in their original, historical spelling and in a manually modernised and validated spelling. A modern translation of a historical text is generally not usable, since word order and sentence structure have to remain the same to enable training and evaluation of the proposed methods. The access to such data is very limited, meaning that the data sets used in our experiments vary in size, genres and time periods between the languages.

4.1 English

For training, tuning and evaluation in the English experiments, we use the *Innsbruck Corpus of English Letters*, a manually normalised collection of letters from the period 1386–1698. This corpus is a subset of the *Innsbruck Computer Archive of Machine-Readable English Texts*, ICAMET (Markus, 1999). A subset of the British National Corpus (BNC) is used as the single modern language resource both for the Levenshtein-based and for the SMT-based approach. Table 1 presents in more detail the data sets used in the English experiments.

Resource	Data	Tokens	Types
Training	ICAMET	148,852	18,267
Tuning	ICAMET	16,461	4,391
Evaluation	ICAMET	17,791	4,573
Lev. dict.	BNC	2,088,680	69,153
Lev. freq.	BNC	2,088,680	69,153
SMT lm	BNC	2,088,680	69,153

Table 1: Language resources for English.

4.2 German

For training, tuning and evaluation in the German experiments, we use a manually normalised subset of the *GerManC* corpus of German texts from the period 1650–1800 (Scheible et al., 2011). This subset contains 22 texts from the period 1659–1780, within the genres of drama, newspaper text, letters, sermons, narrative prose, humanities, science och legal documents. The German *Parole* corpus is used as the single modern language resource both for the Levenshtein-based and for the SMT-based approach (Teubert (ed.), 2003). Table 2 presents in more detail the data sets used in the German experiments.

Resource	Data	Tokens	Types
Training	GerManC	39,887	9,055
Tuning	GerManC	5,418	2,056
Evaluation	GerManC	5,005	1,966
Lev. dict.	Parole	18,662,243	662,510
Lev. freq.	Parole	18,662,243	662,510
SMT lm	Parole	18,662,243	662,510

Table 2: Language resources for German.

4.3 Hungarian

For training, tuning and evaluation in the Hungarian experiments, we use a collection of manually normalised codices from the *Hungarian Generative Diachronic Syntax* project, HGDS (Simon, To appear), in total 11 codices from the time period 1440–1541. The Szeged Treebank is used as the single modern language resource both for the Levenshtein-based and for the SMT-based approach (Csendes et al., 2005). Table 3 presents in more detail the data sets used in the Hungarian experiments.

Resource	Data	Tokens	Types
Training	HGDS	137,669	45,529
Tuning	HGDS	17 181	8 827
Evaluation	HGDS	17,214	8,798
Lev. dict.	Szeged	1,257,089	144,248
Lev. freq.	Szeged	1,257,089	144,248
SMT lm	Szeged	1,257,089	144,248

Table 3: Language resources for Hungarian.

[1] For information on how to access the data sets used in our experiments, please contact the authors.

4.4 Icelandic

For training, tuning and evaluation in the Icelandic experiments, we use a manually normalised subset of the *Icelandic Parsed Historical Corpus* (IcePaHC), a manually tagged and parsed diachronic corpus of texts from the time period 1150–2008 (Rögnvaldsson et al., 2012). This subset contains four texts from the 15th century: three sagas (*Vilhjálm's saga*, *Jarlmann's saga*, and *Ector's saga*) and one narrative-religious text (*Miðaldaævintýri*). As a dictionary for Levenshtein calculations we use a combination of *Beygingarlýsing Íslensks Nútímamáls*, BÍN (a database of modern Icelandic inflectional forms (Bjarnadóttir, 2012)), and all tokens occurring 100 times or more in the *Tagged Icelandic Corpus of Contemporary Icelandic texts*, MÍM (Helgadóttir et al., 2012).[2] The frequency-based choice of a final normalisation candidate in the Levenshtein approach, as well as the training of a language model in the SMT approach, are done on all tokens occurring 100 times or more in the MÍM corpus. Table 4 presents in more detail the data sets used in the Icelandic experiments.

Resource	Data	Tokens	Types
Training	IcePaHC	52,440	9,748
Tuning	IcePaHC	6,443	2,270
Evaluation	IcePaHC	6,384	2,244
Lev. dict.	BÍN+MÍM	27,224,798	2,820,623
Lev. freq.	MÍM	21,339,384	9,461
SMT lm	MÍM	21,339,384	9,461

Table 4: Language resources for Icelandic.

4.5 Swedish

For training, tuning and evaluation in the Swedish experiments, we use balanced subsets of the Gender and Work corpus (GaW) of court records and church documents from the time period 1527–1812 (Ågren et al., 2011). As a dictionary for Levenshtein calculations we use SALDO, a lexical resource developed for present-day written Swedish (Borin et al., 2008). For frequency-based choice of a final normalisation candidate, we use the Stockholm Umeå corpus (SUC) of text representative of the Swedish language in the 1990s (Ejerhed and Källgren, 1997). The SUC corpus is also used to train a language model in the SMT-based approach. Table 5 presents in more detail the data sets used in the Swedish experiments.

Resource	Data	Tokens	Types
Training	GaW	28,237	7,925
Tuning	GaW	2,590	1,260
Evaluation	GaW	33,544	8,859
Lev. dict.	SALDO	1,110,731	723,138
Lev. freq.	SUC	1,166,593	97,670
SMT lm	SUC	1,166,593	97,670

Table 5: Language resources for Swedish.

5 Results

Table 6 presents the results for different languages and normalisation methods, given in terms of *normalisation accuracy*, i.e. the percentage of tokens in the normalised text with a spelling identical to the manually modernised gold standard, and *character error rate (CER)*, providing a more precise estimation of the similarity between the normalised token and the gold standard version at a character level. Table 7 summarises the results in terms of *Precision (Pre)*, *Recall (Rec)* and *F-score (F)* for the filtering approach, the Levenshtein-based approach (with and without filtering), and the best-performing SMT-based approach.

For the Levenshtein experiments, we have used context-sensitive weights, as described in Section 3.2. In the SMT approach, we run GIZA with standard word alignment models for character unigrams (un) and bigrams (bi). The m2m aligner is implemented with single character edit operations (1:1) and multi-character operations (2:2).

The baseline case shows the proportion of tokens in the original, historical text that already have a spelling identical to the modern gold standard spelling. In the Hungarian text, only 17.1% of the historial tokens have a modern spelling, with a character error rate of 0.85. For German on the other hand, accuracy is as high as 84.4%, with a character error rate of only 0.16. At a first glance, the historical spelling in the Hungarian corpus appears to be very similar to the modern spelling. A closer look however reveals recurrent differences involving single letter substitutions and/or the use of accents, as for *fiayval* → *fiaival*, *mèghalanac* → *meghalának* and *hazaba* → *házába*.

[2] The BÍN database alone is not sufficient for Levenshtein calculations, since it only contains content words.

	English		German		Hungarian		Icelandic		Swedish	
	Acc	CER	Acc	CER	Acc	CER	Acc	CER	Acc	CER
baseline	75.8	0.26	84.4	0.16	17.1	0.85	50.5	0.51	64.6	0.36
filter	91.7	0.20	94.6	0.26	75.0	0.30	81.7	0.25	86.2	0.27
Lev	82.9	0.19	87.3	0.13	31.7	0.71	67.3	0.35	79.4	0.22
Lev+filter	92.9	0.09	95.1	0.06	76.4	0.35	84.6	0.19	90.8	0.10
giza un	94.3	0.07	96.6	0.04	79.9	0.21	71.8	0.30	92.9	0.07
giza bi	92.4	0.09	95.5	0.05	80.1	0.21	71.5	0.30	92.5	0.08
m2m 1:1 un	90.6	0.11	96.0	0.04	79.4	0.21	71.2	0.31	92.3	0.08
m2m 1:1 bi	88.0	0.14	95.6	0.05	79.5	0.21	71.5	0.30	92.2	0.08
m2m 2:2 un	90.7	0.11	96.4	0.04	77.3	0.24	71.0	0.31	91.3	0.09
m2m 2:2 bi	87.5	0.14	95.5	0.05	79.1	0.22	71.4	0.31	92.1	0.08

Table 6: Normalisation results given in accuracy (Acc) and character error rate (CER).

	English			German			Hungarian			Icelandic			Swedish		
	Pre	Rec	F	Pre	Rec	F	Pre	Rec	F	Pre	Rec	F	Pre	Rec	F
filter	93.6	97.8	95.7	95.0	99.6	97.2	77.4	96.0	85.7	89.3	90.6	89.9	87.5	98.3	92.6
Lev	92.7	88.6	90.7	91.0	95.6	93.2	68.0	37.3	48.2	85.4	76.1	80.5	90.5	86.6	88.5
Lev+filter	97.4	95.2	96.3	97.3	97.7	97.5	96.2	78.8	86.7	95.6	88.0	91.7	96.6	93.8	95.2
SMT	98.2	95.9	97.0	98.7	97.9	98.3	98.3	81.3	89.0	82.0	85.2	83.6	98.6	94.1	96.3

Table 7: Normalisation results given in precision (Pre), recall (Rec) and F-score (F).

The Icelandic corpus also has a relatively low number of tokens with a spelling identical to the modern spelling. Even though the Hungarian and Icelandic texts are older than the English, German, and Swedish texts, the rather low proportion of tokens with a modern spelling in the Icelandic corpus is rather surprising, since the Icelandic language is generally seen as conservative in spelling. A closer inspection of the Icelandic corpus reveals the same kind of subtle single letter divergences and differences in the use of accents as for Hungarian, e.g. *ad* → *að* and *hun* → *hún*.

The simplistic filtering approach (filter), relying solely on previously seen tokens in the training data, captures frequently occurring word forms and works surprisingly well, improving normalisation accuracy by up to 63 percentage units. The Levenshtein-based approach (Lev) in its basic version, with no parallel training data available, also improves normalisation accuracy as compared to the baseline. However, for all languages, the simplistic filtering approach yields significantly higher normalisation accuracy than the more sophisticated Levenshtein-based approach does. This could be partly explained by the fact that frequently occurring word forms have a high chance of being captured by the filtering approach, whereas the Levenshtein-based approach runs the risk of consistently normalising high-frequent word forms incorrectly. For example, in the English Levenshtein normalisation process, the high-frequent word form *stonde* has consistently been normalised to *stone* instead of *stand*, due to the larger edit distance between *stonde* and *stand*. The even more common word form *ben*, which should optimally be normalised to *been*, has consistently been left unchanged as *ben*, since the BNC corpus, which is used for dictionary lookup in the English setup, contains the proper name *Ben*. The issue of proper names would not be a problem if a modern dictionary were used for Levenshtein comparisons instead of a corpus, or if casing was taken into account in the Levenshtein comparisons. There would however still be cases left like *stonde* being incorrectly normalised to *stone* as described above, which would be disadvantageous to the Levenshtein-based method. The low recall figures, especially for Hungarian, also indicates that there may be old word forms that are not present in modern dictionaries and thus are out of reach for the Levenshtein-based method, as for the previously discussed Hungarian word form *meghalának*.

In the Lev+filter setting, the filter is used as a first step in the normalisation process. Only tokens that could not be matched through dictionary lookup based on the training corpus are normalised by Levenshtein comparisons. The idea is that combining these two techniques would perform better than one approach only, since high-frequent word forms are consistently normalised correctly by the filter, whereas previously unseen tokens are handled through Levenshtein comparisons. This combination does indeed perform better for all languages, and for Icelandic this is by far the most successful normalisation method of all.

For the SMT-based approach, it is interesting to note that the simple unigram models in many cases perform better than the more advanced bigram and multi-character models. We also tried adding the filter to the SMT approach, so that only tokens that could not be matched through dictionary lookup based on the training corpus, would be considered for normalisation by the SMT model. This did however not have a positive effect on normalisation accuracy, probably because the training data has already been taken care of by the SMT model, so adding the filter only led to redundant information and incorrect matches, deteriorating the results. For four out of five languages, the GIZA unigram setting yields the highest normalisation accuracy of all SMT models evaluated. For Hungarian, the GIZA bigram modell performs marginally better than the unigram model.

From the presented results, it is not obvious which normalisation approach to choose for a new language. For Icelandic, the Levenshtein-based approach combined with the filter leads to the highest normalisation accuracy. For the rest of the languages, the SMT-based approach with the GIZA unigram or bigram setting gives the best results. Generally, the Levenshtein-based method could be used for languages lacking access to annotated historical data with information on both original and modernised spelling. If, on the other hand, such data is available, the filtering approach, or the combination of filtering and Levenshtein calculations, would be likely to improve normalisation accuracy. Moreover, the effort of training a character-based SMT system for normalisation would be likely to further improve the results.

It would be interesting to also compare the results between the languages, in a language evolution perspective. This is however not feasible within the scope of this study, due to the differences in corpus size, genres and covered time periods, as discussed in Section 4.

6 Conclusion

We have performed a multilingual evaluation of three approaches to spelling modernisation of historical text: a simplistic filtering model, a Levenshtein-based approach and a character-based statistical machine translation method. The results were evaluated on historical texts from five languages: English, German, Hungarian, Icelandic and Swedish. We see that all approaches are successful in increasing the proportion of tokens in the historical text with a spelling identical to the modernised gold standard spelling. We conclude that the proposed methods have the potential of enabling us to use modern NLP tools for analysing historical texts. Which approach to choose is not clear, since the results vary for the different languages in our study, even though the SMT-based approach generally works best. If no historical training data is available, the Levenshtein-based approach could still be used, since only a modern dictionary is required for edit distance comparisons. If there is a corpus of token pairs with historical and modern spelling available, training an SMT model could however result in improved normalisation accuracy. Since the SMT models are character-based, only a rather small amount of training data is needed for this task, as discussed in Section 3.3.

We believe that our results would be of interest to several research fields. From a language evolution perspective, future research would include a thorough investigation of why certain approaches work better for some languages but not for other languages, and what the results would be if the data sets for the different languages were more similar with regard to time period, size, genre etc. The latter could however be problematic, due to data sparseness. For historians interested in using modern NLP tools for analysing historical text, an extrinsic evaluation is called for, comparing the results of tagging and parsing using modern tools, before and after spelling normalisation. Finally, the proposed methods all treat words in isolation in the normalisation process. From a language technology perspective, it would be interesting to also explore ways of handling grammatical and structural differences between historical and modern language as part of the normalisation process. This would be particularly interesting when evaluating subsequent tagging and parsing performance.

References

Maria Ågren, Rosemarie Fiebranz, Erik Lindberg, and Jonas Lindström. 2011. Making verbs count. The research project 'Gender and Work' and its methodology. *Scandinavian Economic History Review*, 59(3):271–291. Forthcoming.

Alistair Baron and Paul Rayson. 2008. Vard2: A tool for dealing with spelling variation in historical corpora. In *Postgraduate Conference in Corpus Linguistics*, Aston University, Birmingham.

Kristín Bjarnadóttir. 2012. The Database of Modern Icelandic Inflection. In *AfLaT2012/SALTMIL joint workshop on Language technology for normalisation of less-resourced languages*, Istanbul, May.

Alan W. Black and Paul Taylor. 1997. Festival speech synthesis system: system documentation. Technical report, University of Edinburgh, Centre for Speech Technology Research.

Marcel Bollmann, Florian Petran, and Stefanie Dipper. 2011. Rule-based normalization of historical texts. In *Proceedings of the Workshop on Language Technologies for Digital Humanities and Cultural Heritage*, pages 34–42, Hissar, Bulgaria.

Marcel Bollmann. 2013. POS tagging for historical texts with sparse training data. In *Proceedings of the 7th Linguistic Annotation Workshop & Interoperability with Discourse*, pages 11–18, Sofia, Bulgaria, August. Association for Computational Linguistics.

Lars Borin, Markus Forsberg, and Lennart Lönngren. 2008. Saldo 1.0 (svenskt associationslexikon version 2). Språkbanken, University of Gothenburg.

C. Csendes, J. Csirik, T. Gyimóthy, and A. Kocsor. 2005. The Szeged Treebank. In *Proceedings of the Eighth International Conference on Text, Speech and Dialogue (TSD 2005)*, Karlovy Vary, Czech Republic.

Eva Ejerhed and Gunnel Källgren. 1997. Stockholm Umeå Corpus. Version 1.0. Produced by Department of Linguistics, Umeå University and Department of Linguistics, Stockholm University. ISBN 91-7191-348-3.

Bo Han and Timothy Baldwin. 2011. Lexical normalisation of short text messages: Makn sens a #twitter. In Association for Computational Linguistics, editor, *Proceedings of the 49th Annual Meeting of the Association for Computational Linguistics*, pages 368–378, Portland, Oregon, USA, June.

Sigrún Helgadóttir, Ásta Svavarsdóttir, Eiríkur Rögnvaldsson, Kristín Bjarnadóttir, and Hrafn Loftsson. 2012. The Tagged Icelandic Corpus (MÍM). In *Proceedings of the Workshop on Language Technology for Normalisation of Less-Resourced Languages*, pages 67–72.

Sittichai Jiampojamarn, Grzegorz Kondrak, and Tarek Sherif. 2007. Applying many-to-many alignments and hidden markov models to letter-to-phoneme conversion. In *Proceedings of the Annual Conference of the North American Chapter of the Association for Computational Linguistics (NAACL-HLT 2007)*, pages 372–379, Rochester, NY, April.

Bryan Jurish. 2008. Finding canonical forms for historical German text. In Angelika Storrer, Alexander Geyken, Alexander Siebert, and Kay-Michael Würzner, editors, *Text Resources and Lexical Knowledge: Selected Papers from the 9th Conference on Natural Language Processing* (KONVENS 2008), pages 27–37. Mouton de Gruyter, Berlin.

Manfred Markus, 1999. *Manual of ICAMET (Innsbruck Computer Archive of Machine-Readable English Texts).* Leopold-Franzens-Universität Innsbruck.

David Matthews. 2007. Machine transliteration of proper names. Master's thesis, School of Informatics.

Preslav Nakov and Jörg Tiedemann. 2012. Combining word-level and character-level models for machine translation between closely-related languages. In *Proceedings of the 50th Annual Meeting of the Association for Computational Linguistics (Volume 2: Short Papers)*, pages 301–305, Jeju Island, Korea, July. Association for Computational Linguistics.

F. J. Och and H. Ney. 2000. Improved statistical alignment models. pages 440–447, Hongkong, China, October.

Eva Pettersson, Beáta Megyesi, and Tiedemann Jörg. 2013a. An SMT approach to automatic annotation of historical text. In *Proceedings of the NoDaLiDa 2013 workshop on Computational Historical Linguistics*, May.

Eva Pettersson, Beáta Megyesi, and Joakim Nivre. 2013b. Normalisation of historical text using context-sensitive weighted Levenshtein distance and compound splitting. In *Proceedings of the 19th Nordic Conference on Computational Linguistics (NoDaLiDa)*, May.

Paul Rayson, Dawn Archer, and Nicholas Smith. 2005. VARD versus Word – A comparison of the UCREL variant detector and modern spell checkers on English historical corpora. In *Proceedings from the Corpus Linguistics Conference Series on-line e-journal*, volume 1, Birmingham, UK, July.

Eiríkur Rögnvaldsson, Anton Karl Ingason, Einar Freyr Sigurdsson, and Joel Wallenberg. 2012. The Icelandic Parsed Historical Corpus (IcePaHC). In *Proceedings of the Eight International Conference on Language Resources and Evaluation (LREC'12)*, Istanbul, Turkey, May. European Language Resources Association (ELRA).

Silke Scheible, Richard J. Whitt, Martin Durrell, and Paul Bennett. 2011. A Gold Standard Corpus of Early Modern German. In *Proceedings of the 5th Linguistic Annotation Workshop*, pages 124–128, Portland, Oregon, USA, June. Association for Computational Linguistics.

Eszter Simon. To appear. Corpus building from Old Hungarian codices. In Katalin É. Kiss, editor, *The Evolution of Functional Left Peripheries in Hungarian Syntax*. Oxford University Press.

Wolfgang Teubert (ed.). 2003. German Parole Corpus. Electronic resource, Oxford Text Archive.

David Vilar, Jan-Thorsten Peter, and Hermann Ney. 2007. Can we translate letters? In *Proceedings of the Second Workshop on Statistical Machine Translation*, pages 33–39, Prague, Czech Republic, June. Association for Computational Linguistics.

Enhancing the possibilities of corpus-based investigations: Word sense disambiguation on query results of large text corpora

Christian Poelitz
Technical University Dortmund
Artificial Intelligence Group
44227 Dortmund, Germany
poelitz@tu-dortmund.de

Thomas Bartz
Technical University Dortmund
Institute of German Language and Literature
44227 Dortmund, Germany
bartz@tu-dortmund.de

Abstract

Common large digital text corpora do not distinguish between different meanings of word forms, intense manual effort has to be done for disambiguation tasks when querying for homonyms or polysemes. To improve this situation, we ran experiments with automatic word sense disambiguation methods operating directly on the output of the corpus query. In this paper, we present experiments with topic models to cluster search result snippets in order to separate occurrences of homonymous or polysemous queried words by their meanings.

1 Introduction

Large digital text corpora contain text documents from different sources, genres and periods of time as well as often structural and linguistic markups. Nowadays, they provide novel and enhanced possibilities of exploring research questions at the basis of authentic language usage not only in the field of linguistics, but for humanities and social sciences in general. But even though tools for query and analysis are getting more and more flexible and sophisticated (not least thanks to the efforts been done in infrastructure projects like CLARIN), automatically obtained data have to be reviewed manually in most cases because of false positives. Depending on the amount of data, intense manual effort has to be done for cleaning, classification or disambiguation tasks. Hence, many research questions cannot be addressed because of time constraints (Storrer, 2011). A project funded by the German BMBF (Bundesministerium für Bildung und Forschung, "Federal Ministry of Education and Research"), therefore, is investigating benefits and issues of using machine learning technology in order to perform these tasks automatically. In this paper, we focus on the disambiguation task, which is an issue known for a long time in the field of corpus-based lexicography (Engelberg and Lemnitzer, 2009), but has not been satisfactorily solved, yet, and is still highly relevant also to social scientists or historians. In the humanities, researchers usually are not examining word forms, but terms representing relations of word forms and their meanings. While the common large corpora do not distinguish between different meanings of word forms, the disambiguation task has to be carried out manually most of the times. To improve this situation, we ran experiments with word sense disambiguation methods operating directly on the output of the corpus queries, i.e. search result lists containing small snippets with the occurrences of the search keyword, each in a context of about only three sentences. In particular, we used topic modelling to automatically detect clusters of keyword occurrences with similar contexts, that we consider corresponding to a certain meaning of the keyword. In the following, we report our findings from experiments with the German terms *Leiter* and *zeitnah*, both supposed to provide interesting insights into processes of language change. *Der Leiter* "chief", "director" and *die Leiter* "ladder" are homonyms with possible further senses *Energieleiter* "conducting medium" and *Tonleiter* "scale" (in music), whereby *der Leiter* competes against borrowings like *Boss* or *Chef*. *Zeitnah*, a polyseme meaning *zeitgenssisch* "contemporary", *zeitkritisch* "critical of the times" as well as *unverzglich* "prompt", seems to have acquired the latter meaning as a new sense not until the second half of the last century. The basis of our experiments are search result lists derived from the DWDS Kernkorpus core corpus of the 20th century (for *Leiter*) and, in addition, from the ZEIT corpus (for *zeitnah*). The DWDS Kernkorpus, constructed at the Berlin-Brandenburg Academy of Sciences (BBAW), contains approximately 100 million running words, balanced chronologically (over the decades of the 20th century) and by text genre (over the genres journalism, literary texts, scientific literature and other nonfiction; (Geyken, 2007)). The ZEIT corpus covers all the issues of the German weekly newspaper *Die Zeit* from 1946 to 2009, approximately 460 million running words (http://www.dwds.de/ressourcen/korpora).

2 Related Work

Word sense disambiguation is a well studied problem in Machine Learning and Natural Language Processing. For a given word, later mentioned as word of interest, we expect that there exist several meanings. The differences in the meanings are reflected by different words occurring and frequencies together with the word to be disambiguated. A very early statistical approach was proposed by (Brown et al., 1991). The authors proposed to estimate the probability distribution of senses for given words from annotated examples. A general survey about the topic can be found in (Navigli, 2009). Latent Dirichlet Allocation (LDA) introduced by (Blei et al., 2003) can be used to estimate topic distributions for a given document corpus. Each topic represent a sense in which the documents, respectively the words, appear. (Griffiths and Steyvers, 2004) proposed efficient training for LDA using Monte Carlo sampling. They used Gibbs sampling to estimate the topic distribution. The authors in (Brody and Lapata, 2009) extend the generative model by LDA by many parallel feature representations. Hence, beside the pure words, additional features like part of speech tags can be used. Further, the authors perform analysis with different context sizes. Investigations of word sense disambiguation on small snippets have been done before on search engine results. The snippets retrieved after a query has been sent to a search engine are used for disambiguation. In (Navigli and Crisafulli, 2010) for instance, the authors search for word senses of web search results using retrieved snippets.

Our approach differs from these previous ones since we concentrate on snippets from a text corpus for linguistic and lexicographic research purposes (see Section 1). Unlike results from search engines, that refer to documents whose topics are strongly related to the search keyword, result lists from text corpora contain snippets with occurrences of the keyword in each document of the corpus, irrespective of the document topic. That is why keywords can occur in less typical, semantically less definite contexts. In the literary documents, they are not infrequently used as metaphors.

3 Snippet Representation

In order to properly apply Machine Learning methods for word sense disambiguation we need to encode the snippets in an appropriate way. Therefore, we represent each snippet as bag-of-words. This means we build a large vector that contains at the component i the number of times word i - from the overall vocabulary of the document corpus - appears in the snippet. These vectors are very sparse and can be efficiently saved as hash tables.

Since we want to investigate different context information for the disambiguation, we generate for each snippet many different bag-of-words representations. First, we use only those words that appear in close proximity to the word we want to disambiguate. This means, we place a window on the text, that contains a certain number of words that appear before and after the word of interest. Next, we filter out words that are not immediate constituents (or immediate constituents of the 1st, 2nd, nth superordinate node) of the word of interest. In this case the proximity is not crucial but the syntactical relatedness to the word of interest.

These word vectors are used for the word sense disambiguation.

4 Disambiguation

For the word sense disambiguation we use Latent Dirichlet Allocation (LDA) as introduced by (Blei et al., 2003). LDA estimates the probability distributions of words and documents, respectively snippet, over a number of different topics. The topics will be used to disambiguate the word of interest. These distributions are drawn from Dirichlet distributions that depend on given meta parameters α and β.

The probability of a topic, given a snippet is modelled as Multinomial distribution that depends on a Dirichlet distributed distribution of the snippets over the topics. Formally we have: $\phi \sim Dirichlet(\beta)$ the probability distribution of a snippet and $p(z_i|\phi(j)) \sim Multi(\phi(j))$ the probability of topic z_i for a given snippet j.

To estimate the distributions we use a Gibbs

Leiter	w10	w40	w80	all	syntax
NMI	0.2086	0.2579	0.2414	0.2573	0.1944
zeitnah	w10	w40	w80	all	syntax
NMI	0.1012	0.1926	0.1656	0.2230	0.0456

Table 1: NMI of the extracted senses with respect to the given annotations of the text snippets.

Leiter	w10	w40	w80	all	syntax
F1	0.7271	0.7487	0.7405	0.7416	0.6904
zeitnah	w10	w40	w80	all	syntax
F1	0.7773	0.6919	0.7630	0.7488	0.4584

Table 2: F1 score of the extracted senses with respect to the given annotations of the text snippets.

sampler as proposed by (Griffiths and Steyvers, 2004). The Gibbs sampler models the probability distributions of a given topic z_i, depending on all other topics and the words in the snippet as Markov chain. This Markov chain converges to the posterior distribution of the topics given the words in a certain snippet. This posterior can be used to estimate the most likely topic for a given snippet.

Further, we use the author topic model as introduced by (Steyvers et al., 2004). This model integrates additional indications about the author for each snippet into the topic modelling process. This method can also be used to model the text categories instead of authors. We simply treat the categories as the authors. Now, the probability distribution of the topics additionally depends on the random variable c over the categories. This can be leveraged to estimate the probability of category c for a given topic z_i, hence $p(c|z_i)$.

Using the author topic model, we estimate the topic distribution over words and categories. Based on these distributions the stochastic process of generating topics is simulated. Depending on the number of times a topic is drawn for a given snippet and category, we extract the most likely words and categories for the topics. The topics represent the different senses of the word of interest.

5 Experiments

We performed experiments on two data sets that consist of short snippets retrieved by corpus queries for the words *Leiter* and *zeitnah* in the DWDS Kernkorpus `www.dwds.de` and the ZEIT corpus (see Section 1). Each snippet consists of the three sentences, whereby the second sentence contains the search keyword (the word to disambiguate) in each case. The snippets belong to the different text categories covered by the mentioned corpora: journalism, literary texts, scientific literature and other nonfiction (see Section 1). For each snippet, we have information to which category it belongs to. This information is used only for validation, not for the topic extraction. For each data set, 30 percent of snippets were disambiguated manually by two independent annotators, whereby doubtful cases were clarified by a third person. The annotations are not used for disambiguation, but for the validation of the method.

For each snippet we generate bag-of-words vectors using contexts of 10, 40, 80 or all words around the word of interest. Hence, for context size 10 we use the ten words before the token, the token itself and the ten following tokens, as representation of the snippet. For further experiments we used the Stanford Constituent Parser (Klein and Manning, 2003) to get only the words that syntactically depend on the words of interest. For the extraction of the topics and distribution over the text categories we used the Gibbs sampler for LDA and the author topic model from the Matlab library Topictoolbox (Griffiths and Steyvers, 2004).

Based on the annotation mentioned above we can estimate the Normalized Mutual Information (NMI) as score for the goodness of the method. NMI measures how many snippets that are annotated as being from different topics are placed into the same topic based on the extracted topics from LDA. It is defined as the fraction of the sum of the entropies of the distributions of the annotations and the disambiguation results, and the entropy of the joint distribution of annotations and results (Manning et al., 2008) (p. 357f). Further, we use one of the standard measures to estimate the goodness of a word sense disambiguation result, the F1 score. The F1 score is the weighted average of the precision and recall of the disambiguation results for the given annotations. This and further evaluation methods are described in (Navigli and Vannella, 2013).

In the Tables 1 and 2 we show the NMI and F1 score for the extracted topics, respectively senses, by LDA. We tested different context sizes from 10 to 80 words around the word of interest. Compared to the results when we use the whole snippets, we see that a context size of 40 results in the

Sense 1	Sense 2	Sense 3	Sense 4
music	standing	GDR [1]	government
Berlin	saw	SED [2]	got
Prof	up	party	Berlin
Comp	above	political	ZK [3]

Table 3: Translation of the most frequent words for each of the extracted senses for the word *Leiter*.

Sense 1	Sense 2	Sense 3	Sense 4
question	society	German	publisher
DM [4]	just	time	book
years	examples	film	literature
music	questions	Berlin	year

Table 4: Translation of the most frequent words for each of the extracted senses for the word *zeitnah*.

best performance. Less context decrease the performance and the filtering by constituencies give the worst results. The experiments show that a windowing approach is well suited to represent documents for a word sense disambiguation task. The size of the window seems to be crucial and must be chosen a priori. Optimal window size could be found by cross validation techniques using annotated snippets.

Next, we investigated the distribution of the topics over the text categories. We used the author topic model as described above to estimate how the categories distribute over the sense. Tables 3 and 4 show the most likely words to appear in the corresponding senses translated into English for four extracted topics. In the Tables 5 and 6 the distribution of the senses over the given categories are presented. Based on the posterior distribution of the categories, we simulated the process of assigning topics to categories for each word in the snippets. In the tables we present the number of times we assign sense i to category c.

For the word *Leiter* in Table 5, we see that in each category always one certain sense for the word is prominent. For instance sense 2, here

Leiter	Sense 1	Sense 2	Sense 3	Sense 4
Literature	597	23818	7464	6718
Non-fiction	3031	5295	63708	8733
Science	41564	3269	1216	1046
Journalism	5527	8845	23104	78645

Table 5: The distribution of the senses among the text categories during the simulation for the word *Leiter*.

zeitnah	Sense 1	Sense 2	Sense 3	Sense 4
Literature	23	0	12	6
Non-fiction	1	0	574	10
Science	211	0	478	1
Journalism	2150	2438	1691	2924

Table 6: The distribution of the senses among the text categories during the simulation for the word *zeitnah*.

Leiter appears in the context of a ladder. In this context, the word is more likely to appear in a fictional text than in the other categories. For *zeitnah* in Table 6 the results are not very clear. First, the word is most likely to appear in news papers rather than in literature or science articles. This is due to the fact that we have much more snippets from news papers. Only in sense 3, the word is also likely to appear in other categories. This context seems to be German films. In contrast, we see sense 2 that is about social questions appears only in news papers.

6 Conclusion and Future Work

We used topic models to cluster search result snippets received by queries in two large digital text corpora in order to separate occurrences of homonymous or polysemous queried words by their meanings. We showed that LDA performs well in extracting the senses in which the words appear. Finally, we found that the author topic model can be used to estimate how the extracted senses distribute over document categories.

For the future, we want to further investigate the distribution of the topics over different categories and time periods, as first experiments showed potential benefit of the author topic model. An important point for future work is, moreover, the integration of syntactic features not only for filtering important words but also for enhancement of our simple bag-of-words representation. Especially, the integration of constituency and dependency information will be further investigated.

Aknowledgements

The authors are supported by the Bundesministerium für Bildung und Forschung (BMBF) in project KobRA[5].

[5]http://www.kobra.tu-dortmund.de/

References

David M. Blei, Andrew Y. Ng, and Michael I. Jordan. 2003. Latent dirichlet allocation. *J. Mach. Learn. Res.*, 3:993–1022, March.

Samuel Brody and Mirella Lapata. 2009. Bayesian word sense induction. In *Proceedings of the 12th Conference of the European Chapter of the Association for Computational Linguistics*, EACL '09, pages 103–111, Stroudsburg, PA, USA. Association for Computational Linguistics.

Peter F. Brown, Stephen A. Della Pietra, Vincent J. Della Pietra, and Robert L. Mercer. 1991. Word-sense disambiguation using statistical methods. In *Proceedings of the 29th Annual Meeting on Association for Computational Linguistics*, ACL '91, pages 264–270, Stroudsburg, PA, USA. Association for Computational Linguistics.

Stefan Engelberg and Lothar Lemnitzer. 2009. *Lexikographie und Woerterbuchbenutzung*. Stauffenburg, Tuebingen.

Alexander Geyken. 2007. The DWDS corpus. A reference corpus for the German language of the twentieth century. In Christiane Fellbaum, editor, *Idioms and collocations. corpus-based linguistic and lexicographic studies*, pages 23–40. Continuum, London.

T. L. Griffiths and M. Steyvers. 2004. Finding scientific topics. *Proceedings of the National Academy of Sciences*, 101(Suppl. 1):5228–5235, April.

Dan Klein and Christopher D. Manning. 2003. Accurate unlexicalized parsing. In *Proceedings of the 41st Annual Meeting on Association for Computational Linguistics - Volume 1*, ACL '03, pages 423–430, Stroudsburg, PA, USA. Association for Computational Linguistics.

Christopher D. Manning, Prabhakar Raghavan, and Hinrich Schütze. 2008. *Introduction to Information Retrieval*. Cambridge University Press, New York, NY, USA.

Roberto Navigli and Giuseppe Crisafulli. 2010. Inducing word senses to improve web search result clustering. In *Proceedings of the 2010 Conference on Empirical Methods in Natural Language Processing*, EMNLP '10, pages 116–126, Stroudsburg, PA, USA. Association for Computational Linguistics.

Roberto Navigli and Daniele Vannella. 2013. Semeval-2013 task 11: Word sense induction and disambiguation within an end-user application. In *Second Joint Conference on Lexical and Computational Semantics (*SEM), Volume 2: Proceedings of the Seventh International Workshop on Semantic Evaluation (SemEval 2013)*, pages 193–201, Atlanta, Georgia, USA, June. Association for Computational Linguistics.

Roberto Navigli. 2009. Word sense disambiguation: A survey. *ACM Comput. Surv.*, 41(2):10:1–10:69, February.

Mark Steyvers, Padhraic Smyth, Michal Rosen-Zvi, and Thomas Griffiths. 2004. Probabilistic author-topic models for information discovery. In *Proceedings of the Tenth ACM SIGKDD International Conference on Knowledge Discovery and Data Mining*, KDD '04, pages 306–315, New York, NY, USA. ACM.

Angelika Storrer. 2011. Korpusgesttzte sprachanalyse in lexikographie und phraseologie. In Karlfried Knapp et al., editor, *Angewandte Linguistik. Ein Lehrbuch*, pages 216–239. Francke Verlag, Tuebingen.

A Hybrid Disambiguation Measure for Inaccurate Cultural Heritage Data

Julia Efremova[1], **Bijan Ranjbar-Sahraei**[2], **Toon Calders**[1,3]
[1]Eindhoven University of Technology, The Netherlands
[2]Maastricht University, The Netherlands
[3]Université Libre de Bruxelles, Belgium
i.efremova@tue.nl, b.ranjbarsahraei@maastrichtuniversity.nl,
toon.calders@ulb.ac.be

Abstract

Cultural heritage data is always associated with inaccurate information and different types of ambiguities. For instance, names of persons, occupations or places mentioned in historical documents are not standardized and contain numerous variations. This article examines in detail various existing similarity functions and proposes a hybrid technique for the following task: among the list of possible names, occupations and places extracted from historical documents, identify those that are variations of the same person name, occupation and place respectively. The performance of our method is evaluated on three manually constructed datasets and one public dataset in terms of precision, recall and F-measure. The results demonstrate that the hybrid technique outperforms current methods and allows to significantly improve the quality of cultural heritage data.

1 Introduction

Inaccurate information and lack of common identifiers are problems encountered when combining information from heterogeneous sources. There are a number of reasons that can cause inaccurate information such as spelling variations, abbreviations, translation from one language into another and modifying long names into shorter ones. Inaccurate information often occurs in many domains, for example, during information extraction from the Web or when attributing a publication to its proper author. Inaccurate information is very typical in cultural heritage data as well. In historical documents a real person could be mentioned many times, for instance in civil certificates such as birth, marriage and death certificates or in property transfer records and tax declarations. The name of the same person, his occupation and the place in such documents varies a lot. When working with such information, researchers have to identify which person references mentioned in different historical documents belong to the same person entity. This problem has been referred to in literature in many different ways but is best known as entity resolution (ER), record linkage or duplicate detection (Lisbach and Meyer, 2013; Christen, 2012; Bhattacharya and Getoor, 2007). The process of ER in historical documents is always accompanied by inaccurate information as well. As an example, there are more than 100 variants of the first name *Jan*, such as *Johan*, *Johannes*, *Janis*, *Jean* or the profession *musician* in historical documents can be spelled as *musikant*, *muzikant* or even *muzikant bij de tiende afd.* The latter means the musician in the 10th department.

The past few decades have seen a large research interest in the problem of inaccurate information. As a result, a large number of methods for comparing string has been developed. These standard methods are called string similarity functions. Some of those well known techniques are character-based, token-based or based on phonetic functions, for instance *Levenshtein Edit distance*, *Jaro Winkler distance*, *Monge Elkan distance*, *Smith Waterman distance*, *Soundex* and *Double Metaphone*. (Elmagarmid et al., 2007; Navarro, 2001; Winkler, 1995). Each of the mentioned similarity functions perform optimally for a particular dataset domain. For example, the phonetic function Soundex works great for encoding names by sound as it pronounced in English, but nevertheless sometimes it is also used to encode names in other European languages. However, only little work has been done in studying combinations of similarity functions, and in their simultaneous use for achieving more reliable results. Bilenko (2003) in his work computes names similarity with affine gaps to train the Support Vector Machines classifier. Ristard and Yianilos (1998) designed a learnable Levenshtein distance for solving the string similarity problem. Tejada et al. (2002) learned weights of different types of string transformations.

In this paper we explore various traditional string similarity functions for solving data ambiguities and also design a supervised hybrid technique. We carry out our experiments on three manually constructed datasets: Dutch names, occupations and places, and also on one publicly available dataset of restaurants. The clarified function, that will allow us to recognize difficult ambiguities in textual fields, later will be incorporated into the overall ER process for a large historical database. The main contributions of this paper is a practical study of existing techniques and the design and the extensive analysis of a hybrid technique that allow us to achieve a significant improvement in results.

The remainder of this paper is structured as follows. In Section 2 we begin by presenting typical ambiguities in real-life cultural heritage data. in Section 3 we give an overview of standard string similarity functions. We describe the general hybrid approach in Section 4. In Section 5 we describe the prediction models that we use in the hybrid approach. In Section 6 we provide details about carrying out the experiments. In Section 7 we present an evaluation of the results. Section 8 offers a discussion about applying the designed approach to real-world data. Concluding remarks are given in Section 9.

2 A Real-Life Cultural Heritage Data

In this paper we use historical documents such as birth, marriage and death certificated provided by Brabants Historisch Informatie Centrum (BHIC) [1] to extract most common person names, occupations and places. Civil certificates are belonging to North Brabant, a province of the Netherlands, in the period 1700 - 1920. To study the name ambiguity we used a subset of data consisting of 10000 randomly selected different documents.Then for each name we obtain its standardized code in the database of Meertens Instituut[2] which has a large collection of Dutch names and last names and their typical variations. In the same way, in the database of The Historical Sample of the Netherlands (HSN) [3], for each occupation and place extracted from civil certificates where possible, we obtain its standardized code (van Leeuwen et al., 2002; Mandemakers et al., 2013). Historians have spent a number of years for creating a database of names, occupations and places variations. Using such data gives us a unique opportunity to explore typical variations in different domains and to design a robust technique which is able to deal with them automatically.

The resulting *Name* variations dataset contains 2170 distinct names that correspond to 1326 standardized forms. Table 1 shows a typical example of the constructed dataset of name variations.

ref_id	Name	name_id
1	Eustachius	1
2	Statius	1
3	Stefan	2
4	Stephan	2
5	Stephanus	2

Table 1: An example of a name variation dataset

The second dataset of *Occupations* contains 1401 occupation records which belong to 1098 standardized occupations.

The third dataset of *Places* contains 1196 locations records belonging to 617 standardized places.

3 Traditional Similarity Functions

There are three main different types of string similarity functions that can be used for variation tasks, namely character-based, phonetic-based and token-based. Each of them we investigate in detail below.

3.1 Character-Based Similarity

Character-based similarities operate on character sequences and their composition which makes them suitable for identifying imprecise names and spelling errors. They compute the similarity between two strings as the difference between their common characters. In this paper, we will consider the *Levenshtein edit distance* (LE), *Jaro* (J), *Jaro Winkler* (JW), *Smith Waterman* (SW), *Smith Waterman with Gotohs backtracing* (GH), *Needleman Wunch* (NW) and *Monge Elkan* (ME) string similarities (Elmagarmid et al., 2007; Christen, 2012; Naumann and Herschel, 2010). All of them return a number between 0 and 1 inclusively,

[1] http://www.bhic.nl

[2] http://www.meertens.knaw.nl/nvb/

[3] http://www.iisg.nl/hsn/data/occupations.html

where the highest value when two names are exactly the same. Table 3 shows an example of computed character-based similarities for three name pair-variants.

3.2 Phonetic-Based Similarity

Phonetic similarity functions analyze the sounds of the names being compared instead of their spelling differences. For example, the two names *Stefan* and *Stephan* barely differ phonetically, but nevertheless they have different spellings. Phonetic functions encode every name with phonetic keys based on a set of rules. For instance, some algorithms ignore all vowels and compare only the groups of consonants, other algorithms analyze consonant combinations and thier sound that describe a large number of sounds. In this paper, we analyze 4 phonetic functions: *Soundex* (SN), *Double Metaphone* (DM), *IBMAlphaCode* (IA) and *New York State Identification and Intelligence System* (NY) (Christen, 2006). The Table 2 shows an example of applied phonetic keys to encode imprecise names.

Name	SN	DM	IA	NYSIIS
Stefan	S315	STFN	00182	STAFAN
Stephan	S315	STFN	00182	STAFPAN
Stephanus	S3152	STFNS	00182	STAFPAN

Table 2: An example of phonetic keys

3.3 Token-Based Similarity

Token-based functions divide two strings into sets of tokens s_1 and s_2, then they compute the intersection between two sets based on the number of equal tokens. Some token-based functions, for instance *Dice similarity* (DS), *Jaccard coefficient*(JS) and *Cosine similarity* (CS) (Cohen et al., 2003), consider as a token the whole word in a string. In our case most of the person names, locations and places are quite different and there are only few intersections between token-words available. Another approach, a *q-gram* (QG) tokenization (McNamee and Mayfield, 2004), divides a string into smaller tokens of size q. QG calculates the similarity between two strings by counting the number of q-grams in common and dividing by the number of q-grams in the longer string. In this paper we consider bigrams ($q = 2$). For example, the name 'stefan' contains the bigrams 'st', 'te', 'ef', 'fa','an'. An example of applied QG and JS similarities is shown in Table 3.

two names	LE	J	JW	SW	GH	NW	ME	QG	JS
(Stefan, Stephan)	0.71	0.85	0.89	0.58	0.57	0.79	0.57	0.5	0
(Stefan, Stephanus)	0.56	0.80	0.86	0.58	0.57	0.61	0.57	0.38	0
(Stephan, Stephanus)	0.78	0.93	0.97	1	1	0.78	1	0.75	0

Table 3: An example of character and token-based similarities

3.4 Exploration of Standard Methods

The goal of this paper is to investigate in how far the terms variation task can be addressed by using standard methods and improve the results by applying a hybrid technique. Fig. 1 shows for each string similarity function the distribution between two non-matching pairs of records on the one hand and two matching pairs of records on the other for different measures. The more discriminative the measure is, the larger is the separation between the distributions. However, in this figure, each of similarity functions is considered independently and can be expected to only perform well in certain situations. Therefore, the goal of this paper is to design an appropriate hybrid technique, which allows to achieve better performance results by using a combination of traditional measures.

4 General Hybrid Approach

In this article we propose a new hybrid approach which takes advantage of a number of existing string similarities. Our method takes into account the most relevant string similarity by obtaining a ranking of each in terms of its importance for a classification task. The outline of the algorithm of the hybrid approach is shown below. The algorithm uses training data $\mathcal{B}$ which is provided in the form of matching and non-matching pairs of terms. First, in steps 1 to 5 the algorithm calculates pairwise similarities between two terms by every string function $(sim^1, sim^2, ..., sim^K)$. In steps 6 to 8 the algorithm computes for every sim_i an importance rate using the Random Forest technique (Genuer et al., 2010; Breiman, 2001). In subsection 4.2 we describe in more detail the process of selecting the most important string similarities. Then, in steps 10 to 22 the algorithm iteratively constructs the set of the similarity functions $\mathcal{T}^*$ which is a subset of Sim. It starts from an empty set $\mathcal{T}^*$ and at each iteration it adds to $\mathcal{T}^*$ the measure that has the highest importance rate and after that it learns the classifier $\mathcal{C}$. After every iteration the algorithm evaluates the performance

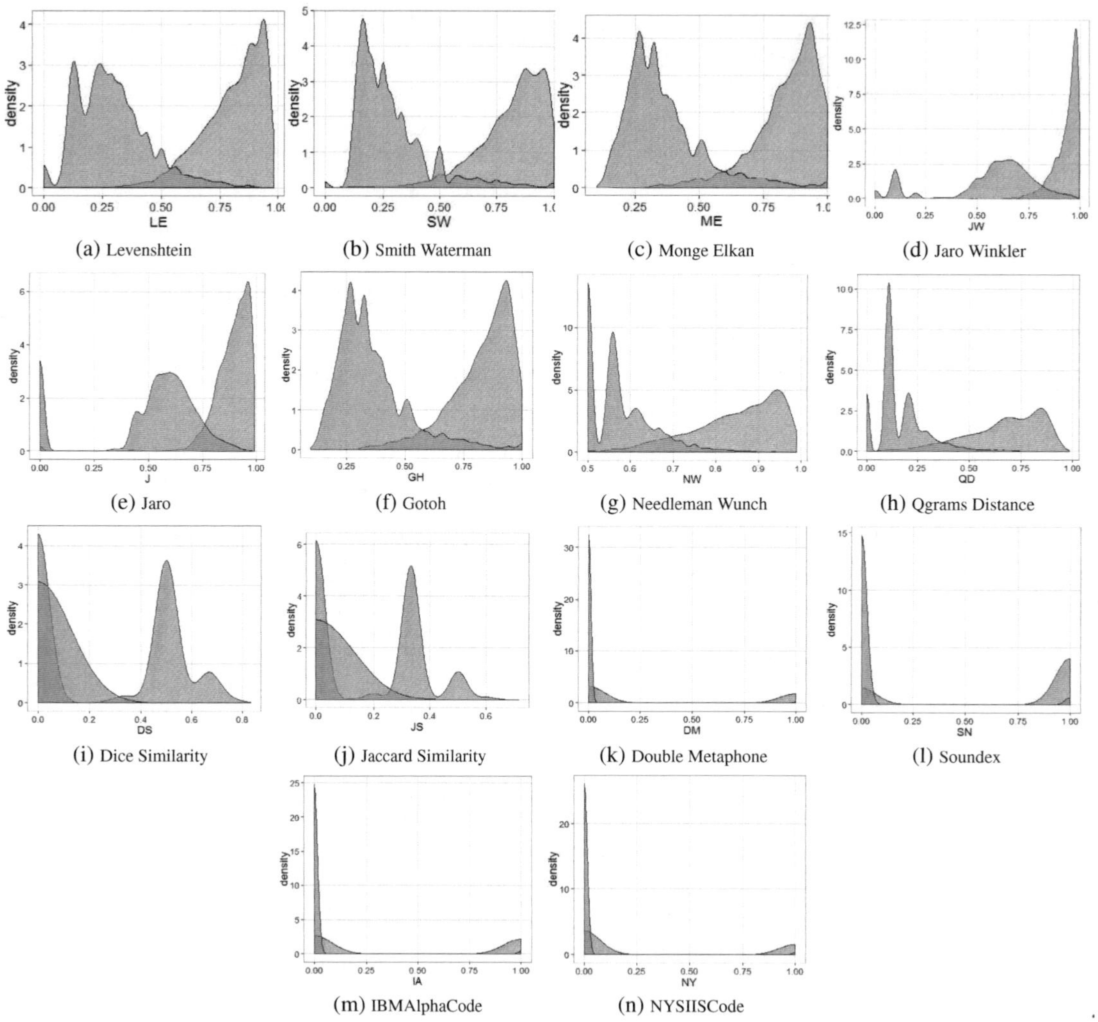

(a) Levenshtein (b) Smith Waterman (c) Monge Elkan (d) Jaro Winkler (e) Jaro (f) Gotoh (g) Needleman Wunch (h) Qgrams Distance (i) Dice Similarity (j) Jaccard Similarity (k) Double Metaphone (l) Soundex (m) IBMAlphaCode (n) NYSIISCode

Figure 1: The distribution between two matching and two non-matching pairs of records for each string similarity function

in term of maximum F measure $Fmeas$ on the validation set $\mathcal{R}$. The algorithm stops if $Fmeas$ doesn't increase anymore or if the size $\mathcal{T}^*$ reaches the parameter η which can be set as a fraction of the total number of string similarity functions.

4.1 Pairwise Similarity Calculation

In order to solve the name ambiguity problem it is necessary to compute the similarity score between two records. Most of the standard string similarity functions and standard classifiers require a pairwise records comparison. We convert each dataset described in Section 2 into a dataset of variant pairs using random combinations of records. Two differently spelled terms are equal when their standardized codes are the same and different otherwise. The example of term pair-variants dataset on is shown in Table 4.

Name1	Name2	class
Statius	Eustachius	1
Statius	Stefan	0
Stefan	Stephanus	1

Table 4: An example of term pair-variants

4.2 Measure Selection

Using only the most important measures for solving the terms variation task can significantly reduce the computational cost. Therefore, we before learning the classifier we apply a selection technique. Generally, there are two common techniques that allow to reduce the number of dimensions: filters and wrappers (Das, 2001). Typically filter-based approaches require only one single scan, whereas wrapper-based ones iteratively look for the set of features which are the most suitable which leads to larger computational over-

Algorithm 1 Hybrid Disambiguation Measure

Input: Training set $\mathcal{B} = \{b_1, ..., b_\beta\}$
Validation set $\mathcal{R} = \{r_1, ..., r_\rho\}$
Set of similarity measures $Sim = (sim^1, ..., sim^K)$
Maximum allowed number of similarity measures η
$\mathcal{L}\{\mathcal{C}, \mathcal{B}, \mathcal{T}^*\}$ classifier $\mathcal{C}$ with learning algorithm $\mathcal{L}$ which is trained on the training set $\mathcal{B}$
Output: A hybrid measure Sim^{hb} based on classifier $\mathcal{C}$

for each b in $\mathcal{B}$ **do**
  for each sim in Sim **do**
    compute $sim(b)$
  end for
end for
for each sim in Sim **do**
  compute $RF_{sim}\{\mathcal{B}\}$
end for
$\mathcal{T}^* \leftarrow \emptyset$
$Fmeas_1\{\mathcal{R}\} \leftarrow 0$
$i \leftarrow 2$
while $|\mathcal{T}^*| \leq \eta$ **do**
  select sim_i that maximizes RF importance rate
  $Sim \leftarrow Sim - \{sim_i\}$
  $\mathcal{T}^* \leftarrow \mathcal{T}^* \cup \{sim_i\}$
  $\mathcal{L}\{\mathcal{C}, \mathcal{B}, \mathcal{T}^*\}$
  Calculate model performance $Fmeas_i\{\mathcal{R}\}$
  if $max(Fmeas_i\{\mathcal{R}\}) > max(Fmeas_{i-1}\{\mathcal{R}\})$ **then**
    break
  end if
  $i \leftarrow i + 1$
end while
$Sim^{hb} \leftarrow \mathcal{L}\{\mathcal{C}, \mathcal{B}, \mathcal{T}^*\}$
return Sim^{hb} corresponding to $\mathcal{T}^*$ and $\mathcal{C}$

heads. For designing a hybrid approach we decided to use *Random Forest* (RF) wrappers to evaluate the weight of every similarity measures. RF, according to many different sources is considered as one of the most reliable methods which is able to deal with high-dimensional and noisy data (Saeys et al., 2007). RF generates a forest of classification trees and then assign an importance rank to each similarity function based on its usefulness for the classification purpose. We use RF results to perform a *stepwise procedure* and to construct the set of measures $\mathcal{T}^*$.

4.3 Hybrid Score Computation and pairwise Classification

We consider the problem of terms variations as a prediction problem. There are many available classification techniques that are suitable for a prediction task. Many of them require a prior training phase on a representative subset of data to make a more efficient prediction on new data. After that, pairs of references are classified into classes *Matched* or *non-Matched* based on a threshold value of the score function. The score function computes the final similarity score between two terms based on results of single comparison measures. For learning the score function we use a training dataset $\mathcal{B}$. We explore 2 robust classifiers that could be applied to cultural heritage dataset domains. They are the *Logistic Regression* (LG) and the *Support Vector Machine* (SVM) (Hastie et al., 2003; Cristianini and Shawe-Taylor, 2000). They are two of the most widely-used classifiers that are suitable for the prediction task (James et al., 2013). It is important to add that we also carried out our experiments and applied three more classifiers, namely *Linear Discriminant Analysis*, *Quadratic Discriminant Analysis* and *k-nearest neighbors* (Hastie et al., 2003; Verma, 2012; Zezula et al., 2006). However results were not improved significantly on all of our datasets, so we do not include those classifiers in the designed hybrid approach.

5 The Prediction Models

In this Section we will briefly describe models that we incorporated into our hybrid approach to address the problem of inaccurate cultural heritage data.

5.1 Logistic regression

We apply a logistic regression as a predictive model and calculate the score function as follows:

$$Sim^{hb}(a_i, a_j) = \frac{1}{1 + e^{-z}}, \quad (1)$$

where $z = \omega_0 + \omega_1 * sim^1(a_i, a_j) + \omega_2 * sim^2(a_i, a_j) + \cdots + \omega_n * sim^K(a_i, a_j)$ is an utilization of a linear regression model with parameters represented by ω_1 to ω_k. The parameters ω_0 to ω_n are learned in a training phase. The functions $sim^1(a_i, a_j)$ to $sim^K(a_i, a_j)$ represent single similarity measures between two terms a_i and a_j.

5.2 Support Vector Machines

We apply and explore SVM as a predictive model. The basic idea of SVM is that the training data is mapped into a new high dimensional space where it is possible to apply linear models to separate the classes. A kernel function performs the mapping of the training data into the new space. After that, a separation between classes is done by maximizing a separation margin between cases belonging to different classes. In our hybrid approach we use the SVM classifier with a *radial basis kernel function* and train it on the training set $\mathcal{B}$.

6 Experiments

Our experiments are conducted on four datasets. Three datasets, namely names, occupations and places variations are manually constructed from Cultural Heritage Data. They are discussed in detail in Section 2.

The fourth dataset is a public dataset called *Restaurant*. It is a standard benchmark dataset which is widely used in data matching studies (Christen, 2012; Bilenko et al., 2003). It contains information about 864 restaurant names and addresses where 112 records are duplicated. It was obtained by integrating records from two sources: Fodors and Zagats guidebooks. The *Restaurant* dataset was taken from the *SecondString* toolkit[4].

We carried out our experiments in accordance to the algorithm described in Section 4. At first, we convert each dataset into a dataset of variant pairs using random combinations of records. Then for each pair of records we compute string similarity functions. We randomly divided all available data into two subsets, namely training and test sets. To construct the set of string similarities we use 70% of the training set to learn RF importance rate and the other 30% of the training set to validate results under stepwise selection procedure as it was described in the algorithm in Section 4. The resulting set of selected string similarities for each dataset is shown in Table 5. After constructing the set of string similarities we learn the classifier on the complete training set and then evaluate it on the test set. In order to assess the performance of our results, we apply a 10-fold cross-validation method. We randomly partition the available dataset into 10 equal size subsets. Then one subset was chosen as the validation data for testing the classifier, and the remaining subsets are used for training the classifier. Then the cross-validation process is repeated 10 times, with each of the 10 subsets used exactly once as the validation dataset.

Dataset					
Names	IA	SN	DM	LE	SW
Occupations	JW	J	LE	NW	QG
Places	QG	JW	LE	SW	J
Restaurants	QG	JW	CS	NW	

Table 5: Selected string similarities during the stepwise procedure

[4] http://secondstring.sourceforge.net/

7 Evaluation Results

In order to evaluate the performance of standard string similarity functions and the applied hybrid approach, we compute the sets of True Positives (TP), False Positives (FP) and False Negatives (FN) as the correctly identified, incorrectly identified and incorrectly rejected matches, respectively. Fig. 2 demonstrates the performance of standard and hybrid approaches on four examined datasets.

The logistic regression as well as SVM classifiers which are used in the hybrid approach on each of the dataset outperform standard string similarities. The improvement in results is significant, especially it is clearly seen on the dataset of occupations. For a more detailed analysis, Fig. 3 shows the evaluation of results in terms of F-measure and the threshold value for all continuous methods. Moreover, Table 6 shows the maximum values of the F-measure for the five best performing methods for each of the datasets. Two upper rows of the table belong only to the hybrid approach. SVM and logistic regression in the combination with the RF selection technique both demonstrate robustness on the multiple datasets domains.

Names		Occupations		Places		Restaurants	
Method	Max.F	Method	Max.F	Method	Max.F	Method	Max.F
SVM	0.94	SVM	0.93	SVM	0.95	LG	0.95
LG	0.92	LG	0.86	LG	0.93	SVM	0.91
LE	0.89	J	0.82	QG	0.88	JW	0.87
J	0.87	LE	0.77	JW	0.87	QG	0.81
SW	0.86	JW	0.71	J	0.85	GH	0.76

Table 6: The maximum F-Measure values for the five best-performing methods

In addition to analyzing the hybrid approach, in this section we investigate in more detail functions which demonstrate not the typical behavior on the precision and recall plots. For instance, on Fig. 2 for SW, GH and ME similarities the simultaneous growth of the precision is accomplished by the growth in the recall on the interval (0, 0.3). The same situation occurs for SW and GH similarities on datasets of occupations and places. In Table 7 for SW similarity on the dataset on names for three levels of the threshold we show its performance indicators, namely TP, FP and FN values and calculated the precision and recall. With the maximum similarity score SW incorrectly identify as positive 99 pairs of names. With the slightly decrease in the threshold value, the larger number of pairs are identified correctly as the variation of

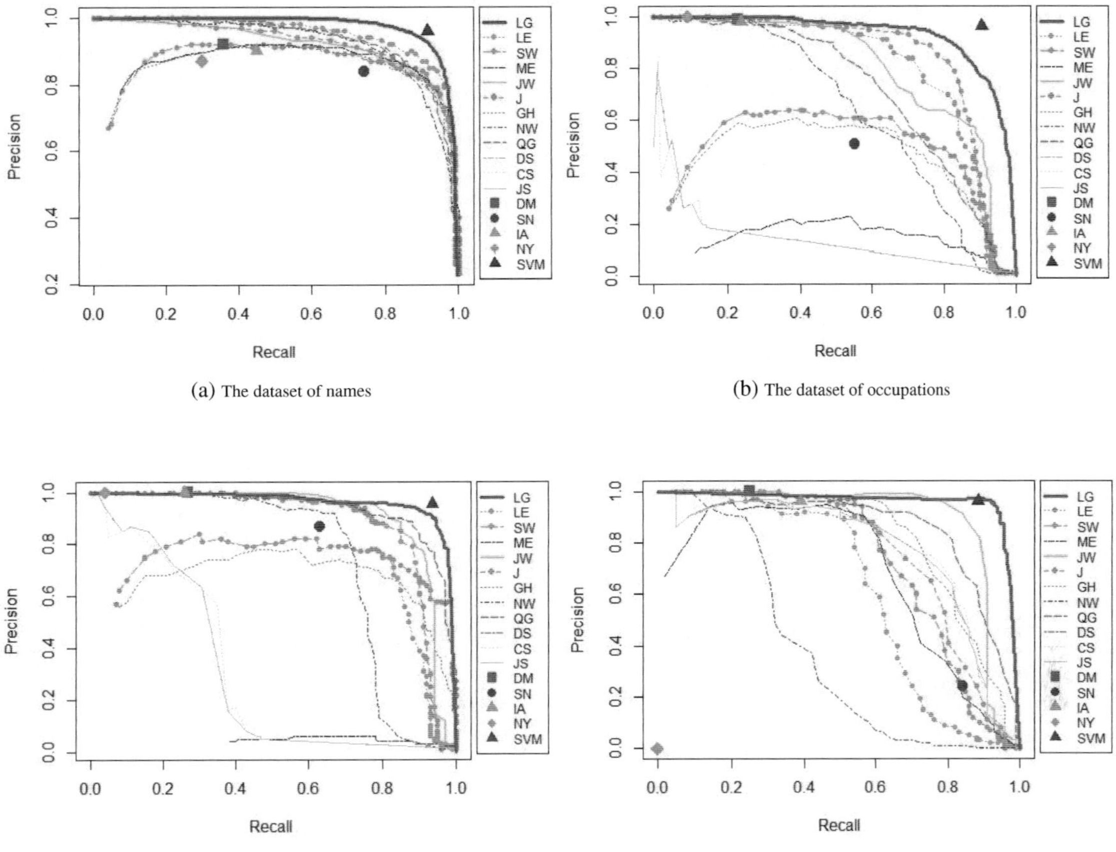

(a) The dataset of names

(b) The dataset of occupations

(c) The dataset of places

(d) Public dataset of restaurants

Figure 2: Evaluation of single string similarities and the hybrid approach in terms of precision and recall

Threshold	TP	FP	FN	Precision	Recall
0.96	809	99	3853	0.89	0.17
0.98	355	99	4307	0.78	0.08
1	200	99	4462	0.67	0.04

Table 7: Evaluation measures for SW similarity for 3 levels of the threshold

Name1	Name2	SW	GH	ME
Peternella	Peter	1	1	1
Pauline	Paul	1	1	1
Henriette	Henri	1	1	1

Table 8: Example of FP pairs of names according to the maximum value of SW, GH and ME functions

the same name. Therefore, to make it absolutely clear, in Table 8 we gave an example of such pairs of names that are included into 99 FP and cause the simultaneous grows of precision and recall.

8 Discussion

The proposed hybrid approach shows very good results in performing the pairwise terms comparison for completely different dataset domains. Nevertheless, the bottleneck of the algorithm is that it is expensive to apply it to real-world data and compare all possible combinations of records.

There are various available techniques for reducing the amount of candidate pairs to be compared. Common techniques are partitioning data into smaller subsets and comparing only records with the same partition. Two widely used partition approaches are blocking and windowing methods (Naumann and Herschel, 2010; Bilenko et al., 2003). The blocking technique assigns to each record a special blocking key, for instance year, place of the documents or the first 3 letters of the last name. The windowing technique such as

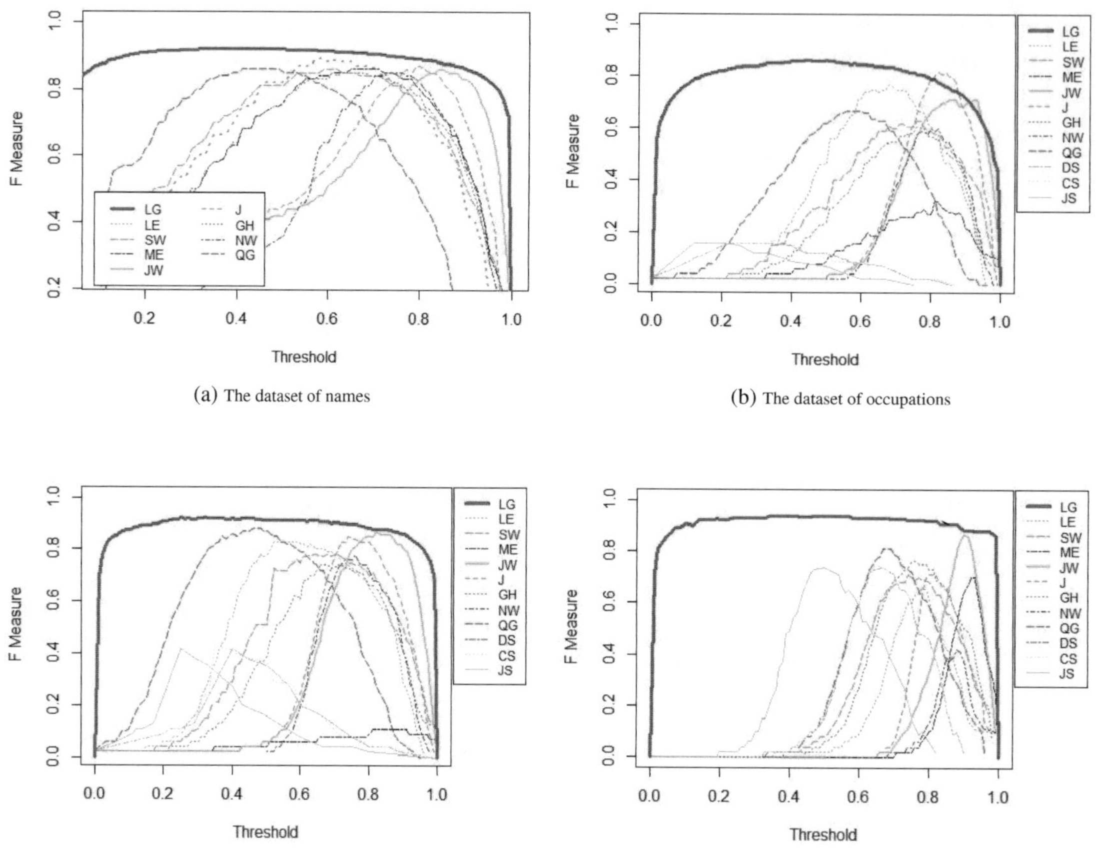

(a) The dataset of names

(b) The dataset of occupations

(c) The dataset of places

(d) Public dataset of restaurants

Figure 3: Evaluation of single string similarities and the hybrid approach in terms of F-Measure and Threshold

Sorted Neighborhood method sorts data according to some key, for instance year of the documents, and then slides a window of fixed size across the sorted data. Reducing the number of candidate pairs may result that two references that refer to the same entity appear in different partitions and then they will never be compared. Therefore, our next work will focus on searching the best partition method (or best hybrid methods) that allows to reduce the number of potential candidate pairs and keep all references referring to the same entity within the same partition.

9 Conclusion

In this paper we studied a number of traditional string similarities and proposed the hybrid approach applied on different cultural heritage dataset domains. It is obvious that dealing with historical documents, where attributes information is often imprecise, is not possible by using only one string similarity. Therefore, we investigated how to improve the performance by using a number of string similarities and applied supervised learning technique.

As future step, the authors are working on incorporating the hybrid approach into overall entity resolution process in a large genealogical database (Efremova et al., 2014), which aims to discover which of the person references mentioned in different historical documents refer to the same person entity. The genealogical database contains a collection of historical documents where names, occupations and places are the essential attributes. Therefore it is very important to find a robust and reliable approach which is able to compare main personal information in the noisy data.

10 Acknowledgments

The authors are grateful to the BHIC Center, in particular to Rien Wols and Anton Schuttelaars for the support in data gathering, data analysis and direction.

References

Indrajit Bhattacharya and Lise Getoor. 2007. Collective entity resolution in relational data. *ACM Trans. Knowl. Discov. Data*, 1(1).

Mikhail Bilenko and Raymond J. Mooney. 2003. Adaptive duplicate detection using learnable string similarity measures. In *Proceedings of the Ninth ACM SIGKDD International Conference on Knowledge Discovery and Data Mining*, KDD '03, pages 39–48. ACM.

Mikhail Bilenko, Raymond Mooney, William Cohen, Pradeep Ravikumar, and Stephen Fienberg. 2003. Adaptive name matching in information integration. *Intelligent Systems*, 18(5):16–23.

Leo Breiman. 2001. Random forests. *Machine Learning*, 45(1):5–32.

Peter Christen. 2006. A comparison of personal name matching: techniques and practical issues. In *Proceedings of the Workshop on Mining Complex Data (MCD06), held at IEEE ICDM06*, pages 290–294.

Peter Christen. 2012. *Data matching*. Springer Publishing Company, Incorporated.

William W. Cohen, Pradeep Ravikumar, and Stephen E. Fienberg. 2003. A comparison of string distance metrics for name-matching tasks. In *Proceedings of IJCAI-03 Workshop on Information Integration*, pages 73–78.

Nello Cristianini and John Shawe-Taylor. 2000. *An introduction to Support Vector Machines: and other kernel-based learning methods*. Cambridge University Press.

Sanmay Das. 2001. Filters, wrappers and a boosting-based hybrid for feature selection. In *Proceedings of the Eighteenth International Conference on Machine Learning*, ICML '01, pages 74–81. Morgan Kaufmann Publishers Inc.

Julia Efremova, Bijan Ranjbar-Sahraei, Frans A. Oliehoek, Toon Calders, and Karl Tuyls. 2014. A baseline method for genealogical entity resolution. In *Proceedings of the Workshop on Population Reconstruction, organized in the framework of the LINKS project*.

Ahmed K. Elmagarmid, Panagiotis G. Ipeirotis, and Vassilios S. Verykios. 2007. Duplicate record detection: A survey. *Knowledge and Data Engineering, IEEE Transactions on*, 19(1):1–16.

Robin Genuer, Jean-Michel Poggi, and Christine Tuleau-Malot. 2010. Variable selection using random forests. *Pattern Recognition Letters*, 31(14):2225–2236.

Trevor Hastie, Robert Tibshirani, and Jerome Friedman. 2003. *The elements of statistical learning*. Springer, corrected edition.

Gareth James, Daniela Witten, Trevor Hastie, and Robert Tibshirani. 2013. *An introduction to statistical learning: with applications in R*. Springer Publishing Company, Incorporated.

Bertrand Lisbach and Victoria Meyer. 2013. *Linguistic identity matching*. Springer.

Kees Mandemakers, Sanne Muurling, Ineke Maas, Bart Van de Putte, Richard L. Zijdeman, Paul Lambert, Marco H.D. van Leeuwen, Frans van Poppel, and Andrew Miles. 2013. *HSN standardized, HISCO-coded and classified occupational titles*. IISG Amsterdam.

Paul McNamee and James Mayfield. 2004. Character n-gram tokenization for european language text retrieval. *Information Retrieval*, 7(1-2):73–97.

Felix Naumann and Melanie Herschel. 2010. *An Introduction to Duplicate Detection*. Morgan and Claypool Publishers.

Gonzalo Navarro. 2001. A guided tour to approximate string matching. *ACM Comput. Surv.*, 33(1):31–88.

Eric Sven Ristad, Peter N. Yianilos, and Senior Member. 1998. Learning string edit distance. *IEEE Transactions on Pattern Analysis and Machine Intelligence*, 20:522–532.

Yvan Saeys, Iñaki Inza, and Pedro Larrañaga. 2007. A review of feature selection techniques in bioinformatics. *Bioinformatics*, 23(19):2507–2517, September.

Sheila Tejada, Craig A. Knoblock, and Steven Minton. 2002. Learning domain-independent string transformation weights for high accuracy object identification. In *Proceedings of the eighth ACM SIGKDD international conference on Knowledge discovery and data mining*, KDD '02, pages 350–359. ACM.

Marco H. D. van Leeuwen, Ineke Maas, and Andrew Miles. 2002. *HISCO. Historical international standard classification of occupations*. Leuven University Press.

J P Verma. 2012. *Data Analysis in Management with SPSS Software*. Springer.

William E. Winkler. 1995. Matching and record linkage. In *Business Survey Methods*, pages 355–384. Wiley.

Pavel Zezula, Giuseppe Amato, Vlastislav Dohnal, and Michal Batko. 2006. *Similarity search: the metric space approach*. Springer.

Automated Error Detection in Digitized Cultural Heritage Documents

Kata Gábor
INRIA & Université Paris 7
Domaine de Voluceau - BP 105
78153 Le Chesnay Cedex
FRANCE
kata.gabor@inria.fr

Benoît Sagot
INRIA & Université Paris 7
Domaine de Voluceau - BP 105
78153 Le Chesnay Cedex
FRANCE
benoit.sagot@inria.fr

Abstract

The work reported in this paper aims at performance optimization in the digitization of documents pertaining to the cultural heritage domain. A hybrid method is proposed, combining statistical classification algorithms and linguistic knowledge to automatize post-OCR error detection and correction. The current paper deals with the integration of linguistic modules and their impact on error detection.

1 Introduction

Providing wider access to national cultural heritage by massive digitization confronts the actors of the field with a set of new challenges. State of the art optical character recognition (OCR) software currently achieve an error rate of around 1 to 10% depending on the age and the layout of the text. While this quality may be adequate for indexing, documents intended for reading need to meet higher standards. A reduction of the error rate by a factor of 10 to 100 becomes necessary for the diffusion of digitized books and journals through emerging technologies such as e-books. Our paper deals with the automatic post-processing of digitized documents with the aim of reducing the OCR error rate by using contextual information and linguistic processing, by and large absent from current OCR engines. In the current stage of the project, we are focusing on French texts from the archives of the French National Library (Bibliothèque Nationale de France) covering the period from 1646 to 1990.

We adopted a hybrid approach, making use of both statistical classification techniques and linguistically motivated modules to detect OCR errors and generate correction candidates. The technology is based on a symbolic linguistic preprocessing, followed by a statistical module which adpots the noisy channel model (Shannon, 1948). Symbolic methods for error correction allow to target specific phenomena with a high precision, but they typically strongly rely on presumptions about the nature of errors encountered. This drawback can be overcome by using the noisy channel model (Kernighan et al., 1990; Brill and Moore, 2000; Kolak and Resnik, 2002; Mays et al., 1991; Tong and Evans, 1996). However, error models in such systems work best if they are created from manually corrected training data, which are not always available. Other alternatives to OCR error correction include (weighted) FSTs (Beaufort and Mancas-Thillou, 2007), voting systems using the output of different OCR engines (Klein and Kope, 2002), textual alignment combined with dictionary lookup (Lund and Ringger, 2009), or heuristic correction methods (Alex et al., 2012). While correction systems rely less and less on pre-existing external dictionaries, a shift can be observed towards methods that dinamically create lexicons either by exploiting the Web (Cucerzan and Brill, 2004; Strohmaier et al., 2003) or from the corpus (Reynaert, 2004).

As to linguistically enhanced models, POS tagging was succesfully applied to spelling correction (Golding and Schabes, 1996; Schaback, 2007). However, to our knowledge, very little work has been done to exploit linguistic analysis for post-OCR correction (Francom and Hulden, 2013). We propose to apply a shallow processing module to detect certain types of named entities (NEs), and a POS tagger trained specifically to deal with NE-tagged input. Our studies aim to demonstrate that linguistic preprocessing can efficiently contribute to reduce the error rate by 1) detecting false corrections proposed by the statistical correction module, 2) detecting OCR errors which are unlikely to be detected by the statistical correction module. We argue that named entity grammars can be adapted to the correction task at a low cost and they allow to target specific types of errors with a very high precision.

In what follows, we present the global architecture of the post-OCR correction system (2), the named entity recognition module (3), as well as our experiments in named entity-aware POS tagging (4). The predicted impact of the linguistic modules is illustrated in section 5. Finally, we present ongoing work and the conclusion (6).

2 System Architecture

Our OCR error detection and correction system uses a hybrid methodology with a symbolic module for linguistic preprocessing, a POS tagger, followed by statistical decoding and correction modules. The SxPipe toolchain (Sagot and Boullier, 2008) is used for shallow processing tasks (tokenisation, sentence segmentation, named entity recognition). The NE-tagged text is input to POS tagging with MElt-h, a hybrid version of the MElt tagger (Denis and Sagot, 2010; Denis and Sagot, 2012). MELT-h can take both NE tagged texts and raw text as input.
The decoding phase is based on the noisy channel model (Shannon, 1948) adapted to spell checking (Kernighan et al., 1990). In a noisy channel model, given an input string s, we want to find the word w which maximizes $P(w|s)$. Using Bayes theorem, this can be written as:

$$argmax(w)P(s|w) * P(w) \quad (1)$$

where P(w) is given by the language model obtained from clean corpora. Both sentence-level (Tong and Evans, 1996; Boswell, 2004) and word-level (Mays et al., 1991) language models can be used. $P(s|w)$ is given by the error model, represented as a confusion matrix calculated from our training corpus in which OCR output is aligned with its manually corrected, noiseless equivalent. The post-correction process is summarized in 1.
The integration of a symbolic module for NE recognition and the use of part of speech and named entity tags constitute a novel aspect in our method. Moreover, linguistic preprocessing allows us to challenge tokenisation decisions prior

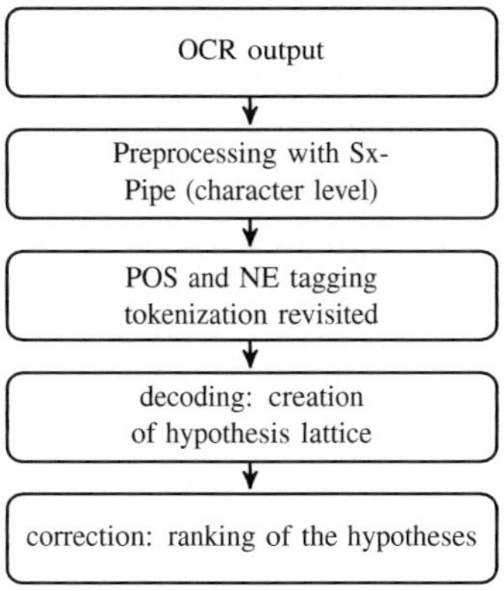

Figure 1: Architecture

to and during the decoding phase (similarly to Kolak (2005)) ; this constitutes a significant feature as OCR errors often boil down to a fusion or split of tokens.

The corpus we use comes from the archives of the French National Library and contains 1 500 documents (50 000 000 tokens). This corpus is available both as a "reference corpus", i.e., in a manually corrected, clean version, and as a "contrast corpus", i.e., a noisy OCR output version. These variants are aligned at the sentence level.

3 Named entity tagging

3.1 NE recognition methodology

As a first step in error detection, the OCR output is analysed in search of "irregular" character sequences such as named entities. This process is implemented with SxPipe (Sagot and Boullier, 2008), a freely available[1], robust and modular multilingual processing chain for unrestricted text. SxPipe contains modules for named entity recognition, tokenization, sentence segmentation, non-deterministic multi-word expression detection, spelling correction and lexicon-based patterns detection. The SxPipe chain is fully customizable with respect to input language, domain, text type and the modules to be used. Users are also free to add their own modules to the chain.

In accordance with our purposes, we defined named entities as sequences of characters which cannot be analysed morphologically or syntactically, yet follow productive patterns. Such entities do not adhere to regular tokenization patterns

[1] https://gforge.inria.fr/projects/lingwb/

since they often include punctuation marks, usually considered as separators. As compared to the consensual use of the term (Maynard et al., 2001; Chinchor, 1998; Sang and Meulder, 2003), our definition covers a wider range of entities, e.g., numerals, currency units, dimensions.[2] The correct annotation of these entities has a double relevance for our project:

- NE tagging prior to POS tagging helps to improve the accuracy of the latter.
- NE tagging allows to detect and, eventually, correct OCR errors which occur inside NEs. Conversely, it can also contribute to detect false correction candidates when the sequence of characters forming the NE would otherwise be assigned a low probability by the language model.

The named entity recognition module is implemented in Perl as a series of local grammars. Local grammars constitute a simple and powerful tool to recognize open classes of entities (Friburger and Maurel, 2004; Maynard et al., 2002; Bontcheva et al., 2002); we are concerned with time expressions, addresses, currency units, dimensions, chemical formulae and legal IDs. Named entity grammars are applied to the raw corpus before tokenization and segmentation. Our grammars are robust in the sense that they inherently recognize and correct some types of frequent OCR errors in the input.[3] SxPipe's architecture allows to define an OCR-specific correction mode as an input parameter and hence apply robust recognition and correction to noisy output, while requiring exact matching for clean texts. However, maximizing precision remains our primary target, as a false correction is more costly than the non-correction of an eventual error at this stage. Therefore, our grammars are built around unambiguous markers.

3.2 Evaluation of NE tagging

A manual, application-independent evaluation was carried out, concentrating primarily on precision for the reasons mentioned in 3. For four types of NEs, we collected a sample of 200 sentences expected to contain one or more instances of the given entity category, based on the presence of category-specific markers (lexical units, acronyms etc.)[4]. However, chemical formulae were evaluated directly on sentences extracted from the archives of the European Patent Office; no filtering was needed due to the density of formulae in these documents.
Legal IDs were evaluated on a legal corpus from the Publications Office of the European Union, while the rest of the grammars were evaluated using the BNF corpus.

Entity Type	Precision	Recall
DATE	0.98	0.97
ADDRESS	0.83	0.86
LEGAL	0.88	0.82
CHEMICAL	0.94	-

Table 1: Evaluation of NE grammars

4 POS tagging

4.1 MElt$_{\mathrm{FR}}$ and MElt-h

The following step in the chain is POS tagging using a named entity-aware version of the MElt tagger. MElt (Denis and Sagot, 2010; Denis and Sagot, 2012) is a maximum entropy POS tagger which differs from other systems in that it uses both corpus-based features and a large-coverage lexicon as an external source of information. Its French version, MElt-FR was trained on the *Lefff* lexicon (Sagot, 2010) and on the French TreeBank (FTB) (Abeillé et al., 2003). The training corpus uses a tagset consisting of 29 tags. MElt$_{\mathrm{FR}}$ yields state of the art results for French, namely 97.8% accuracy on the test set.

In order to integrate MElt into our toolchain, the tagger needed to be trained to read NE-tagged texts as output by SxPipe. We thus extended the FTB with 332 manually annotated sentences (15 500 tokens) containing real examples for each type of NE covered by our version of SxPipe. SxPipe's output format was slightly modified to facilitate learning: entities covered by the grammars were replaced by pseudo-words corresponding to their category. The training corpus is the union

[2] Our current experiments do not cover single-word proper names.

[3] E.g., A numerical 0 inside a chemical formula is presumed in most cases to be an erroneous hypothesis for alphabetical O.

[4] Although this sampling is biased towards entities with a certain type of marker, it gives an approximation on the recall, as opposed to simply extracting hits of our grammars and evaluating only their precision.

of the FTB and the small NE corpus annotated with 35 categories (29 POS and 6 named entity categories). We used this corpus to train MElt-h, a hybrid tagger compatible with our OCR post-processing toolchain. MElt-h can tag both raw corpora (using the 29 POS categories learnt from the FTB), and NE-annotated texts (preprocessed with SxPipe or any other tool, as long as the format is consistent with the output of SxPipe).
Training a tagger on a heterogeneous corpus like the one we used is theoretically challengeable. Therefore, careful attention was paid to evaluating it on both NE-annotated data and on the FTB test corpus. The latter result is meant to indicate whether there is a decrease in performance compared to the "original" MElt_{FR} tagger, trained solely on FTB data.

4.2 Evaluation of POS and NE tagging

A set of experiments were performed using different sections of the NE-annotated training data. First, we cut out 100 sentences at random and used them as a test corpus. From the rest of the sentences, we created diverse random partitionings using 50, 100, 150 and all the 232 sentences as training data. We trained MElt-h on each training corpus and evaluated it on the test section of the FTB as well as on the 100 NE-annotated sentences.

#sentences	Prec on FTB	Prec on PACTE-NE
0	97.83	—
50	97.82	95.61
100	97.80	95.71
150	97.78	95.76
200	97.78	95.84
232	97.75	96.20

Table 2: Evaluation of MElt-h on the FTB and on the NE-annotated corpus

The results confirm that adding NE-annotated sentences to the training corpus does not decrease precision on the FTB itself. Furthermore, we note that the results on the NE corpus are slightly inferior to the results on the FTB, but the figures suggest that the learning curve did not reach a limit for NE-annotated data: adding more NE-annotated sentences will probably increase precision.

5 Expected impact on OCR error reduction

While the major impact of named entity tagging and NE-enriched POS tagging is expected to result from their integration into the language model, series of experiments are currently being carried out to estimate the efficiency of the symbolic correction module and the quantity of the remaining OCR errors inside named entities. A sample of 500.000 sentences (15.500.000 tokens) was extracted from the BNF corpus to be used for a comparison and case studies, both in the noisy OCR output version and in the editorial quality version. Both types of texts were tagged for NEs with SxPipe, using the "clean input" mode (without tolerance for errors and correction candidates). Only 65% of the recognized NEs are identical, implying that 35% of the named entities are very likely to contain an OCR error.[5] To investigate further, we applied the grammars one by one in "noisy input" mode. This setting allows to detect certain types of typical OCR errors, with an efficiency ranging from 0 (no tolerance) to 10% i.e., up to this quantity of erroneous input can be detected and correctly tagged with certain named entity grammars. Detailed case studies are currently being carried out to determine the exact precision of the correction module.

6 Conclusion and Future Work

We described an architecture for post-OCR error detection in documents pertaining to the cultural heritage domain. Among other characteristics, the specificity of our model consists in a combination of linguistic analysis and statistical modules, which interact at different stages in the error detection and correction process. The first experiments carried out within the project suggest that linguistically informed modules can efficiently complement statistical methods for post-OCR error detection. Our principal future direction is towards the integration of NE-enriched POS tagging information into the language models, in order to provide a finer grained categorization and account for these phenomena. A series of experiences are planned to be undertaken, using different combinations of token-level information.

[5]In the less frequent case, divergences can also be due to errors in the editorial quality text.

References

Anne Abeillé, Lionel Clément, and François Toussenel. 2003. Building a treebank for French. In Anne Abeillé, editor, *Treebanks*. Kluwer, Dordrecht.

Bea Alex, Claire Grover, Ewan Klein, and Richard Tobin. 2012. Digitised historical text: Does it have to be mediOCRe? In *Proceedings of KONVENS 2012 (LThist 2012 workshop)*, pages 401–409, Vienna, Austria.

Richard Beaufort and Céline Mancas-Thillou. 2007. A weighted finite-state framework for correcting errors in natural scene OCR. In *Proceedings of the Ninth International Conference on Document Analysis and Recognition*, pages 889–893, Washington, DC, USA.

Kalina Bontcheva, Marin Dimitrov, Diana Maynard, Valentin Tablan, and Hamish Cunningham. 2002. Shallow methods for named entity coreference resolution. In *Proceedings of the TALN 2002 Conference*.

Dustin Boswell. 2004. Language models for spelling correction. *CSE*, 256.

Eric Brill and Robert C. Moore. 2000. An Improved Error Model for Noisy Channel Spelling Correction. In *Proceedings of the 38th ACL Conference*, pages 286–293.

Nancy Chinchor. 1998. Muc-7 named entity task definition. In *Seventh Message Understanding Conference (MUC-7)*.

Silviu Cucerzan and Eric Brill. 2004. Spelling correction as an iterative process that exploits the collective knowledge of web users. In *Proceedings of Proceedings of the 2004 Conference on Empirical Methods in Natural Language Processing (EMNLP'04)*, pages 293–300, Barcelona, Spain.

Pascal Denis and Benoît Sagot. 2010. Exploitation d'une ressource lexicale pour la construction d'un étiqueteur morphosyntaxique état-de-l'art du français. In *Traitement Automatique des Langues Naturelles : TALN 2010*, Montréal, Canada.

Pascal Denis and Benoît Sagot. 2012. Coupling an annotated corpus and a lexicon for state-of-the-art POS tagging. *Language Resources and Evaluation*, 46(4):721–736.

Jerid Francom and Mans Hulden. 2013. Diacritic error detection and restoration via part-of-speech tags. In *Proceedings of the 6th Language and Technology Conference*.

Nathalie Friburger and Denis Maurel. 2004. Finite-state transducer cascades to extract named entities in texts. *Theoretical Computer Science*, 313:94–104.

Andrew Golding and Yves Schabes. 1996. Combining trigram-based and feature-based methods for context-sensitive spelling correction. In *ACL*, pages 71–78.

Mark Kernighan, Kenneth Church, and William Gale. 1990. A spelling correction program based on a noisy channel model. In *Proceedings of the 13th conference on Computational linguistics*, pages 205–210.

Samuel Klein and Miri Kope. 2002. A voting system for automatic OCR correction. In *Proceedings of the Workshop On Information Retrieval and OCR: From Converting Content to Grasping Meaning*, pages 1–21, Tampere, Finland.

Okan Kolak and Philip Resnik. 2002. OCR error correction using a noisy channel model. In *Proceedings of the Second International Conference on Human Language Technology Research (HLT'02)*, pages 257–262, San Diego, USA.

Okan Kolak and Philip Resnik. 2005. OCR post-processing for low density languages. In *Proceedings of the HLT-EMNLP Conference*, pages 867–874.

William Lund and Eric Ringger. 2009. Improving optical character recognition through efficient multiple system alignment. In *Proceedings of the 9th ACM/IEEE-CS Joint Conference on Digital Libraries (JCDL'09)*, pages 231–240, Austin, USA.

Diana Maynard, Valentin Tablan, Cristian Ursu, Hamish Cunningham, and Yorick Wilks. 2001. Named entity recognition from diverse text types. In *In Proceedings of the Recent Advances in Natural Language Processing Conference*, pages 257–274.

Diana Maynard, Valentin Tablan, Hamish Cunningham, Cristian Ursu, Horacio Saggion, Kalina Bontcheva, and Yorick Wilks. 2002. Architectural elements of language engineering robustness. *Journal of Natural Language Engineering - Special Issue on Robust Methods in Analysis of Natural Language Data*, 8:257–274.

Eric Mays, Fred Damerau, and Robert Mercer. 1991. Context based spelling correction. *Information Processing and Management*, 23 (5):517–522.

Martin Reynaert. 2004. Multilingual text induced spelling correction. In *Proceedings of the Workshop on Multilingual Linguistic Ressources (MLR'04)*, pages 117–117.

Benoît Sagot and Pierre Boullier. 2008. SxPipe 2: architecture pour le traitement pré-syntaxique de corpus bruts. *Traitement Automatique des Langues*, 49(2):155–188.

Benoît Sagot. 2010. The lefff, a freely available and large-coverage morphological and syntactic lexicon for french. In *Proceedings of LREC 2010, La Valette, Malte*.

Erik Tjong Kim Sang and Fien De Meulder. 2003. Introduction to the conll-2003 shared task: Language-independent named entity recognition. In *In Proceedings of Computational Natural Language Learning*, pages 142–147. ACL Press.

Johannes Schaback. 2007. Multi-level feature extraction for spelling correction. In *IJCAI Workshop on Analytics for Noisy Unstructured Text Data*, pages 79–86.

Claude Shannon. 1948. A Mathematical Theory of Communication. *Bell System Technical Journal*, 27 (3):379–423.

Christan Strohmaier, Cristoph Ringlstetter, Klaus Schulz, and Stoyan Mihov. 2003. Lexical post-correction of OCR-results: the web as a dynamic secondary dictionary? In *Proceedings of the Seventh International Conference on Document Analysis and Recognition (ICDAR'03)*, page 11331137, Edinburgh, Royaume-Uni.

Xiang Tong and David Evans. 1996. A statistical approach to automatic OCR error correction in context. In *Proceedings of the Fourth Workshop on Very large Corpora*, pages 88–100.

Mining the Twentieth Century's History from the Time Magazine Corpus

Mike Kestemont
University of Antwerp
Prinsstraat 13, D.188
B-2000, Antwerp
Belgium
mike.kestemont@uantwerpen.be

Folgert Karsdorp
Meertens Institute
Postbus 94264
1090 GG Amsterdam
The Netherlands
Folgert.Karsdorp@meertens.knaw.nl

Marten Düring
University of North-Carolina
551 Hamilton Hall
CB 3195, Chapel Hill
North Carolina 27599
United States
marten@live.unc.edu

Abstract

In this paper we report on an explorative study of the history of the twentieth century from a lexical point of view. As data, we use a diachronic collection of 270,000+ English-language articles harvested from the electronic archive of the well-known *Time Magazine* (1923–2006). We attempt to automatically identify significant shifts in the vocabulary used in this corpus using efficient, yet unsupervised computational methods, such as Parsimonious Language Models. We offer a qualitative interpretation of the outcome of our experiments in the light of momentous events in the twentieth century, such as the Second World War or the rise of the Internet. This paper follows up on a recent string of frequentist approaches to studying cultural history ('Culturomics'), in which the evolution of human culture is studied from a quantitative perspective, on the basis of lexical statistics extracted from large, textual data sets.

1 Introduction: Culturomics

Although traditionally, the Humanities have been more strongly associated with qualitative rather than quantitative methodologies, it is hard to miss that 'hipster' terms like 'Computational Analysis', 'Big Data' and 'Digitisation', are currently trending in Humanities scholarship. In the international initiative of Digital Humanities, researchers from various disciplines are increasingly exploring novel, computational means to interact with their object of research. Often, this is done in collaboration with researchers from Computational Linguistics, who seem to have adopted quantitative approaches relatively sooner than other Humanities disciplines. The subfield of Digital History (Zaagsma, 2013), in which the present paper is to be situated, is but one of the multiple Humanities disciplines in which rapid progress is being made as to the application of computational methods. Although the vibrant domain of Digital History cannot be exhaustively surveyed here due to space limits, it is nevertheless interesting to refer to a recent string of frequentist lexical approaches to the study of human history, and the evolution of human culture in particular: 'Culturomics'.

This line of computational, typically data-intensive research seeks to study various aspects of human history, by researching the ways in which (predominantly cultural) phenomena are reflected in, for instance, word frequency statistics extracted from large textual data sets. The field has been initiated in a lively, yet controversial publication by Michel et al. (2011), which – while it has invited a lot of attention in popular media – has not gone uncriticized in the international community of Humanities.[1] In this paper, the authors show how a number of major historical events show interesting correlations with word counts in a vast corpus of *n*-grams extracted from the Google Books, allegedly containing 4% percent of all books ever printed.

In recent years, the term 'Culturomics' seems to have become an umbrella term for studies engaging, often at an increasing level of complexity, with the seminal, publicly available Google Books NGram Corpus (Juola, 2013; Twenge et al., 2012; Acerbi et al., 2013b). Other studies, like the inspiring contribution by Leetaru (2011) have independently explored other data sets for similar purposes, such as the retroactive prediction of the Arab Spring Revolution using news data. In

[1] Consult, for instance, the critical report by A. Grafton on the occasion of a presentation by Michel and Lieberman Aiden at one of the annual meetings of the American Historical Association (https://www.historians.org/publications-and-directories/perspectives-on-history/march-2011/loneliness-and-freedom).

the present paper, we seek to join this recent line of Culturomics research: we will discuss a series of quantitative explorations of the *Time Magazine Corpus* (1923–2006), a balanced textual data set covering a good deal of the twentieth (and early twenty-first) century.

The structure of the paper is as follows: in the following section 2, we will discuss the data set used. In section 3, we will introduce some of the fundamental assumptions underlying the Culturomics approach for Big Data, and report on an experiment that replicates an earlier sentiment-related analysis of the Google Books Corpus (Acerbi et al., 2013b) using our *Time* data. Subsequently, we will apply a Parsimonious Language Model to our data (section 4) and assess from a qualitative perspective how and whether this technique can be used to extract the characteristic vocabulary from specific time periods. To conclude, we will use these Parsimonious Language Models in a variability-based neighbor clustering (section 5), in an explorative attempt to computationally identify major turning points in the twentieth century's history.

2 Data: Time Magazine Corpus

For the present research, we have used a collection of electronic articles harvested from the archive of the well-known weekly publication *Time Magazine*. The magazine's online archive is protected by international copyright law and it can only be consulted via a paying subscription.[2] Therefore, the corpus cannot be freely redistributed in any format. To construct the corpus, we have used metadata provided by corpus linguist Mark Davies who has published a searchable interface to the Time Corpus (Davies, 2013). For the present paper, we were only dependent on the unique identification number and publication year which Davies provides for each article. Users who are interested in downloading (a portion of) the corpus which we used, can use this metadata to replicate our findings.

We have used the Stanford CoreNLP Suite to annotate this collection (with its default settings for the English language).[3] We have tokenized and lemmatized the corpus with this tool suite. Additionally, we have applied part-of-speech tagging (Toutanova et al., 2003) and named entity recognition (Finkel et al., 2005). In the end, our reconstructed version of the Time Corpus in total amounted to 270,695 individual articles. In its entirety, the corpus counted 191,743,541 distinct word forms (including punctuation marks), 867,399 forms of which proved unique in their lowercased format. Some general statistics about our reconstructed version of the Time Corpus are given in Table 1. In addition to the cumulative word count statistics about the corpus, we have included the frequency information per decade (1920s, 1930s, etc.), as this periodisation will prove important for the experiments described in section 4.

Period	# Documents	# Word forms	# Unique forms
1920s	24,332	11,155,681	158,443
1930s	32,788	20,622,526	222,777
1940s	41,832	22,547,958	234,918
1950s	42,249	25,638,032	251,658
1960s	35,440	27,355,389	258,276
1970s	27,804	25,449,488	218,322
1980s	25,651	24,185,889	208,678
1990s	23,300	20,637,179	204,393
2000s	17,299	14,151,399	176,515
Overall	**270,695**	**191,743,541**	**867,399**

Table 1: General word frequency statistics on the reconstructed version of the Time Corpus (1923-2006).

In its entirety, the corpus covers the period March 1923 throughout December 2006. It only includes articles from the so-called 'U.S. edition' of *Time* (i.e., it does not contain articles which only featured in the e.g. European edition of the Magazine). Because of *Time*'s remarkably continuous publication history, as well as the considerable attention the magazine traditionally pays to international affairs and politics, the Time Corpus can be expected to offer an interesting, albeit exclusively American perspective on the recent world history. As far as we know, the corpus has only been used so far in corpus linguistic publications and we do not know of any advanced studies in the field of cultural history that make extensive use of the corpus.

3 Assumption: Lexical frequency

Previous contributions to the field of Culturomics all have in common that they attempt to establish a correlation between word frequency statistics and cultural phenomena. While this is rarely explicitly voiced, the broader assumption underlying these studies is that frequency statistics extracted from

[2] `http://content.time.com/time/archive.`

[3] `http://nlp.stanford.edu/software/corenlp.shtml`

the texts produced by a society at specific moment in history, will necessarily reflect that society's cultural specific (e.g. cultural) concerns at that time. As such, it can for instance be expected that the frequency of conflict-related terminology will tend to be more elevated in texts produced by a society at war than one at peace. (Needless to say, this need not imply that a society e.g. supports that war, since the same conflict-related terminology will be frequent in texts that oppose a particular conflict.) Obviously, the resulting assumption is that the study of developments in the vocabulary of a large body of texts should enable the study of the evolution of the broader historical concerns that exist(ed) in the culture in which these texts were produced.

Frequency has been considered a key measure in recent studies into cultural influence (Skiena and Ward, 2013). The more frequent a word in a corpus, the more weighty the cultural concerns which that word might be related to. A naive illustration of this frequency effect can be gleaned from Figure 1. In the subplots of the figure, we have plotted the absolute frequency with which the last names of U.S. presidents have been yearly mentioned throughout the Time Corpus (in their lowercased form, and only when tagged as a named entity). The horizontal axis represents time, with grey zones indicating start and end dates of the administration periods. The absolute frequencies have been normalised in each year, by taking their ratio over the frequency of the definite article *the*. Before plotting, these relative frequencies have been mean-normalised. (Readers are kindly requested to zoom in on the digital PDF to view more detail for all figures.) Although this is by no means a life-changing observation, each presidential reign is indeed clearly characterised by a significant boost in the frequency of the corresponding president's last name. Nevertheless, the graph also displays some notable deficiencies, such the confusion of father and son Bush, or the increase in frequency right before an administration period, which seems related to the presidential election campaigns.

Figure 1: Diachronic visualisation of mean-normalised frequencies-of-mention of the last names of U.S. presidents in the Time corpus, together with their administration periods.

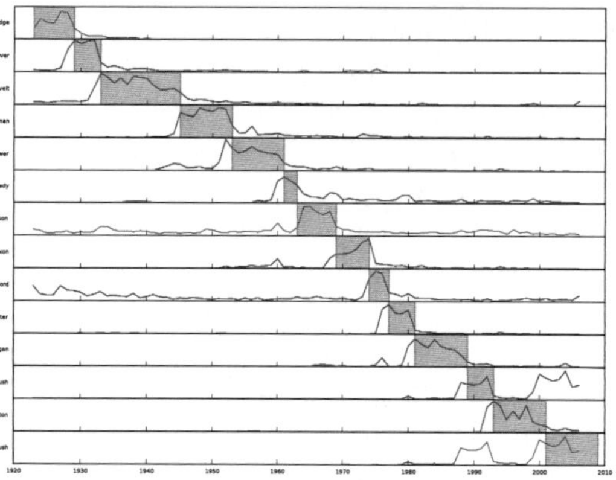

Importantly, it has been stressed that reliable frequency information can only be extracted from large enough corpora, in order to escape the bias caused by limiting oneself to e.g. too restricted a number of topics or text varieties. This has caused studies to stress the importance of so-called 'Big Data' when it comes to Culturomics, reviving the old adagium from the field of Machine Learning 'There's no data like more data', attributed to Mercer. In terms of data size, it is therefore an important question whether the Time Corpus is a reliable enough resource for practicing Culturomics. While the Time Corpus (just under 200 million tokens) is not a small data set, it is of course orders of magnitude smaller than the Google Books corpus with its intimidating 361 billion words. As such, the Time Corpus might hardly qualify as 'Big Data' in the eyes of many contemporary data scientists. One distinct advantage which the Time Corpus might offer to counter-balance the disadvantage of its limited size, is the high quality, both of the actual text, as well as the metadata (OCR-errors are for instance extremely rare).

In order to assess whether a smaller, yet higher-quality corpus like the Time Corpus might yield valid results when it comes to Culturomics we have attempted to replicate an interesting experiment reported by Acerbi et al. (2013b) in the context of a paper on the expression of emotions in twentieth century books. For their research, they used the publicly available Google Books unigram corpus. In our Figure 2 we have reproduced their 'Figure 1: Historical periods of positive and negative moods'. For this analysis, they used the so-called LIWC-procedure: a methodology which attempts to measure the presence of particular emotions in texts by calculating the relative occurrences of a set of key words (Tausczik and Pennebaker, 2010).[4] In the authors' own words, the graph "shows that moods tracked broad historical trends, including a 'sad' peak corresponding to Second World War, and two 'happy' peaks, one in the 1920's and the other in the 1960's."

We have exactly re-engineered their methodology and applied it to the Time Corpus. The result of this entirely parallel LIWC-analysis (Tausczik and Pennebaker, 2010) of the Time Corpus is visualized in Figure 3. While our data of course only starts in 1923 instead of 1900 (cf. grey area), it is clear that our experiment has produced a surprisingly similar curve, especially when it comes to the 'sad' and 'happy' periods in the 1940s and 1960s respectively. These pronounced similarities are especially remarkable because, to our knowledge, the Time Corpus is not only much smaller but also completely unrelated to the Google Books corpus. This experiment thus serves to emphasise the remarkable stability of certain cultural trends as reflected across various text types and unrelated text corpora.[5] Moreover, these results suggest that the Time Corpus, in spite of limited size, might still yield interesting and valid results in the context of Culturomics research.

4 Parsimonious Language Models

As discussed above, Michel et al. (2011) have proposed a methodology in their seminal paper, whereby, broadly speaking, they try to establish a correlation between historical events and word counts in corpora. They show, for instance, that the term 'Great War' is only frequent in their data until the 1940s: at that point the more distinctive terms 'World War I' and 'World War II' suddenly become more frequent. One interesting issue here is that this methodology is characterised by a modest form a 'cherry picking': with this way of working, a researcher will only try out word frequency plots of which (s)he expects beforehand that they will display interesting trends. Inevitably, this fairly supervised approach might lower one's chance to discover new phenomena, and thus reduces the chance for scientific serendipity to occur. An equally interesting, yet much less

Figure 2: Figure reproduced from Acerbi et al. (2013b): 'Figure 1: Historical periods of positive and negative moods'. Also see Figure 3.

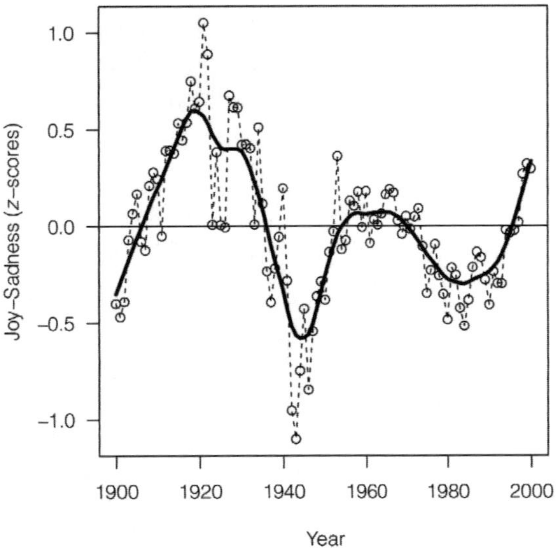

supervised approach might therefore be to *automatically* identify which terms are characteristic for a given time span in a corpus.

In this respect, it is interesting to refer to Parsimonious Language Models (PLMs), a fairly recent addition to the field of Information Retrieval (Hiemstra et al., 2004). PLMs can be used to create a probabilistic model of a text collection, describing the relevance of words in individual documents in contrast to all other texts in the collection. From the point of view of indexing in Information Retrieval, the question which a PLM in reality tries to answer is: 'Suppose that in the future, a user will be looking for this document, which search terms is (s)he most likely to use?' As such, PLMs offers a powerful alternative to the established TF-IDF metric, in that they are also able to estimate which words are most characteristic of a given document. While PLMs are completely unsupervised (i.e. no manual annotation of documents is needed), they do require setting the λ parameter beforehand. The λ parameter will of course have a major influence on the final results, since it will control the rate at which the language of each document will grow different from that of all other documents, during the subsequent updates of the model. (For the mathematical details on λ, consult Hiemstra et al. (2004).) Thus, PLMs can be expected to single out more characteristic vocab-

[4] We would like to thank Ben Verhoeven for sharing his LIWC-implementation. The methodology adopted by Acerbi et al. (2013b) has been detailed in the following blog post: `http://acerbialberto.wordpress.com/tag/emotion/`.

[5] Acerbi et al. (2013a) have studied the robustness of their own experiments recently, using different metrics.

Figure 3: LIWC-analysis carried on the Time Corpus (cf. Figure 2), attempting to replicate the trends found by Acerbi et al. (2013b). Plotted is the absolute difference between the z-scores for the LIWC-categories 'Positive emotions' and 'Negative emotions'. The same smoother ('Friedman's supersmoother') has been applied (R Core Team, 2013).

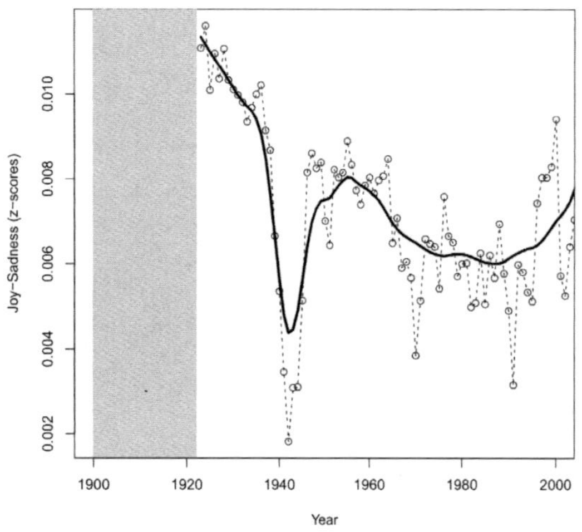

ulary than simpler frequentist approaches and, interestingly, they are more lightweight to run than e.g. temporal topic models.

In a series of explorative experiments, we have applied PLMs to the Time Corpus. In particular, we have build PLMs for this data, by combining individual articles into much larger documents: both for each year in the data, as well as all 'decades' (e.g. $1930 = 1930 - 1939$) we have constructed such large, multi-article documents. For both document types (years and decades), we have subsequently generated PLMs. In Figure 4 to Figure 12 we have plotted the results for the PLMs based on the decade documents (for $\lambda = 0.1$). In the left subpanel, we show the 25 words (technically, the lowercased lemma's) which the PLM estimated to be most discriminative for a given decade. In the right subpanel, we have plotted the evolution of the relevance scores for each of these 25 words in the year-based PLM (the grey zone indicates the decade). Higher scores indicate a more pronounced relevance for a given decade. For the sake of interpretation, we have restricted our analysis to words which were tagged as nouns ('NN'

Figure 4: PLM for the 1920s.

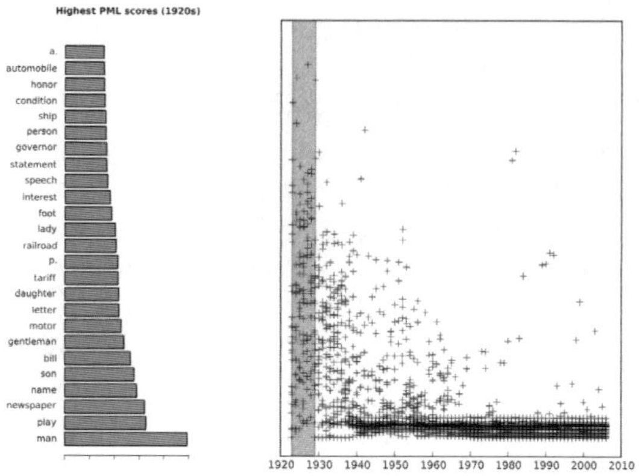

Figure 5: PLM for the 1930s.

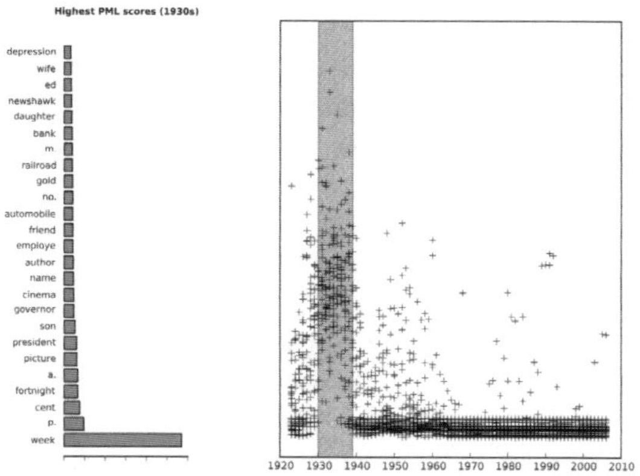

& 'NNS').

It is not immediately clear how the output of these PLMs can be evaluated using quantitative means. A concise qualitative discussion seems most appropriate to assess the results. For this reason, we have combined individual articles into larger decade documents in these experiments, since this offers a very intuitive manner of arranging the available sources from a historical, interpretative point of view. Often, when people address the periodisation of the twentieth century they will use decades, where terms like e.g. 'the seventies' or 'the twenties' refer to a fairly well-delineated concept in people's minds, associated with a particular set of political events, people and cultural phenomena, etc. By sticking to this decade-based periodisation, we can verify fairly easily to what extent the top 25 yielded by the PLM corresponds to commonplace historical

Figure 6: PLM for the 1940s.

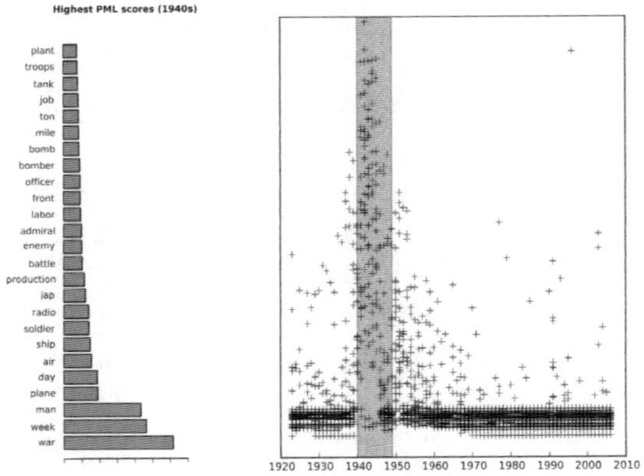

Figure 7: PLM for the 1950s.

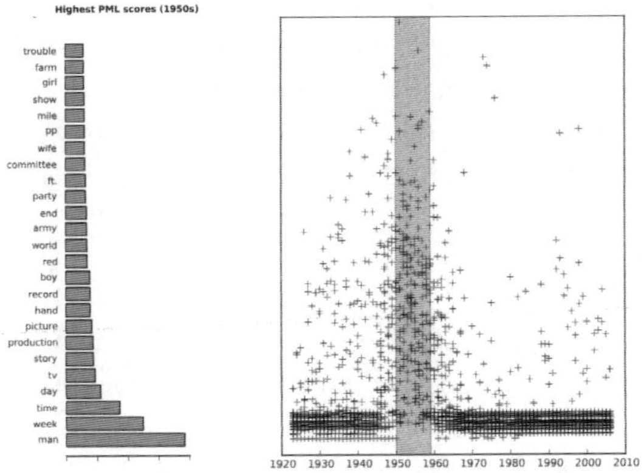

Figure 8: PLM for the 1960s.

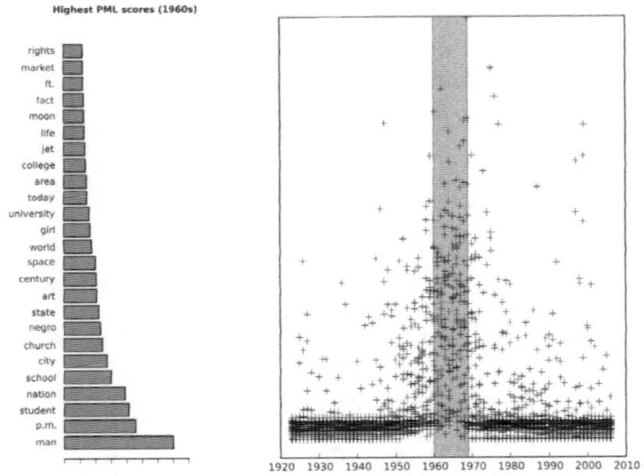

Figure 9: PLM for the 1970s.

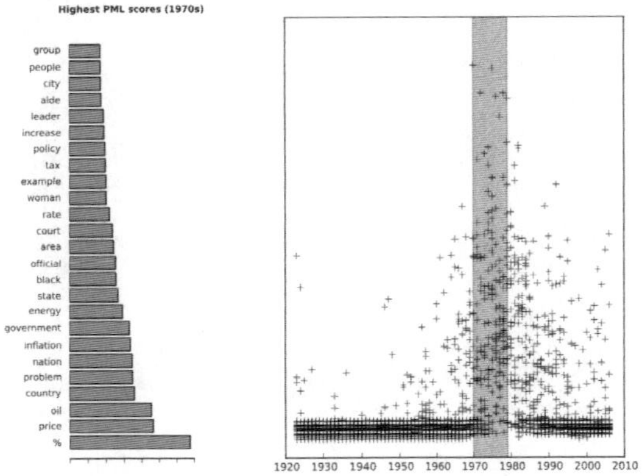

Figure 10: PLM for the 1980s.

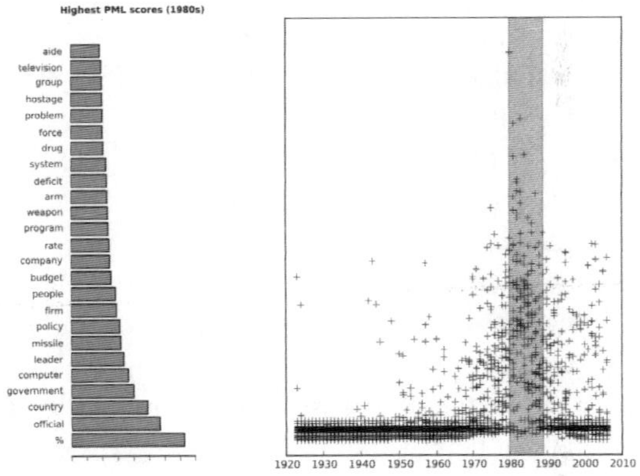

Figure 11: PLM for the 1990s.

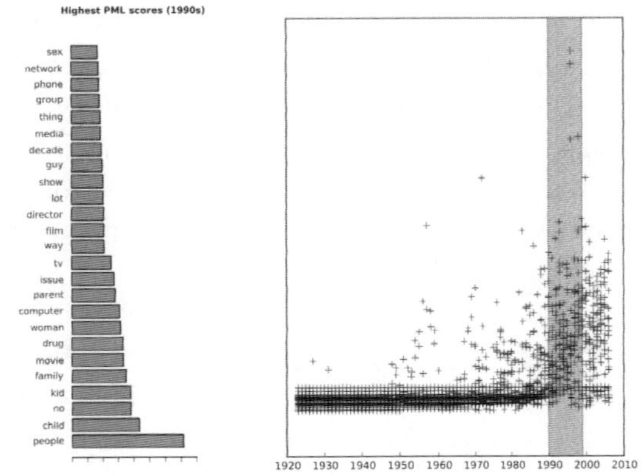

Figure 12: PLM for the 2000s.

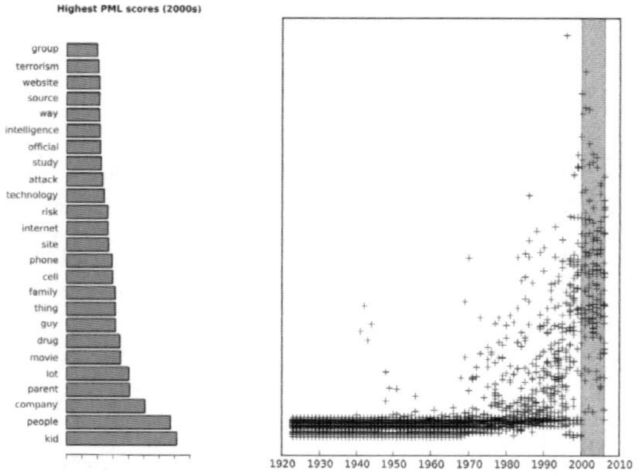

stereotypes about the decades in the twentieth century.

Let us start by inspecting the top 25 for the 1940s, a decade in which the Second War II naturally played a major role. Already at first glance, it is clear that the top 25 is dominated by war-related terminology (*war*, *soldier*, *enemy*, ...). Interestingly, the list also contains words referring to WWII, but not from the politically correct jargon which we would nowadays use to address the issue (e.g. *jap*). Remarkable is the pronounced position of aviary vocabulary (*bomber*, *air*, *plane*, ...), which is perhaps less surprising if we consider the fact that WWI was one of the first international conflicts in which aircrafts played a major military role.

Interestingly, the 1920s are hardly characterised by an equally focused set of relevant words. Although mobility does seem to play an important role (cf. the recently invented *automobile*, but also *ship* and *railroad*), a number of less meaningful abbreviations (such as *p.* for 'page') pop up that seem connected to superficial changes in *Time*'s editorial policies, rather than cultural developments. (Future analyses might want to remove such words manually.) On the other hand, the use of the terms *lady* and *honour* might be rooted in a cultural climate that is different from ours ('lady' seems the equivalent of woman today). A number of parallel observations can be made for the 1930s, although here, the high ranking word *depression* is of course striking (cf. the economic crisis of 1929). Fascinatingly, a variety of denominations for (popular) media play a major role throughout the decade PLMs. Note, that while the 1920s' top 25 mentioned the *radio* as the primary communication medium, the popular *cinema* and (moving?) *picture* show up in the 1930s. Interestingly, the popular media of *tv* and *record* make their appearance in the 1950s. (In the 1980s and 1990s top 25, *television* moreover continues to show up.)

The PLM also seems to offer an excellent cultural characterisation of the 1960s and the associated baby boom, with an emphasis on the controversies of the time, debate involving human rights (*rights*, *negro*, *nation*), and in particular educational (*college*, *university*, *school*). The use of 'educational' words might well be related to the social unrest, much of which took place in and around universities. Does the striking presence of the word 'today' in the list reveal an elevated *hic et nunc* mentality in the contemporary States? America's well-documented interest in space traveling at the time is also appropriately reflected (*space*, *moon*). Perhaps unexpectedly, this seemingly optimistic 'Zeitgeist' is more strongly associated in the Time Corpus with the sixties, than with the seventies: in the flower-power era, *Time* displays a remarkable focus on political and especially economic issues. Rather, the oil crisis seems to dominate Time's lexis in the seventies.

In the 1990s and 2000s, we can observe a focus on what one might unrespectfully call 'first-world problems', involving for instance family relations (*family*, *kid*, *parent*, *child*, etc.). Apart from the fact that *Time*'s vocabulary seems to grow more colloquial in general in this period (at least in our eyes, e.g. *guy*, *lot*, *thing*), a number of controversial taboo subjects seem to have become discussable: *sex*, *drug*. 'Terrorism' and 'intelligence' seem to have become major concerns in post-09/11 America, and perhaps the presence of the word 'attack' and 'technology' might be (partially) interpreted in the same light. Again, we see how vocabulary related to media absolutely dominates the final rankings in the corpus: Hollywood seems to have enjoyed an increasing popularity (*film*, *director*, *movie*, ...) but it is information technology that seems to have had the biggest cultural impact: mobile communication devices (*phone*, *cell*) and Internet-related terminology (*network*, *computer*, *internet*, ...) seem to have caused a major turning point in Time's lexis.[6]

[6]Due to lack of space, we only report results for $\lambda = 0.1$ applied to nouns, but highly similar results could be obtained

5 Twentieth Century Turning Points?

An interesting technique in this respect is a clustering method called VNC or 'Variability-Based Neighbor Clustering' (Gries and Hilpert, 2008). The technique has been introduced in the field of historical linguistics as an aid in the automated identification of temporal stages in diachronic data. The method will apply a fairly straightforward clustering algorithm to a data set (with e.g. Ward linkage applied to a Cosine distance matrix) but, importantly, it will add the connectivity constraint that (clusters of) data points can only merge with each other at the next level in a dendrogram, if they are immediately adjacent. That is to say that e.g. in a series of yearly observations 1943 would be allowed to merge with 1942 and 1944, but not with 1928 (even if 1943 would be much more similar to 1928 than to 1943). We have applied VNC (with Ward linkage applied to a plain Cosine distance table) to a series of vectors which for each year in our data (1923-2006) contained the PML scores of 5,000 words deemed most relevant for that year by the model.

The dendrogram resulting from the VNC procedure is visualised in Figure 13. The early history of *Time Magazine* (1923-1927) does not really seem to fit in with the rest and takes up a fairly deviant position. However, the most attention-grabbing feature of this tree structure is the major divide which the dendrogram suggests (cf. red vs. green-blue cluster) between the years before and after 1945, the end of the Second World War. Another significant rupture seem to be present before and after 1996: the discussion leaves us to wonder whether this turning point might related to the recent introduction of new communication technologies, in particular the rise of the Internet.

Historically speaking, these turning points do not come as a surprise. There is, for instance, widespread acceptance among historians WWII has indeed been the single most influential event in the twentieth century. What does surprise, however, is the relative easy with which a completely unsupervised procedure has managed to suggest this identification. Arguably, this is where we leave the realm of the obvious when it comes to the computational study of cultural history. The identification of major events and turning points in human history is normally a task which requires a good deal of formal education and some advanced reasoning skills. Here, we might be nearing a modest form of Artificial Intelligence when we apply computational methods to achieve a fairly similar goal. Hopefully, these analyses, as well as the ones reported above, illustrate the huge potential of computational methods in the study of cultural history, even if only as a discovery tool.

using other part-of-speech categories and settings for λ. An interesting effect was associated with 'fiddling the knob' of this last parameter: for lower values (0.01, 0.001 etc.), the model would come up with perhaps increasingly characteristic, but also increasingly obscure and much less frequent vocabulary. For the fourties, for instance, instead of returning the word 'bomber' the analysis would return the exact name of a particular bomber type which was used at the time. This parameter setting deserves further exploration.

Figure 13: Dendrogram resulting from applying Variability-Based Neighbor Analysis to vectors which contain for each year the 5,000 words deemed most relevant by the PML.

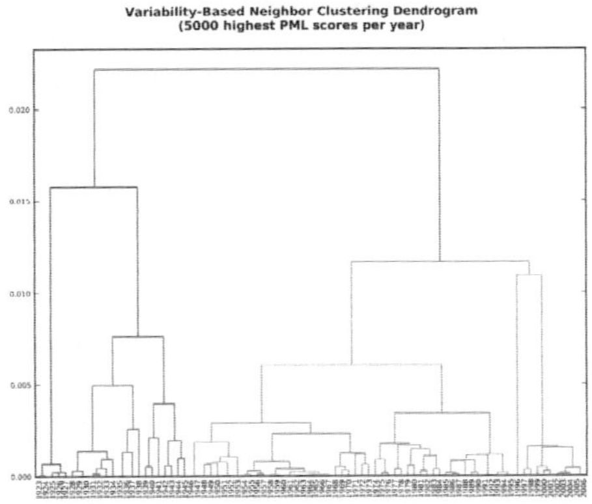

6 Conclusion and criticism

In this paper we have discussed a series of analyses that claim to mine a data-driven cultural characterization of the 'Zeitgeist' of some of the main periods in the twentieth century. Nevertheless, we must remain vigilant not to overstate the achievement of these techniques: it remains to be determined to which extent can we truly call these applications Digital History and whether these analyses have taught us anything which we did not know before. Because the twentieth century is so well known to most of us, the evidence often tends to be self-referential and self-explanatory, and merely confirms that which we already knew intuitively. Like with most distant reading approaches, the results urge us to go back to the original material for the close reading of individual sources in their historical context, in order to verify the macro-hypotheses that might be suggested at a higher level. Therefore, the proposed method might in fact be more suitable for the study of time periods and corpora of which we know less.

Nevertheless, our methodology seems promising for future applications in Digital History: our naïve periodisation in decades, for instance, might be hugely fine-tuned by processing the results of a VNC-dendrogram. Breaking up history into meaningful units is a much more complex, and often controversial matter (e.g. 'When does modernity start?'). In this light, it would be helpful to have at our disposal unbiased, computational tools that might help us to identify cultural ruptures or even turning points in history. Our results reported in the final section do show that this application yields interesting results, and again, the method seems promising for the analysis of lesser known corpora.

Acknowledgments

The authors would like to thank the anonymous reviewers and Kalliopi Zervanou for their valuable feedback on earlier drafts of this paper, as well as Walter Daelemans and Antal van den Bosch for the inspiring discussions on the topic. For this study, Mike Kestemont was funded as a postdoctoral research fellow for the Research Foundation of Flanders (FWO). Folgert Karsdorp was supported as a Ph.D. candidate by the Computational Humanities Programme of the Royal Netherlands Academy of Arts and Sciences, as part of the Tunes & Tales project.

References

Alberto Acerbi, Vasileios Lampos, and Alexander R. Bentley. 2013a. Robustness of emotion extraction from 20th century English books. In *BigData '13*. IEEE, IEEE.

Alberto Acerbi, Vasileios Lampos, Philip Garnett, and Alexander R. Bentley. 2013b. The Expression of Emotions in 20th Century Books. *PLoS ONE*, 8(3):e59030.

Mark Davies. 2013. TIME Magazine Corpus: 100 million words, 1920s-2000s.

Jenny Rose Finkel, Trond Grenager, and Christopher Manning. 2005. Incorporating Non-local Information into Information Extraction Systems by Gibbs Sampling. In *Proceedings of the 43rd Annual Meeting on Association for Computational Linguistics*, ACL '05, pages 363–370, Stroudsburg, PA, USA. Association for Computational Linguistics.

Stefan Th. Gries and Martin Hilpert. 2008. The identification of stages in diachronic data: variability-based neighbour clustering. *Corpora*, 3(1):59–81.

Djoerd Hiemstra, Stephen E. Robertson, and Hugo Zaragoza. 2004. Parsimonious language models for information retrieval. In Mark Sanderson, Kalervo Jrvelin, James Allan, and Peter Bruza, editors, *SIGIR*, pages 178–185. ACM.

Patrick Juola. 2013. Using the Google N-Gram corpus to measure cultural complexity. *Literary and Linguistic Computing*, 28(4):668–675.

Kalev H. Leetaru. 2011. Culturomics 2.0: Forecasting large-scale human behavior using global news media tone in time and space. *First Monday*, 16(9).

Jean-Baptiste Michel, Yuan Kui Shen, Aviva Presser Aiden, Adrian Veres, Matthew K. Gray, The Google Books Team, Joseph P. Pickett, Dale Hoiberg, Dan Clancy, Peter Norvig, Jon Orwant, Steven Pinker, Martin A. Nowak, and Erez Lieberman Aiden. 2011. Quantitative Analysis of Culture Using Millions of Digitized Books. *Science*, 331(6014):176–182.

R Core Team, 2013. *R: A Language and Environment for Statistical Computing*. R Foundation for Statistical Computing, Vienna, Austria.

Steve Skiena and Charles Ward. 2013. *Who Belongs in Bonnie's Textbook?* Cambridge University Press.

Yla R. Tausczik and James W. Pennebaker. 2010. The Psychological Meaning of Words: LIWC and Computerized Text Analysis Methods. *Journal of Language and Social Psychology*, 29(1):24–54.

Kristina Toutanova, Dan Klein, Christopher Manning, and Yoram Singer. 2003. Feature-rich Part-of-speech Tagging with a Cyclic Dependency Network. In *Proceedings of the 2003 Conference of the North American Chapter of the Association for Computational Linguistics on Human Language Technology - Volume 1*, NAACL '03, pages 173–180, Stroudsburg, PA, USA. Association for Computational Linguistics.

Jean M. Twenge, Keith W. Campbell, and Brittany Gentile. 2012. Increases in Individualistic Words and Phrases in American Books, 19602008. *PLoS ONE*, 7(7):e40181.

Gerben Zaagsma. 2013. On Digital History. *BMGN – Low Countries Historical Review*, 128(4):3–29.

Social and Semantic Diversity: Socio-semantic Representation of a Scientific Corpus

Elisa Omodei
LATTICE and ISC-PIF
CNRS & ENS & U. Sorbonne Nouvelle
1 rue Mauriece Arnoux
92120 Montrouge France
elisa.omodei@ens.fr

Yufan Guo
University of Washington
Computer Science
Engineering
Box 352350 Seattle, WA 98195-2350
yufanguo@cs.washington.edu

Jean-Philippe Cointet
INRA Sens and ISC-PIF
Cité Descartes, 5 boulevard Descartes
77454 Marne-la-Vallée Cedex France
75013 Paris France
jphcoi@yahoo.fr

Thierry Poibeau
LATTICE
CNRS & ENS & U. Sorbonne Nouvelle
1 rue Mauriece Arnoux
92120 Montrouge France
thierry.poibeau@ens.fr

Abstract

We propose a new method to extract keywords from texts and categorize these keywords according to their informational value, derived from the analysis of the argumentative goal of the sentences they appear in. The method is applied to the ACL Anthology corpus, containing papers on the computational linguistic domain published between 1980 and 2008. We show that our approach allows to highlight interesting facts concerning the evolution of the topics and methods used in computational linguistics.

1 Introduction

Big data makes it possible to observe in vivo the dynamics of a large number of different domains. It is particularly the case in the scientific field, where researchers produce a prolific literature but also other kinds of data like numbers, figures, images and so on. For a number of domains, large scientific archives are now available over several decades.

This is for example the case for computational linguistics. The ACL Anthology contains more than 24,500 papers, for the most part in PDF format. The oldest ones date back to 1965 (first edition of the COLING conference) but it is mostly after 1980 that data are available in large volumes so that they can be exploited in evolution studies. The volume of data increases over time, which means there is a wide diversity in the number of papers available depending on the given period of time. There are similar archives for different domains like, e.g. physics (the APS database provided by the American Physical Society) or the bio-medical domain (with Medline).

These scientific archives have already given birth to a large number of different pieces of work. Collaboration networks have for example been automatically extracted so as to study the topology of the domain (Girvan and Newman, 2002) or its morphogenesis (Guimera et al., 2005). Referencing has also been the subject of numerous studies on inter-citation (Garfield, 1972) and co-citation (Small, 1973). Other variables can be taken into account like the nationality of the authors, the projects they are involved in or the research institutions they belong to, but it is the analysis of the textual content (mostly titles, abstracts and keywords provided with the papers) that have attracted the most part of the research in the area since the seminal work of Callon (Callon et al., 1986; Callon et al., 1991).

In this paper, our goal is to investigate the evolution of the field of computational linguistics, which means that text will play a crucial role. Textual analysis is then mixed with the study of individual trajectories in the semantic space: our goal is to propose possible avenues for the study of the dynamics of innovation in the computational linguistics domain.

The ACL Anthology has been the subject of several studies in 2012, for the 50 years of the ACL. More specifically, a workshop called "Rediscovering 50 Years of Discoveries" was organized to examine 50 years of research in NLP (but, for the reasons given above, the workshop mostly focused on the evolution of the domain since 1980). This workshop was also an opportunity to study a large scientific collection with recent NLP techniques and see how these techniques can be applied to study the dynamics of a scientific domain.

The analysis of this kind of data is generally based on the extraction of key information (authors, keywords) and the discovery of their relationships. The data can be represented as a graph, therefore graph algorithmics can be used to study the topology and the evolution of the graph of collaborations or the graph of linked authors. It is thus possible to observe the evolution of the domain, check some hypotheses or common assumptions about this evolution and provide a strong empirical basis to epistemology studies.

The paper "Towards a computational History of the ACL: 1980-2008" is very relevant from this point of view (Anderson et al., 2012). The authors try to determine the evolution of the main sub-domains of research within NLP since 1980 and they obtain very interesting results. For example, they show the influence of the American evaluation campaigns on the domain: when a US agency sponsored a sub-domain of NLP, one can observe a quick concentration effect since a wide number of research groups suddenly concentrated their efforts on the topic; when no evaluation campaign was organized, research was much more widespread across the different sub-domains of NLP. Even if this is partially predictable, it was not obvious to be able to show this in a collection of papers as large as the ACL Anthology.

Our study has been profoundly influenced by the study by Anderson et al. However, our goal here is to characterize automatically the keywords based on the information they carry. We will thus combine keyword extraction with text zoning so as to categorize the keywords depending on their context of use.

The rest of the paper is organized as follows. We first present an analysis of the structure of abstracts so as to better characterize their content by mixing keyword extraction with text zoning. We show how these techniques can be applied to the ACL Anthology in order to examine specific facts, more specifically concerning the evolution of the techniques used in the computational linguistics domain.

2 A Text Zoning Analysis of the ACL Anthology

The study of the evolution of topics in large corpora is usually done through keyword extraction. This is also our goal, but we would like to be able to better characterize these keywords and make a difference, for example, between keywords referring to concepts and keywords referring to methods. Hence, the context of these keywords seems highly important. Consequently, we propose to use Text Zoning that can provide an accurate characterization of the argumentative goal of each sentence in a scientific abstract.

2.1 Previous work

The first important contributions in text zoning are probably the experiments by S. Teufel who proposed to categorize sentences in scientific papers (and more specifically, in the NLP domain) according to different categories (Teufel, 1999) like BKG: General scientific background, AIM: Statements of the particular aim of the current paper or CTR: Contrastive or comparative statements about other work. This task is called Rhetorical zoning or Argumentative zoning since the goal is to identify the rhetoric or argumentative role of each sentence of the text.

The initial work of Teufel was based on the manual annotation of 80 papers representing the different areas of NLP (the corpus was made of papers published within the ACL conferences or Computational Linguistics). A classifier was then trained on this manually annotated corpus. The author reported interesting results despite "a 20% diference between [the] system and human performance" (Teufel and Moens, 2002). The learning method used a Naive Bayesian model since more sophisticated methods tested by the author did not obtain better results. Teufel in subsequent publications showed that the technique can be used to produce high quality summaries (Teufel and Moens, 2002) or precisely characterize the different citations in a paper (Ritchie et al., 2008).

The seminal work of Teufel has since then given

rise to different kinds of works, on the one hand to refine the annotation method, and on the other hand to check its applicability to different scientific domains. Concerning the first point, research has focused on the identification of relevant features for classification, on the evaluation of different learning algorithms for the task and more importantly on the reduction of the volume of text to be annotated. Concerning the second point, it is mostly the biological and bio-medical domains that have attracted attention, since scientists in these domains often have to access the literature "vertically" (i.e. experts may need to have access to all the methods and protocols that have been used in a specific domain) (Mizuta et al., 2006; Tbahriti et al., 2006).

Guo has since developed a similar trend of research to extend the initial work of Teufel (Guo et al., 2011; Guo et al., 2013): she has tested a large list of features to analyze the zones, evaluated different learning algorithms for the task and proposed new methods to decrease the number of texts to be annotated. The features used for learning are of three categories: *i*) positional (location of the sentence inside the paper), *ii*) lexical (words, classes of words, bigrams, etc. are taken into consideration) and *iii*) syntactic (the different syntactic relations as well as the class of words appearing in subject or object positions are taken into account). The analysis is thus based on more features than in Teufel's initial work and requires a parser.

2.2 Application to the ACL Anthology corpus

In our experiment, we only used the abstracts of the papers. Our hypothesis is that abstracts contain enough information and are redundant enough to study the evolution of the domain. Taking into consideration the full text would probably give too many details and thus introduce noise in the analysis.

The annotation scheme includes five different categories, which are the following: OBJECTIVE (objectives of the paper), METHOD (methods used in the paper), RESULTS (main results), CONCLUSION (conclusion of the paper), BACKGROUND (general context), as in (Reichart and Korhonen, 2012). These categories are also close to those of (Mizuta et al., 2006; Guo et al., 2011; Guo et al., 2013) and have been adapted to abstracts (as opposed to full text[1]). It seems relevant to take into consideration an annotation scheme that has already been used by various authors so that the results are easy to compare to others.

Around one hundred abstracts from the ACL Anthology have then been manually annotated using this scheme ($\sim$500 sentences; ACL abstracts are generally quite short since most of them are related to conference papers). The selection of the abstracts has been done using stratified sampling over time and journals, so as to obtain a representative corpus (papers must be related to different periods of time and different sub-areas of the domain). The annotation has been done according to the annotation guideline defined by Y. Guo, especially for long sentences when more than one category could be applied (preferences are defined to solve complex cases[2]).

The algorithm defined by (Guo et al., 2011) is then adapted to our corpus. The analysis is based on positional, lexical and syntactic features, as explained above. No domain specific information was added, which makes the whole process easy to reproduce. As for parsing, we used the C&C parser (James Curran and Stephen Clark and Johan Bos, 2007). All the implementation details can be found in (Guo et al., 2011), especially concerning annotation and the learning algorithm. As a result, each sentence is associated with a tag corresponding to one of the zones defined in the annotation scheme.

2.3 Results and Discussion

In order to evaluate the text zoning task, a number of abstracts were chosen randomly ($\sim$300 sentences that do not overlap with the training set). CONCLUSION represented less than 3% of the sentences and was then dropped for the rest of the analysis. The four remaining zones are unequaly represented: 18.05 % of the sentences refer to BACKGROUND, 14.35% to OBJECTIVE, 14.81 % to RESULT and 52.77 % to METHOD. Just by looking at these numbers, one can see how

[1]The categories used in (Teufel, 1999) were not relevant since this model focused on full text papers, with a special emphasis on the novelty of the author's work and the attitude towards other people's work, which is not the case here.

[2]The task is to assign the sentence only a single category. The choice of the category should be made according to the following priority list: Conclusion > Objective > Result > Method > Background. The only exception is that when 75% or more of the sentence belongs to a less preferred category, then that category will be assigned to the sentence.

Table 1: Result of the text zoning analysis (precision)

Category	Precision
Objective	83,87 %
Background	81,25 %
Method	71,05 %
Results	82,05 %

Figure 1: An abstract annotated with text zoning information. Categories are indicated in bold face.

Most of errors in Korean morphological analysis and POS (Part-of-Speech) tagging are caused by unknown morphemes . **BACKGROUND**
This paper presents a generalized unknown morpheme handling method with POSTAG(POStech TAGger) which is a statistical/rule based hybrid POS tagging system . **OBJECTIVE**
The generalized unknown morpheme guessing is based on a combination of a morpheme pattern dictionary which encodes general lexical patterns of Korean morphemes with a posteriori syllable tri-gram estimation . **METHOD**
The syllable tri-grams help to calculate lexical probabilities of the unknown morphemes and are utilized to search the best tagging result . **METHOD**
In our scheme , we can guess the POS's of unknown morphemes regardless of their numbers and positions in an eojeol , which was not possible before in Korean tagging systems . **RESULTS**
In a series of experiments using three different domain corpora , we can achieve 97% tagging accuracy regardless of many unknown morphemes in test corpora . **RESULTS**

methodological issues are important for the domain.

We then calculate for each of the categories, the percentage of sentences that received the right label, which allows us to calculate precision. The results are given in table 1.

These results are similar to the state of the art (Guo et al., 2011), which is positive taking into consideration the small number of sentences annotated for training. The diversity of the features used makes it easy to transfer the technique from one domain to the other without any heavy annotation phase. Results are slightly worse for the METHOD category, probably because this category is more diverse and thus more difficult to recognize. The fact that NLP terms can refer either to objectives or to methods also contributes rendering the recognition of this category more difficult.

Figure 1 shows an abstract annotated by the text zoning module (the paper is (Lee et al., 2002): it has been chosen randomly between those containing the different types of zones). One category is associated with each sentence but this is sometimes problematic: for example the fact that a hybrid method is used is mentioned in a sentence that is globally tagged as OBJECTIVE by the system. However, sentences tagged as METHOD contain relevant keywords like *lexical pattern* or *tri-gram estimation*, which makes it possible to infer that the approach is hybrid. One can also spot some problems with digitization, which are typical of this corpus: the ACL Anthology contains automatically converted files to PDF, which means texts are not perfect and may contain some digitization errors.

3 Contribution to the Study of the Evolution ACL Anthology

As said above, we are largely inspired by (Anderson et al., 2012). We think the ACL Anthology is typical since it contains papers spanning over more than 30 years: it is thus interesting to use it as a way to study the main evolutions of the computational linguistics domain. The method can of course also be applied to other scientific corpora.

3.1 Keyword extraction and characterization

The first step consists in identifying the main keywords of the domain. We then want to more precisely categorize these keywords so as to identify the ones specifically referring to methods for example. From this perspective, keywords appearing in the METHOD sections are thus particularly interesting for us. However, one major problem is that there is no clear-cut difference between goals and methods in NLP since most systems are made of different layers and require various NLP techniques. For example, a semantic analyzer may use a part-of-speech tagger and a parser, which means NLP tools can appear as part of the method.

Keyword extraction aims at automatically extracting relevant keywords from a collection of texts. A popular approach consists in first extracting typical sequences of tags that are then filtered according to specific criteria (these criteria can include the use of external resources but they are more generally based on scores mixing frequency and specificity (Bourigault and Jacquemin, 1999; Frantzi and Ananiadou, 2000)). In this study, we voluntarily used a minimal approach for keyword extraction and filtering since we want to keep most

Table 2: Most specific keywords found in the METHOD sections.

	Methods	
Category	Method	N-grams
Machine learning	Bayesian methods	baesyan
	Vector Space model	space model, vector space, cosine
	Genetic algorithms	genetic algorithms
	HMM	hidden markov models, markov model
	CRF	conditional random fields
	SVM	support vector machines
	MaxEnt	maximum entropy model, maximum entropy approach, maximum entropy
	Clustering	clustering algorithm, clustering method, word clusters, classification problem
Speech & Mach. Trans.	Language models	large-vocabulary, n-gram language model, Viterbi
	Parallel Corpora	parallel corpus, bilingual corpus, phrase pairs, source and target languages, sentence pairs, word pairs, source sentence
	Alignment	phrase alignment, alignment algorithm, alignment models, ibm model, phrase translation, translation candidates, sentence alignment
NLP Methods	POS tagging	part-of-speech tagger, part-of-speech tags
	Morphology	two-level morphology, morphological analyzer, morphological rules
	FST	finite-state transducers, regular expressions, state automata, rule-based approach
	Syntax	syntactic categories, syntactic patterns, extraction patterns
	Dependency parsing	dependency parser, dependency graphs, prague dependency, dependency treebank, derivation trees, parse trees
	Parsing	grammar rules, parser output, parsing process, parsed sentences, transfer rules
	Semantics	logical forms, inference rules, generative lexicon, lexical rules, lexico-syntactic, predicate argument
Applications	IE and IR	entity recognition, answer candidates, temporal information, web search, query expansion, google, user queries, keywords, query terms, term recognition
	Discourse	generation component, dialogue acts, centering theory, lexical chains, resolution algorithm, generation process, discourse model, lexical choice
	Segmentation	machine transliteration, phonological rules, segmentation algorithm, word boundaries
Words and Resource	Lexical knowledge bases	lexical knowledge base, semantic network, machine readable dictionaries, eurowordnet, lexical entries, dictionary entries, lexical units, representation structures, lookup
	Word similarity	word associations, mutual information, semantic relationships, word similarity, semantic similarity, semeval-2007, word co-occurrence, synonymy
	Corpora	brown corpus, dialogue corpus, annotation scheme, tagged corpus
Evaluation	Evaluation	score, gold standard, evaluation measures, estimation method
Calculation & complexity	Software	tool development, polynomial time, software tools, series of experiments, system architecture, runtime, programming language
	Constraints	relaxation, constraint satisfaction, semantic constraints

of the information for the subsequent text zoning phase. We thus used NLTK for part-of-speech tagging and from this result extracted the most common noun phrases. We used a pre-defined set of grammatical patterns to extract noun phrases defined as sequences of simple sequences (e.g. adjectives + nouns, "phrase pairs", "dependency graph", etc.) possibly connected to other such patterns through propositions to form longer phrases (e.g. "series of experiments"). Only the noun phrases appearing in more than 10 papers are kept for subsequent processing.

Candidate keywords are then ranked per zone, according to their specificity (the zone they are the most specific of) . Specificity corresponds to the Kolmogorov-Smirnov test that quantifies a distance between the empirical distribution functions of two samples. The test is calculated as follows:

$$D = \max_x |S_{N_1}(x) - S_{N_2}(x)| \quad (1)$$

where $S_{N_1}(x)$ et $S_{N_2}(x)$ are the empirical distribution function of the two samples (that correspond in our case to the number of occurrences of the keyword in a given zone, and to the total number of occurrences of all the keywords in the same zone, respectively) (Press et al., 2007). A high value of D for a given keyword means that it is highly specific of the considered zone. At the opposite, a low value means that the keyword is spread over the different zones and not really specific of any zone.

The first keywords of each category are then categorized by an expert of the domain. For the METHOD category, we obtain Table 2. Logically, given our approach, the table does not contain all the keywords relevant for the computational linguistics domain, but it contains the mots specific ones according to the above approach. One should thus not be surprised not to see all the keywords used in the domain.

3.2 Evolution of methods over time

The automatic analysis of the corpus allows us to track the main evolutions of the field over time. During the last 30 years, the methods used have changed to a large extent, the most notable fact being probably the generalization of machine learning methods since the late 1990s. This is outlined by the fact that papers in the domain nowadays nearly always include a section that describes an experiment and some results.

To confirm this hypothesis, we observe the relative frequency of sentences tagged as RESULTS in the papers over time. In the figure 3, we see that the curve increases almost linearly from the early 1980s until the late 2000s.

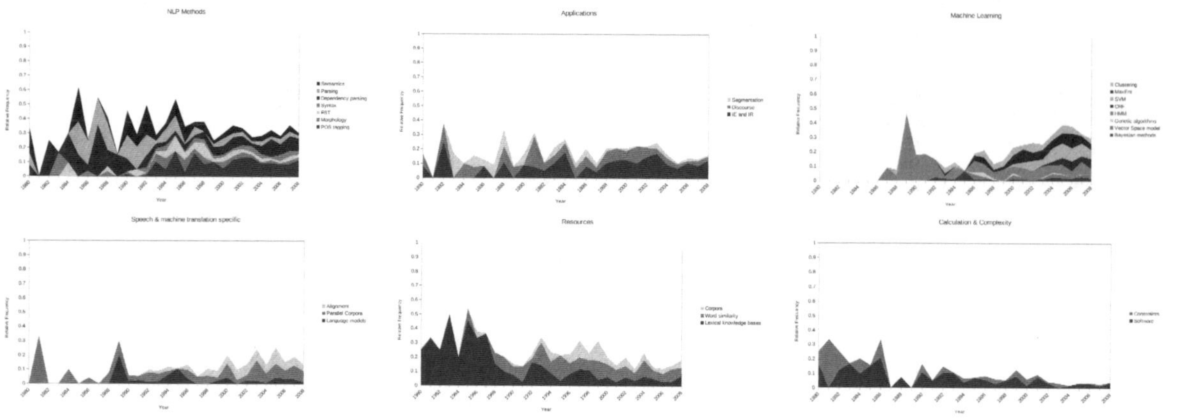

Figure 2: Evolution of the relative frequency of the different groups of methods over time.

It is also possible to make more fine-grained observations, for example to follow over time the different kinds of methods under consideration. The results are shown in figure 2. Rule based methods and manually crafted resources are used all over the period, while machine learning based methods are more and more successful after the late 1990s. This is not surprising since we know that machine learning is now highly popular within the field. However, symbolic methods are still used, sometimes in conjunction with learning methods. The two kinds of methods are thus more complementary than antagonistic.

One could observe details that should be checked through a more thorough study. We observe for example the success of dependency parsing in the end of the 1980s (probably due to the success of the Tree Adjoining Grammars at the time) and the new popularity of this area of research in the early 2000s (dependency parsing has been the subject of several evaluation campaigns in the 2000s, see for example for the CONLL shared tasks from 2006 to 2009).

Different machine learning methods have been popular over time but each of them continues to be used after a first wave corresponding to their initial success. Hidden Markov Models and n-grams are highly popular in the 1990s, probably thanks to the experiments made by Jelinek and his colleagues, which will open the field of statistical machine translation (Brown et al., 1990). SVM and CRF have had a more recent success as everybody knows.

We are also interested in the distribution of these methods between papers and authors. Figure 4 shows the average number of keywords

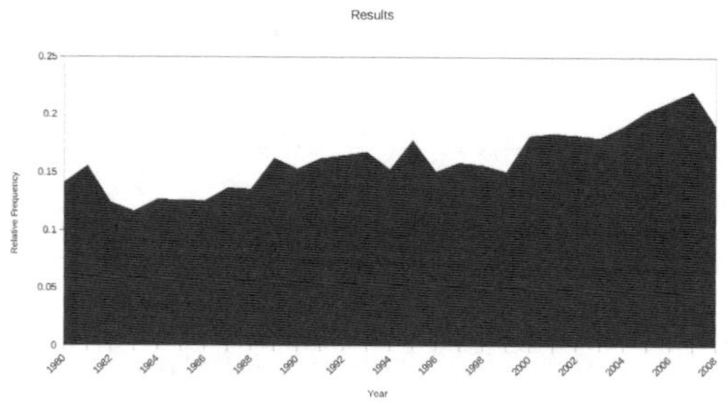

Figure 3: Evolution of the relative frequency of sentences tagged as RESULTS in the abstracts of the papers

appearing in the METHOD section of the papers over time. We see that this number regularly increases, especially during the 1980s, showing possibly a gradually increasing complexity of the systems under consideration.

Lastly, figure 5 shows the number of authors who are specialists of one or several methods. Most of the authors just mention one method in their papers and, logically, the curves decrease, which means that there are few authors who are really specialists of many methods. This result should be confirmed by a larger scale study taking into account a larger number of keywords but the trend seems however interesting.

3.3 The dynamics of the authors in the method space

One could say that the results we have reported in the previous section are not new but rather confirm some already well known facts. Our method allows to go one step further and try to answer more

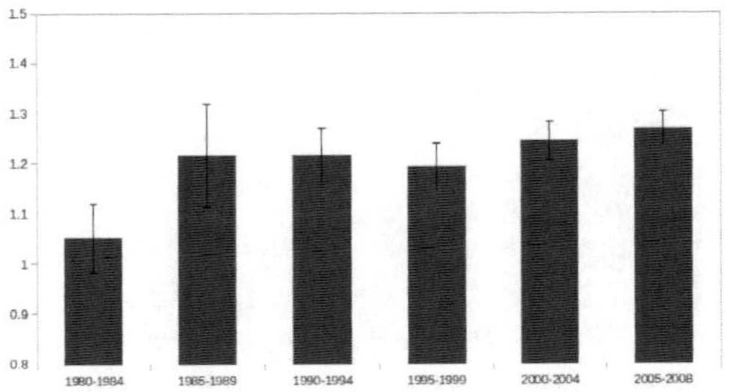

Figure 4: Evolution of the number of keywords related to methods over time.

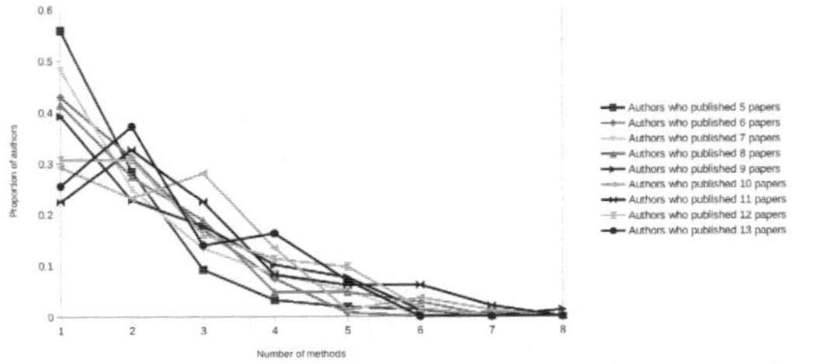

Figure 5: Proportion of authors specialized in a given number of methods (i.e. mentioning frequently the name of the method in the abstracts), for different categories of researchers.

challenging questions. How are new methods introduced in the field? Are they mainly brought by young researchers or is it mainly confirmed researchers who develop new techniques (or import them from related fields)? Are NLP experts specialized in one field or in a wide variety of different fields?

These questions are of course quite complex. Each individual has his own expertise and his own history but we think that automatic methods can provide some interesting trends over time. For example, (Anderson et al., 2012) show that evaluation campaigns have played a central role at certain periods of time, which does not mean of course that there was no independent research outside these campaigns at the time. Our goal is thus to exhibit some tendencies that could be interpreted or even make it possible to compare the evolution of the computational linguistics field with other fields. Out tools provide some hypotheses that must of course be confirmed by further observations and analysis. We do not claim that they provide an exact and accurate view of the domain.

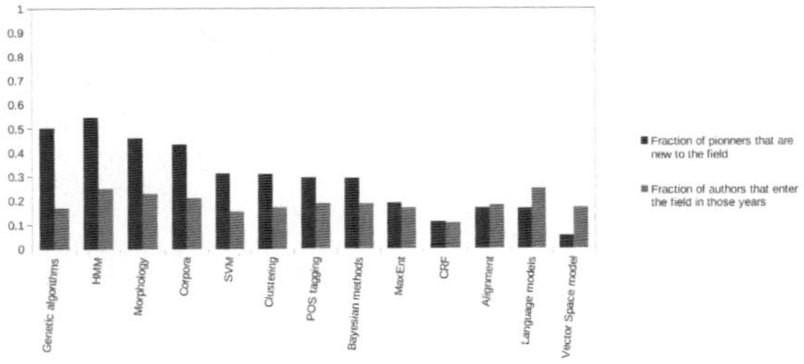

Figure 6: For each "new method", number of "pioneers" not having published any paper before (compared to the total number of new authors during the same period of time).

For this study we only take into account authors who have published at least 5 papers in the ACL Anthology, in order to take into consideration authors who have contributed to the domain during a period of time relevant for the study. We consider as "pioneers" the authors of the first 25% of papers in which a keyword referring to a method is introduced (for example, the first papers where the keywords *support vector machine* or *SVM* appear). We then calculate, among this set of authors, the ones who can be considered as new authors, which means people who have not published before in the field. Since there are every year a large number of new authors (who use standard techniques) we compare the ratio of new authors using new techniques with the number of authors using already known techniques over the considered period. Results are visible in figure 6.

Results are variable depending on the method under consideration but some of them seem interesting. Papers with the keyword Hidden Markov Model in the 1990s seem to be largely written by new comers, probably by researchers having tested this method in related fields before (and we know that it was the case of Jelinek's team who was largely involved in speech processing, a domain not so well represented in the ACL Anthology before the 1990s. Of course, Jelinek and colleague were confirmed and even highly established researchers already at the beginning of the 1990s). We observe a similar patten for genetic algorithms but the number of authors is too limited to say if the trend is really meaningful. SVM also seem to have been popularized by new comers but it is not the case of language models or of the vector space model. A more thorough study is of course needed to confirm and better understand

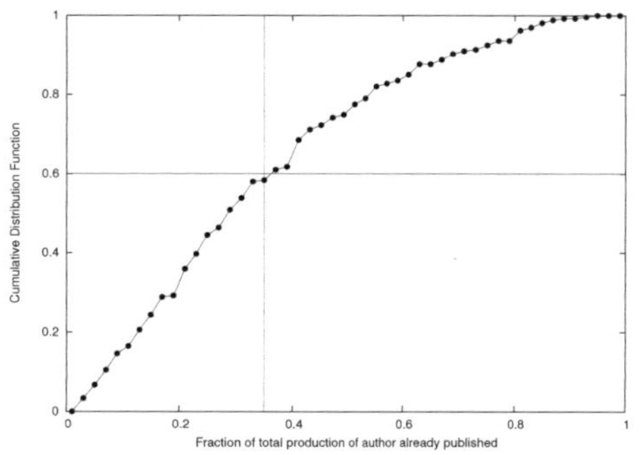

Figure 7: Distribution function of the number of papers already published by "pioneers" when they have published their paper on the new method, compared to the total production of their career.

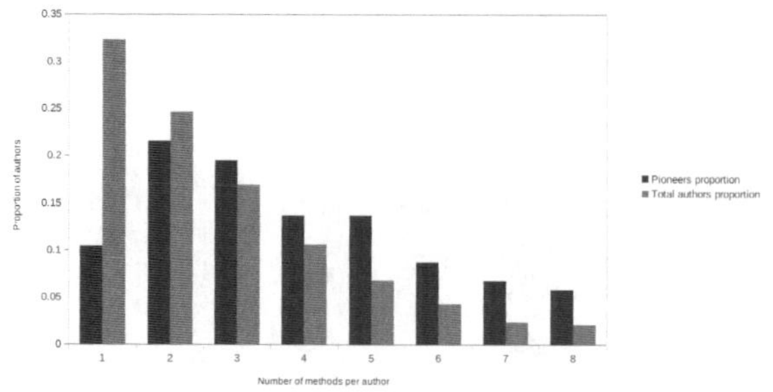

Figure 8: Proportion of "pioneers" experts in a given number of methods compared to all the other authors in the corpus.

these results.

We then do a similar experiment to try to determine when, during their career, researchers use new methods. Practically, we examine at what point of their career the authors who are characterized as "pioneers" in our study (what refers to the first authors using a new method) have published the papers containing new methods (for example, if an author is one of the first who employed the keyword SVM, has he done this at the beginning of his career or later on?). The result is visible in figure 7 and shows that 60% of pioneers had published less than a third of their scientific production when they use the new method. We thus observe a similar set of authors between the pioneers and researchers having published so far in related but nevertheless different communities. To confirm this result, it would be useful to study other domains and other corpora (in computer science, linguistics, cognitive sciences) so as to get a better picture of the domain, but the task is then highly challenging.

One may want then to observe the diversity of methods employed in the domain, especially by the set of people called "pioneers" in our study. Figure 8 shows in blue the number of methods detected for the pioneers and in red the number of methods used by all the authors.

We see that pioneers, when taking into consideration the whole set of papers in the ACL Anthology, are using a larger number of methods. They are over represented among authors using 3 methods and more. This group of people also contribute to a larger number of sub-areas in the domains compared to the set of other authors.

4 Conclusion

We have presented in this paper an analysis of the ACL Anthology corpus. Our analysis is based on the identification of keywords which are categorized according to their informational status. Categorization is done according to a Text Zoning analysis of the papers' abstracts, which provides very relevant information for the study. We have shown that coupling keyword extraction with Text Zoning makes it possible to observe fine grained facts in the dynamics of a scientific domain.

These tools only give pieces of information that should be confirmed by subsequent studies. It is necessary to go back to the texts themselves, consult domain experts and probably the larger context to be able to get a really accurate picture of the evolution of a scientific domain. This multi-disciplinary research means that to collaborate with people from other fields is needed, especially with the history of science and epistemology. However, the platforms and the techniques we have described in this paper are now available and can be re-used for other kinds of studies, making it possible to reproduce similar experiments across different domains.

References

Ashton Anderson, Dan Jurafsky, and Daniel A. McFarland. 2012. Towards a computational history of the acl: 1980-2008. In *Proceedings of the ACL-2012 Special Workshop on Rediscovering 50 Years of Discoveries*, pages 13–21, Jeju Island, Core. Association for Computational Linguistics.

Didier Bourigault and Christian Jacquemin. 1999. Term extraction + term clustering: An integrated platform for computer-aided terminology. In *Proceedings of the Ninth Conference on European*

Chapter of the Association for Computational Linguistics, EACL '99, pages 15–22.

Peter F. Brown, John Cocke, Stephen A. Della Pietra, Vincent J. Della Pietra, Fredrick Jelinek, John D. Lafferty, Robert L. Mercer, and Paul S. Roossin. 1990. A statistical approach to machine translation. *Computational Linguistics*, 16(2):79–85.

Michel Callon, John Law, and Arie Rip. 1986. *Mapping the dynamics of science and technology*. McMillan, London.

Michel Callon, Jean-Pierre Courtial, and Françoise Laville. 1991. Co-word analysis as a tool for describing the network of interaction between basic and technological research: The case of polymer chemistry. *Scientometrics*, 22(1):155–205.

Katarina Frantzi and Sophia Ananiadou. 2000. Automatic recognition of multi-word terms:. the C-value/NC-value method. *International Journal on Digital Libraries*, 3(2):115–130.

Eugene Garfield. 1972. Citation Analysis as a Tool in Journal Evaluation. *Science*, 178(4060):471–479.

Michelle Girvan and Mark E J Newman. 2002. Community structure in social and biological networks. *Proceedings of the National Academy of Sciences of the United States of America*, 99:7821–7826.

Roger Guimera, Brian Uzzi, Jarrett Spiro, and Luis A. Nunes Amaral. 2005. Team Assembly Mechanisms Determine Collaboration Network Structure and Team Performance. *Science*, 308(5722):697–702.

Yufan Guo, Anna Korhonen, and Thierry Poibeau. 2011. A weakly-supervised approach to argumentative zoning of scientific documents. In *Proceedings of the 2011 Conference on Empirical Methods in Natural Language Processing*, pages 273–283, Edinburgh.

Yufan Guo, Roi Reichart, and Anna Korhonen. 2013. Improved information structure analysis of scientific documents through discourse and lexical constraints. In *Proceedings of Human Language Technologies: Conference of the North American Chapter of the Association of Computational Linguistics (HLT-NAACL)*, pages 928–937.

James Curran and Stephen Clark and Johan Bos. 2007. Linguistically Motivated Large-Scale NLP with C&C and Boxer. In *Proceedings of the 45th Meeting of the Association for Computation Linguistics (ACL)*, pages 33–36.

Gary Geunbae Lee, Jong-Hyeok Lee, and Jeongwon Cha. 2002. Syllable-pattern-based unknown-morpheme segmentation and estimation for hybrid part-of-speech tagging of korean. *Computational Linguistics*, 28(1):53–70.

Yoko Mizuta, Anna Korhonen, Tony Mullen, and Nigel Collier. 2006. Zone analysis in biology articles as a basis for information extraction. *International Journal of Medical Informatics*, 75(6):468–487.

William H. Press, Saul A. Teukolsky, William T. Vetterling, and Brian P. Flannery. 2007. *Numerical Recipes 3rd Edition: The Art of Scientific Computing*. Cambridge University Press, New York, NY, USA, 3 edition.

Roi Reichart and Anna Korhonen. 2012. Document and corpus level inference for unsupervised and transductive learning of information structure of scientific documents. In *Proceedings of COLING (Posters)*, pages 995–1006, Mumbai.

Anna Ritchie, Stephen Robertson, and Simone Teufel. 2008. Comparing citation contexts for information retrieval. In *Proeedings of the 17th Conference on Information and Knowledge Management (CIKM)*, pages 213–222, Napa Valley.

Henry G Small. 1973. Co-citation in the scientific literature: A new measure of the relationship between two documents. *Journal of American Society for Information Science*, 24(4):265–269.

Imad Tbahriti, Christine Chichester, Frédérique Lisacek, and Patrick Ruch. 2006. Using argumentation to retrieve articles with similar citations: An inquiry into improving related articles search in the medline digital library. *I. J. Medical Informatics*, 75(6):488–495.

Simone Teufel and Marc Moens. 2002. Summarizing scientific articles: Experiments with relevance and rhetorical status. *Computational Linguistics*, 28(4):409–445.

Simone Teufel. 1999. *Argumentative Zoning: Information Extraction from Scientific Articles*. University of Edinburgh.

A Tool for a High-Carat Gold-Standard Word Alignment

Drayton C. Benner
Near Eastern Languages & Civilizations Department
University of Chicago
Chicago, IL USA
drayton@uchicago.edu

Abstract

In this paper, we describe a tool designed to produce a gold-standard word alignment between a text and its translation with a novel visualization. In addition, the tool is designed to aid the aligners in producing an alignment at a high level of quality and consistency. This tool is presently being used to align the Hebrew Bible with an English translation of it.

1 Introduction and Background

Gold-standard word alignments have been produced for a variety of purposes, but the machine translation community has been the most interested in aligned texts. For this community, aligning texts is not an end in and of itself. Rather, gold-standard aligned texts have served to train and also evaluate machine translation algorithms or their components, especially automatic alignment algorithms. However, there are other scholarly endeavors in which gold-standard word alignments are useful in and of themselves. Within linguistics they are certainly helpful to the subfields of contact linguistics, corpus linguistics, and historical linguistics, but they are also useful in humanistic inquiry more broadly, especially in in studies of translation technique, textual criticism, philology, and lexicography. In addition, presenting gold-standard aligned texts can make texts more accessible to a broader audience, especially to an audience that has limited skill in either the source or target language.

A gold-standard alignment that is designed to aid the humanist is likely to have different requirements with regard to quality, consistency, and visualization than a gold-standard alignment designed as an input to a machine translation algorithm. Results from research into the effect of the quality of alignments above a certain level on machine translation quality has been mixed (Fraser and Marcu, 2007; Fossum et al., 2008; Lambert et al., 2012). Thus, the extra cost of making a good alignment excellent might outweigh its benefits if its only purpose is to aid in machine translation. Put differently, a 14 carat gold-standard alignment may be sufficient for the purposes of machine translation. However, for the humanistic endeavors enumerated above, incremental improvements in quality continue to be useful to scholars; a 24 carat gold-standard alignment is highly desirable. Similarly, consistency is important for many of these humanistic endeavors. For example, a scholar researching the way in which a particular word or class of words is translated needs the alignment to be done consistently across the translated corpus. Finally, when the translation and alignment themselves are an object of study, the alignment needs to be presented visually in an appealing manner, and the researcher needs to be able to access additional information easily.

2 Alignment Project and Tool

Achieving a high level of quality and consistency requires a software tool designed to facilitate this, and the visualization techniques for this software tool can be similar to the visualization of the final alignment. In what follows, we present a manual alignment tool that has been built as a Java application for desktop operating systems in order to achieve these goals for an ongoing project to align the Hebrew Bible with an English translation of it. For the Hebrew Bible, we use the *Westminster Leningrad Codex* (*WLC*) and

Westminster Hebrew Morphology (*WHM*), both version 4.18. *WLC* is a diplomatic edition of *Codex Leningradensis*, the oldest complete manuscript of the Hebrew Bible in the Tiberian tradition. *WHM* tokenizes the text and provides a lemma and morphology codes for each token. *WLC* and *WHM* are presently maintained by the *J. Alan Groves Center for Advanced Biblical Research*. For an English translation, we use the *English Standard Version*, 2011 text edition. Its tokenization is straightforward and was done at the word level.

While various groups have aligned the Hebrew Bible with various English translations, beginning with (Strong, 1890), and even to the Greek Septuagint translation (Tov, 1986), this project is unparalleled in its focus on quality and consistency in the alignment, and the alignment tool reflects that. The Alignment Panel provides the primary visualization of the alignment and allows for its manipulation while several other panels provide data to aid the aligner with regard to quality and consistency. The aligners follow a lengthy document outlining consistency standards.

2.1 Alignment Panel

Several types of visualizations have typically been used to display aligned texts. Most commonly, lines have been used to show links between aligned tokens (Melamed, 1998; Daume III; Smith and Jahr, 2000; Madnani and Hwa, 2004; Grimes et al., 2010; Hung-Ngo and Winiwarter, 2012). While this is helpful, the lines become difficult to follow when the word order differs significantly between the source text and its translation or even if one text requires significantly more tokens than the other. The second common approach uses an alignment matrix (Tiedemann, 2006; Germann, 2007; Germann, 2008). Again, this is a helpful visualization technique, but it takes time for the user to see which source tokens link to which target tokens at a glance, and it is easy to accidentally move over a row or column with one's eye. A third approach involves coloring linked words using distinguishable colors (Merkel, 2003; Ahrenberg et al., 2002; Ahrenberg et al., 2003). When used by itself, this is helpful but slow for the eye to find which source token links to which target token. A fourth approach requires the user to place the mouse over a particular token of interest to see links for just that token (Germann, 2007; Germann, 2008). This removes the clutter but is cumbersome for a user trying to see the entirety of the alignment.

The approach taken here, shown in Figure 1, combines the first and third of these visualization techniques but modifies them in order to make the alignment easier to read and to enable the aligner to align quickly while maintaining high quality. In addition, the Alignment Panel includes language helps to speed up the human aligner. Tokens are displayed vertically. While previous alignment tools have more conventionally displayed the tokens horizontally, whether as a flowing text or as separated tokens, Hebrew is written right-to-left, while English is written left-to-right, so a vertical display, as done by (Grimes et al., 2010) for an Arabic-English alignment, makes more sense: both languages can be read top to bottom. The Hebrew tokens are grouped by the human aligner into token sets, and these token sets form a partition over all the Hebrew tokens. The same is true for the English tokens. Hebrew token sets can then be aligned with English token sets. In addition, in token sets with two or more tokens, the human aligner can optionally declare precisely one token in the token set to have primary status if it is most basic to the token set on a semantic level. For example, in Figure 1, the Hebrew word רשׁעים ("wicked") is linked to an English token set consisting of two tokens: *the* and *wicked*. The aligner has correctly identified *wicked* as the primary token in this English token set. In token sets containing just one token, the one token always has primary status.

Alignment visualizations using lines can be difficult to process if the word order differs sharply between the source text and its translation. In order to combat this issue, a key innovation of this tool is that blank rows are inserted at times on both the source and target sides. The blank rows are inserted in such a way that the number of straight, horizontal lines linking source token sets to target token sets is maximized. That is, the maximum possible number of aligned token sets are aligned horizontally. Subject to this constraint, blank rows are inserted so as to minimize the sum of the length of the vertical components of the lines, including both the lines joining multiple tokens into a token set and the lines indicating links between source and target token sets. When the user changes the alignment, which is done primarily using drag-and-drop, the tool immediately recalculates the optimal blank rows and redraws if necessary, all the while remaining responsive. While multiple formats are supported for exporting the alignment data, all of the data is imported into memory during application startup. This requires more updating of complex internal

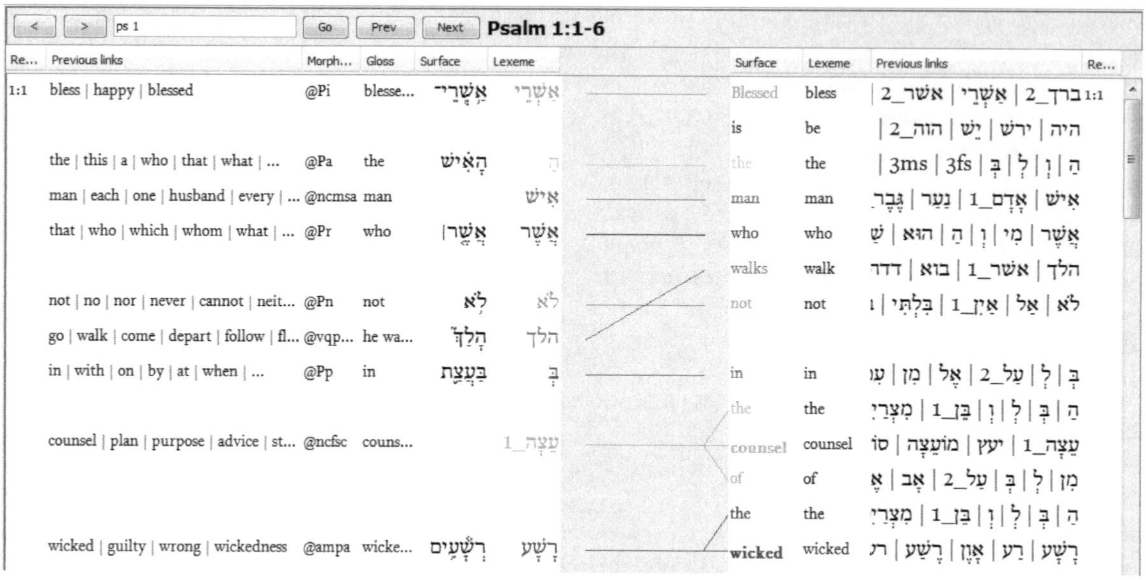

Figure 1. Alignment Panel

data structures during execution than if an external database were used, but the approach taken here supports responsiveness. Deciding where to put the blank rows is analogous to the more familiar problem of finding the weighted minimum edit distance between two strings with backtrace and thus can be done using the Wagner–Fischer algorithm, a dynamic programming algorithm that is $O(mn)$ in both time and memory, where m and n are the number of source and target tokens (Wagner and Fischer, 1974). In addition, the tokens in token sets are connected via lines. For example, in Figure 1, the English tokens *the*, *counsel*, and *of* are connected together with lines. So as to avoid visual clutter, the line linking this English token set to the Hebrew meets at the primary token in the token set. If there is no primary token in the token set, a centrally located token is chosen instead.

The Alignment Panel uses fifteen different, easily distinguishable colors that still show up well on computer monitors for both tokens and lines to make it immediately clear which tokens are linked to one another. A few extremely common function words as well as pronominal suffixes in the source language always get a consistent color when they are linked. These are the tokens that cause Hebrew words often to contain multiple tokens. For the rest of the tokens, the colors are selected in such a way so as to avoid having similar colors near each other and to keep the colors as stable as possible as the user changes the alignment. In token sets containing multiple tokens, primary tokens are bolded.

When aligning modern languages, one might be able to assume that the aligners are fluent in both languages. However, when dealing with ancient languages or ancient dialects with relatively small corpora, language helps are a necessity in order to allow the aligner to work quickly. On the source language side, the Hebrew lemmas and morphology codes from *WHM* are presented to the aligner. The Hebrew lemmas are presented closest to the center rather than the surface forms simply because dividing multi-token Hebrew surface forms would look orthographically inappropriate and would be slower for the human aligner to process. For most languages the surface form should be presented closest to the center. A literal yet contextual gloss of the Hebrew token is also presented. These glosses were produced by Thom Blair using a separate software tool we wrote; they were designed for use in (*Hebrew-English Interlinear*, 2013). The English lemmas to which the Hebrew lemma has been linked elsewhere are also listed. To be listed, both the Hebrew lemma and the English lemma must have primary status. When there are multiple such English lemmas, they are listed in order of frequency of being linked. The target language side mirrors some of the source language side but is less extensive since we assume the aligner is fluent in English. The English lemmas were initially produced using *StanfordCoreNLP* (Toutanova et al., 2003, de Marneffe et al., 2006), with post-processing used to fix errors. The human aligner can edit them in case of errors.

2.2 Other panels aiding quality and consistency

Several other panels, shown in Figures 2-4, are designed to enable the aligner to check the alignment for quality and consistency.

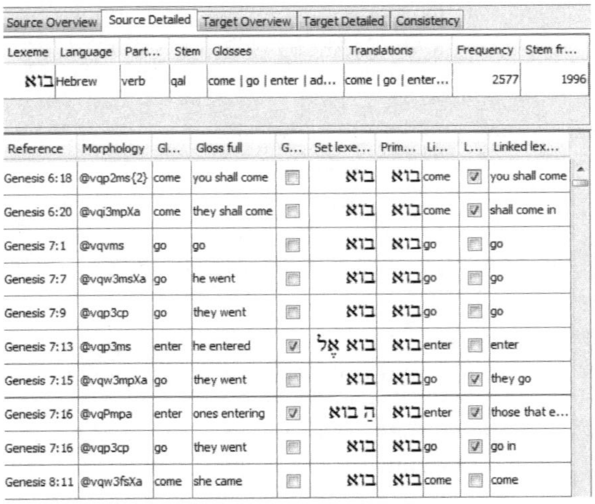

Figure 2. Source Detailed Panel

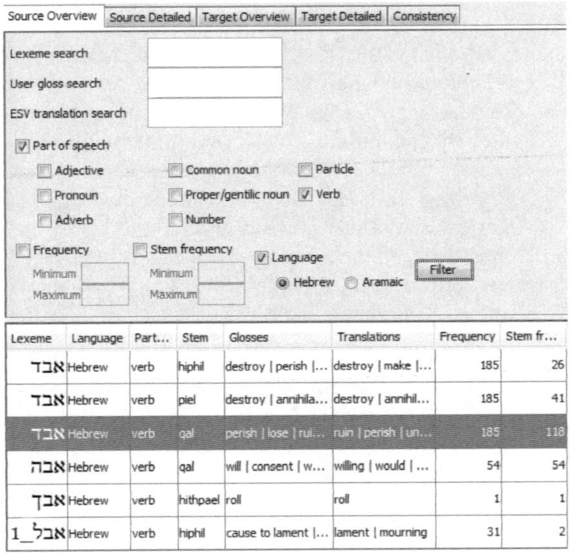

Figure 3. Source Overview Panel

Figure 4. Consistency Panel

The Source Detailed Panel gives detailed information about the alignment for each occurrence of a lemma in the source text in a sortable table. In order to aid the aligner, the third column shows a form of the English gloss that has been shortened, usually to a single lemma, by making use of *WHM*'s morphology information and *WordNet*. The Target Detailed Panel is similar.

The Source Overview Panel briefly presents information concerning how all source tokens are aligned in a sortable, filterable table. The glosses shown are the short forms and are sorted based on frequency. Similarly, the translations are primary lemmas only and are sorted according to frequency. The Target Overview Panel is similar.

The Consistency Panel is oriented toward enforcing the consistency standards. It uses *WHM* as well as information from *StanfordCoreNLP*, including the syntactic dependency tree, to look for probable deviations from the project's consistency standards. It can fix some errors automatically if the human aligner allows it, but the human aligner is not required to follow its suggestions since it sometimes make mistakes, especially when the syntactic dependency tree from *StanfordCoreNLP* contains errors.

3 Conclusions and future work

The alignment tool is enabling a fast production of a high-quality, consistent gold-standard alignment between the Hebrew Bible and an English translation because of the way it provides an easy-to-process visualization of the alignment, provides options for aligners to dig deeper into the data and check their work, and makes changing the alignment easy. At present, the alignment tool is an in-house tool geared toward two specific texts, but with the exception of the consistency rules, which will be specific to particular languages and projects, it could be generalized to align other texts and languages. At that point, the generalized alignment tool could be licensed liberally to researchers.

Acknowledgments

The work presented in this paper has been funded by Crossway Books. The author would like to thank James Covington for his input.

References

Lars Ahrenberg, Mikael Andersson, Magnus Merkel. 2002. A System for Incremental and Interactive Word Linking. In *Proceedings of the 3nd Language Resources and Evaluation Conference (LREC 2002)*, Las Palmas, Spain. ELRA.

Lars Ahrenberg, Magnus Merkel, and Michael Petterstedt. 2003. Interactive Word Alignment for Language Engineering. In *Conference Companion of the 10th Conference of the European Chapter of the Association for Computational Linguistics (EACL 2003)*, pages 49-52, Budapest, Hungary. ACL.

Hal Daume III. HandAlign Documentation. `http://www.umiacs.umd.edu/~hal/HandAlign/`.

Victoria Fossum, Kevin Knight, and Steven Abney. 2008. Using Syntax to Improve Word Alignment Precision for Syntax-Based Machine Translation. In *Proceedings of the Third Workshop on Statistical Machine Translation*, pages 44-52, Columbus, Ohio. ACL.

Alexander Fraser and Daniel Marcu. 2007. Measuring Word Alignment Quality for Statistical Machine Translation. *Computational Linguistics*, 33(3), 293-303.

Ulrich Germann. 2007. Two Tools for Creating and Visualizing Sub-sentential Alignments of Parallel Texts. In *Proceedings of the Linguistic Annotation Worship*, pages 121-124. Prague, Czech Republic. ACL.

Ulrich Germann. 2008 *Yawat*: Yet Another Word Alignment Tool. *Proceedings of the ACL-08: HLT Demo Session (Companion Volume)*, pages 20-23. Columbus, Ohio. ACL.

Stephen Grimes, Xuansong Li, Ann Bies, Seth Kulick, Xiaoyi Ma, and Stephanie Strassel. 2010. Creating Arabic-English Parallel Word-Aligned Treebank Corpora at LDC. In *Proceedings of the 7th International Language Resources and Evaluation Conference (LREC 2010)*, Valletta, Malta. ELRA.

Hebrew-English Interlinear ESV Old Testament: Biblia Hebraica Stuttgartensia (BHS) and English Standard Version (ESV). 2013. Wheaton, Il. Crossway.

Quoc Hung-Ngo and Werner Winiwarter. 2012. A Visualizing Annotation Tool for Semi-Automatically Building a Bilingual Corpus. In *Proceedings of the 8th International Language Resources and Evaluation Conference (LREC 2012)*, pages 67-74, Istanbul, Turkey. ELRA.

Patrik Lambert, Simon Petitrenaud, Yanjun Ma, and Andy Way. 2012. What types of word alignment improve statistical machine translation? *Mach Translat* 26, 289–323.

Nitin Madnani and Rebecca Hwa. 2004. The UMIACS Word Alignment Interface. `http://www.umiacs.umd.edu/~nmadnani/alignment/`.

Marie-Catherine de Marneffe, Bill MacCartney, and Christopher D. Manning. 2006. Generating Typed Dependency Parses from Phrase Structure Parses. In *Proceedings of the 5th International Language Resources and Evaluation Conference (LREC 2006)*, pages 449-454, Genoa, Italy. ELRA.

I. Dan Melamed. 1998. Manual Annotation of Translational Equivalence: The Blinker Project. IRCS Technical Report #98-07. The University of Pennsylvania.

Magnus Merkel, Michael Petterstedt, and Lars Ahrenberg. 2003. Interactive Word Alignment for Corpus Linguistics. In *Proceedings of Corpus Linguistics 2003*, 533-542, Lancaster University, United Kingdom. UCREL technical paper 16.

Noah A. Smith and Michael E. Jahr. 2000. Cairo: An Alignment Visualization Tool. In *Proceedings of the 2nd Language Resources and Evaluation Conference (LREC 2000)*, Athens, Greece. ELRA.

James Strong. 1890. The exhaustive concordance of the Bible: showing every word of the text of the common English version of the canonical books, and every occurrence of each word in regular order: together with A comparative concordance of the Authorized and Revised versions, including the American variations: also brief dictionaries of the Hebrew and Greek words of the original, with references to the English words. Cincinnati: Jennings & Graham.

Jörg Tiedemann. 2006. ISA & ICA – Two Web Interfaces for Interactive Alignment of Bitexts. In *Proceedings of the 5th International Conference on Language Resources and Evaluation (LREC 2006)*, pages 2154-2159, Genoa, Italy. ELRA.

Kristina Toutanova, Dan Klein, Christopher D. Manning, and Yoram Singer. 2003. Feature-Rich Part-of-Speech Tagging with a Cyclic Dependency Network. In *Proceedings of the 2003 Conference of the North American Chapter of the Association for Computational Linguistics on Human Language Technology*, pages 173-180, Edmonton, Canada. ACL.

Emmanuel Tov. 1986. A Computerized Data Base for Septuagint Studies: The Parallel Aligned Text of the Greek and Hebrew Bible. Computer Assisted Tools for Septuagint Studies (CATSS) Vol. 2. Journal of Northwest Semitic Languages Supplement Series 1. Stellenbosch.

Robert A. Wagner and Michael J. Fischer. 1974. The String-to-String Correction Problem. *Journal of the Association for Computing Machinery*, 21(1): 168-173.

CorA: A web-based annotation tool for historical and other non-standard language data

Marcel Bollmann, Florian Petran, Stefanie Dipper, Julia Krasselt
Department of Linguistics
Ruhr-University Bochum, 44780 Bochum, Germany
{bollmann|petran|dipper|krasselt}@linguistics.rub.de

Abstract

We present CorA, a web-based annotation tool for manual annotation of historical and other non-standard language data. It allows for editing the primary data and modifying token boundaries during the annotation process. Further, it supports immediate retraining of taggers on newly annotated data.

1 Introduction[1]

In recent years, the focus of research in natural language processing has shifted from highly standardized text types, such as newspaper texts, to text types that often infringe orthographic, grammatical and stylistic norms normally associated with written language. Prime examples are language data produced in the context of *computer-mediated communication* (CMC), such as Twitter or SMS data, or contributions in chat rooms. Further examples are data produced by learners or historical texts.

Tools trained on standardized data perform considerably worse on "non-standard varieties" such as internet data (cf. Giesbrecht and Evert (2009)'s work on tagging the web or Foster et al. (2011)'s results for parsing Twitter data) or historical language data (Rayson et al., 2007; Scheible et al., 2011). This can mainly be attributed to the facts that tools are applied out of domain, or only small amounts of manually-annotated training data are available.

A more fundamental problem is that common and established methods and categories for language analysis often do not fit the phenomena occurring in non-standard data. For instance, grammaticalization is a process of language evolution where new parts of speech are created or words switch from one class to another. It is difficult to draw strict categorial boundaries between words that take part in a continuous smooth transition of categories. Factors like these can also affect the way the data should be tokenized, along with other problems such as the lack of a fixed orthography.

In the light of the above, we developed a web-based tool for manual annotation of non-standard data. It allows for editing the primary data, e.g. for correcting OCR errors of historical texts, or for modifying token boundaries during the annotation process. Furthermore, it supports immediate retraining of taggers on newly annotated data, to attenuate the problem of sparse training data.

CorA is currently used in several projects that annotate historical data, and one project that analyzes chat data. So far, about 200,000 tokens in 84 texts have been annotated in CorA. Once the annotation process is completed, the transcriptions and their annotations are imported into the ANNIS corpus tool (Zeldes et al., 2009) where they can be searched and visualized.

The paper focuses on the annotation of historical data. Sec. 2 presents the tool, and Sec. 3 describes the data model. Sec. 4 concludes.

2 Tool Description

CorA uses a web-based architecture:[2] All data is stored on a server, while users can access and edit annotations from anywhere using their web browser. This approach greatly simplifies collaborative work within a project, as it ensures that all users are working on the same version of the data at all times, and requires no software installation on the user's side. Users can be assigned to individual project groups and are only able to access documents within their group(s).

2.1 The annotation editor

All annotation in CorA is done on a token level; the currently supported annotation types are part-

[1]The research reported here was financed by Deutsche Forschungsgemeinschaft (DFG), Grant DI 1558/5-1.

[2]It implements a standard AJAX architecture using PHP 5, MySQL, and JavaScript.

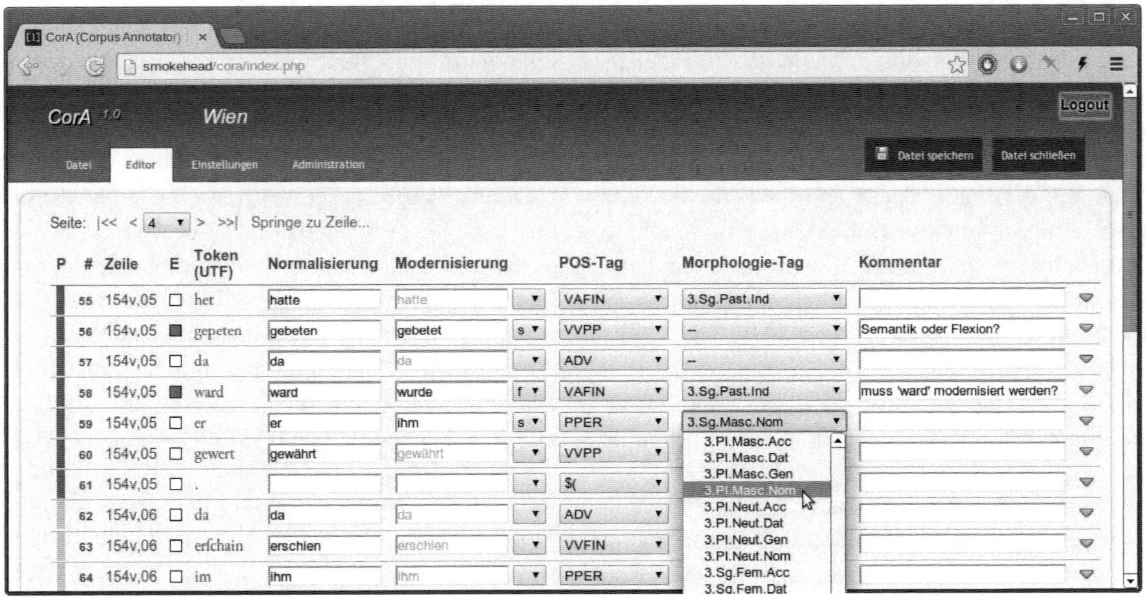

Figure 1: Web interface of CorA showing the annotation editor

of-speech tags, morphology tags, lemmatization, and (spelling) normalization. The tool is designed to increase productivity for these particular annotation tasks, while sacrificing some amount of flexibility (e.g., using different annotation layers, or annotating spans of tokens). Note that this is mainly a restriction of the web interface; the underlying database structure is much more flexible (cf. Sec. 3), facilitating the later addition of other types of annotation, if desired.

Tokens are displayed vertically, i.e., one token per line. This way, the annotations also line up vertically and are always within view. Additionally, a horizontal text preview can be displayed at the bottom of the screen, which makes it easier to read a continuous text passage. Fig. 1 shows a sample screenshot of the editor window.[3] Users can customize the editor, e.g. by hiding selected columns.

Parts-of-speech and morphology Within the editor, both POS and morphology tags can be selected from a dropdown box, which has the advantage of allowing both mouse-based and faster keyboard-based input. Tagsets can be defined individually for each text. If morphology tags are used, the selection of tags in the dropdown box is restricted by the chosen POS tag.

[3]The user interface is only available in German at the time of writing, but an English version is planned.

Lemmatization Lemma forms are entered into a text field, which can optionally be linked to a pre-defined lexicon from which it retrieves auto-completion suggestions. Furthermore, if an identical token has already been annotated with a lemma form elsewhere within the same project, that lemma is always displayed as a highlighted suggestion.

Normalization For corpora of non-standard language varieties, spelling normalization is often found as an annotation layer, see, e.g., Scheible et al. (2011) for historical data and Reznicek et al. (2013) for learner data.

In addition to normalization, an optional modernization layer can be used that defaults to the content of the normalization field. The normalization layer can be used for standardizing spelling, and the modernization layer for standardizing inflection and semantics (Bollmann et al., 2012).

Meta information CorA features a progress indicator which can be used to mark annotations as verified (see the green bar in Fig. 1). Besides serving as a visual aid for the annotator, it is also used for the automatic annotation component (cf. Sec. 2.2). Additionally, tokens can be marked as needing further review (indicated with a red checkbox), and comments can be added.

2.2 Automatic annotation

CorA supports (semi-)automatic annotation by integrating external annotation software on the server side. Currently, RFTagger (Schmid and Laws, 2008) and the Norma tool for automatic normalization (Bollmann, 2012) are supported, but in principle any other annotation tool can be integrated as well. The "retraining" feature collects all verified annotations from a project and feeds them to the tools' training functions. The user is then able to invoke the automatic annotation process using the newly trained parametrizations, which causes all tokens not yet marked as verified to be overwritten with the new annotations.

The retraining module is particularly relevant for non-standard language varieties where appropriate language models may not be available. The idea is that as more data is manually annotated within a corpus, the performance of automatic annotation tools increases when retrained on that data. This in turn makes it desirable to re-apply the automatic tools during the annotation process.

2.3 Editing primary data

In diplomatic transcriptions of historical manuscripts, the transcripts reproduce the manuscripts in the most accurate way, by encoding all relevant details of special graphemes and diacritics, and also preserving layout information. Transcribers often use ASCII-based encodings for special characters, e.g., the dollar sign $ in place of a long s ('ſ').

The data model of CorA (cf. Sec. 3) distinguishes between different types of token representations. In the annotation editor, the user can choose to display either the original transcription layer or the UTF-8 representation.

If an error in the primary data—e.g., a transcription error or wrong tokenization—is noticed during the annotation, it can be corrected directly within the editor. CorA provides functionality to edit, add, or delete existing tokens. Furthermore, external scripts can be embedded to process any changes, by checking an edited token for validity (e.g., if tokens need to conform to a certain transcription format), or generating the UTF-8 representation by interpreting special characters (e.g., mapping $ to ſ).

2.4 Comparison to related tools

There is a range of annotation tools that can be used for enriching data with different kinds of annotations. Prominent examples are GATE, EXMARaLDA, MMAX2, brat, and WebAnno.[4] Many annotation projects nowadays require distributed collaborative working of multiple parties. The currently preferred solution is to use a tool with an underlying database which is operated through a standard web-browser. Among the tools above, only brat and WebAnno are web-based tools. Compared to CorA, these tools are more flexible in that they support more annotation layers and more complex (e.g., multi-word) annotations. WebAnno, in addition, offers facilities for measuring inter-annotator agreement and data curation. However, brat and WebAnno do not allow edits to the source document from within the tool, which is particularly relevant for non-standard language varieties. Similarly, they do not support retraining on newly annotated data.

3 Data Model

The requirements described in Sec. 2 present various challenges to the data storage, which necessitated the development of our own data model. A data model in this context is a conceptual model of the data structure that allows serialization into various representations such as XML or databases. Such a model also allows for easy conversion between serializations and hence facilitates interoperability with existing formats and tools. The complex, multi-layered layout, the differences in tokenization, and the fine-grained description of graphematic pecularities in the primary data cannot be captured well using existing formats. For example, tokenization differences as they are handled by formats such as <tiger2/> (Bosch et al., 2012) pertain only to the contraction of underlying units to original forms, and not the other way around. This means that while a conversion in such formats is easily possible, some of the data structure that is captured by our model is necessarily lost in the process. To come up with a data model that minimizes redundancy and allows for flexibility and extensibility, and accomodates the work flow of our transcriptors and annotators, we employed normalization techniques from database development. A slightly simplified version of the data model is shown in Fig. 2.

[4] GATE: `http://gate.ac.uk/`
EXMARaLDA: `http://www.exmaralda.org/`
MMAX2: `http://mmax2.sourceforge.net/`
brat: `http://brat.nlplab.org/`
WebAnno: `https://code.google.com/p/webanno/`

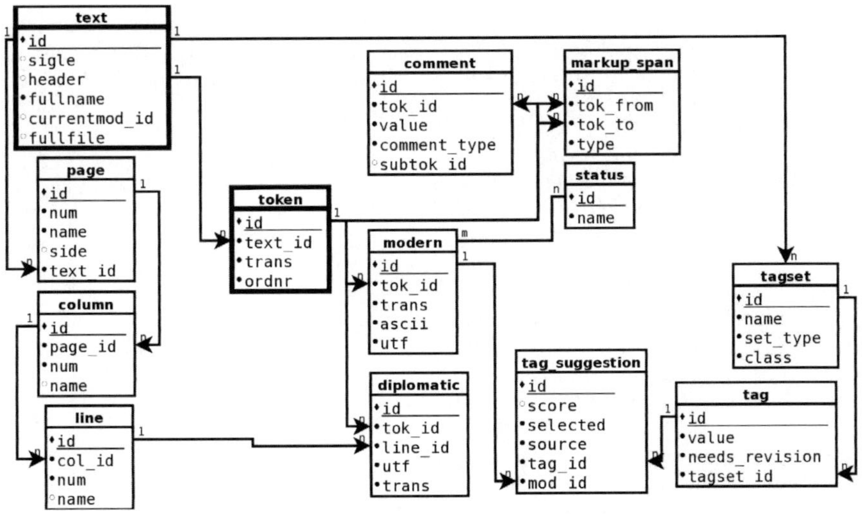

Figure 2: Data model used for CorA

Token and Text The model is centered around two units, a text and a token. A token is a virtual unit that can manifest in two ways, the diplomatic token and the modern token, each of which has a one-to-many relation with a token (cf. Fig. 3). Diplomatic tokens are tokens as they appear in the original, historical text, while modern tokens mirror modern conventions for token boundaries, representing suitable units for further annotations, e.g. with POS tags. All physical layout information on the other hand relates to the diplomatic token.

The text is the entirety of a transcribed document that can be partitioned in various ways. The layout is captured by its relation to the page, column, and line, which in turn relate to the diplomatic tokens. Furthermore, a text can be assigned one or more tagsets. The tagsets in turn can be open, such as lemmatization tags, or closed, such as POS tags. Each text can be assigned different tagsets.

Extensions In addition, the data model also allows for the import of markup annotations with the texts, which may denote layout-related or linguistic peculiarities encoded by the transcriptors, as well as information about its annotation status such as progress, or dubious annotations. The model is easily extendable for user management that can tie in to the text table, e.g., a user can be set as owner or creator of a text.

As XML serialization is not optimized for data which is not strictly hierarchically structured, storage and retrieval is rather inefficient, and extensions are not easily possible. For this reason, we chose to implement the application with an SQL database

```
<token>
    <!-- diplomatic tokenization -->
    <dipl trans="ober"/>
    <dipl trans="czugemich"/>

    <!-- modern tokenization -->
    <mod trans="oberczuge">
        <norm tag="überzeuge"/>
        <pos tag="VVIMP.Sg"/>
    </mod>
    <mod trans="mich">
        <norm tag="mich"/>
        <pos tag="PPER.1.Sg.*.Acc"/>
    </mod>
</token>
```

Figure 3: Example serialization of *ober czugemich* (modern *überzeuge mich* 'convince me') in XML

serialization of the data model.

4 Conclusion

We described CorA, a web-based annotation tool. Its main features are the integration of automatic annotation software, the possibility of making edits to the source document, and the conceptual distinction between diplomatic and modern tokens in the data model. We believe that these features are particularly useful for annotators of non-standard language data such as historical texts, and set CorA apart from other existing annotation tools.

We plan to make the tool available under an open source license eventually. However, we are currently still working on implementing additional functionality. In future work, we plan to integrate features to evaluate annotation quality, such as automatically calculating inter-annotator agreement.

References

Marcel Bollmann, Stefanie Dipper, Julia Krasselt, and Florian Petran. 2012. Manual and semi-automatic normalization of historical spelling – case studies from Early New High German. In *Proceedings of the First International Workshop on Language Technology for Historical Text(s) (LThist2012)*, Vienna, Austria.

Marcel Bollmann. 2012. (Semi-)automatic normalization of historical texts using distance measures and the Norma tool. In *Proceedings of the Second Workshop on Annotation of Corpora for Research in the Humanities (ACRH-2)*, Lisbon, Portugal.

Sonja Bosch, Key-Sun Choi, Éric de la Clergerie, Alex Chengyu Fang, Gertrud Faaß, Kiyong Lee, Antonio Pareja-Lora, Laurent Romary, Andreas Witt, Amir Zeldes, and Florian Zipser. 2012. <tiger2/> as a standardised serialisation for ISO 24615. In *Proceedings of the 11th Workshop on Treebanks and Linguistic Theory (TLT)*, Lisbon, Portugal.

Jennifer Foster, Ozlem Cetinoglu, Joachim Wagner, Joseph Le Roux, Stephen Hogan, Joakim Nivre, Deirdre Hogan, and Josef van Genabith. 2011. #hardtoparse: POS tagging and parsing the twitterverse. In *Proceedings of AAAI-11 Workshop on Analysing Microtext*, San Francisco, CA.

Eugenie Giesbrecht and Stefan Evert. 2009. Part-of-speech tagging — a solved task? An evaluation of POS taggers for the German Web as Corpus. In *Proceedings of the 5th Web as Corpus Workshop (WAC5)*, pages 27–35, San Sebastian, Spain.

Paul Rayson, Dawn Archer, Alistair Baron, Jonathan Culpeper, and Nicholas Smith. 2007. Tagging the Bard: Evaluating the accuracy of a modern POS tagger on Early Modern English corpora. In *Proceedings of Corpus Linguistics 2007*, University of Birmingham, UK.

Marc Reznicek, Anke Lüdeling, and Hagen Hirschmann. 2013. Competing target hypotheses in the Falko Corpus: A flexible multi-layer corpus architecture. In Ana Díaz-Negrillo, Nicolas Ballier, and Paul Thompson, editors, *Automatic Treatment and Analysis of Learner Corpus Data*, pages 101–123. Amsterdam: Benjamins.

Silke Scheible, Richard J. Whitt, Martin Durrell, and Paul Bennett. 2011. Evaluating an 'off-the-shelf' POS-tagger on Early Modern German text. In *Proceedings of the ACL-HLT 2011 Workshop on Language Technology for Cultural Heritage, Social Sciences, and Humanities (LaTeCH 2011)*, pages 19–23, Portland, Oregon, USA.

Helmut Schmid and Florian Laws. 2008. Estimation of conditional probabilities with decision trees and an application to fine-grained POS tagging. In *Proceedings of COLING '08*, Manchester, Great Britain.

Amir Zeldes, Julia Ritz, Anke Lüdeling, and Christian Chiarcos. 2009. ANNIS: a search tool for multi-layer annotated corpora. In *Proceedings of Corpus Linguistics*, Liverpool, UK.

Developing a Tagalog Linguistic Inquiry and Word Count (LIWC) 'Disaster' Dictionary for Understanding Mixed Language Social Media: A Work-in-Progress Paper

Amanda Andrei, Alison Dingwall, Theresa Dillon, Jennifer Mathieu
MITRE Corporation
7515 Colshire Drive
Mclean, Virginia 22042 USA
aandrei@mitre.org

Abstract

In the wake of super typhoon Yolanda (known internationally as Haiyan) in the Philippines in 2013, many individuals in the Philippines turned to social media to express their thoughts and emotions in a variety of languages. In order to understand and analyze the sentiment of populations on the ground, we used a novel approach of developing a conceptual Linguistic Inquiry and Word Count (LIWC) dictionary comprised of Tagalog words relating to disaster. This work-in-progress paper documents our process of filtering and choosing terms and offers suggestions for validating the dictionary. When results on how the dictionary was used are available, we can better assess the process for creating conceptual LIWC dictionaries.

1 Background

By engaging in a variety of social networking and blogging activities, individuals often reveal their "perceptions, attitudes, beliefs, and behaviors" (Maybury, 2010) through multiple social media platforms such as Facebook and Twitter. In addition, social media provides an important source for breaking news, especially during natural disasters and emergencies (Nagar et al., 2012; Crowe, 2012). During events such as the 2010 earthquake in Haiti and the 2011 tsunami in Japan, individuals turned to social media to report injuries, ask for assistance, and publish personal accounts (Gao et al., 2011; Abbasi et al., 2012). Likewise, the 2013 disaster of super typhoon Yolanda (known internationally as Haiyan) in the Philippines triggered a wide use of social media during the period of the storm.

1.1 Philippines

With its two official languages (English and Filipino) and dozens of other local languages and dialects, the Philippines has a complex and politicized history of multilingualism (Gonzalez, 1998; Nical et al., 2004; Ang, 1978). Both the grammar and vocabulary of Filipino (also known as Pilipino) is based primarily from Tagalog, a language originating from the regions surrounding the capital city of Manila, although some scholars argue that Filipino is essentially Tagalog (Ang, 1978; Baumgartner, 1989).

In 2011, the Philippines had the highest percentage of active online users in the world (Global WebIndex, 2011). In 2012, the nation had more than 10 million active Twitter users, which ranked it tenth in countries with the most Twitter users (Abuy, 2012). Tweets from the Philippines are in mixed languages, with 80% in English and the other 20% in Filipino languages (Pilkington, 2011). Furthermore, the Philippines is the most disaster-prone nation in the world (CDRC Admin, 2013; Bankoff, 2002), making it a prime candidate for analyzing sentiment in social media during and following a natural disaster.

1.2 Linguistic Inquiry and Word Count (LIWC)

As social media analysis continues to mature as a field, if social media is to be leveraged more effectively for disaster response and relief there is a need for more quantitative methods to supplement current qualitative techniques and subject matter expertise (Servi and Elson, 2012). Servi & Elson (2012) used the novel approach of combining mathematical algorithms with a social psychology tool, Linguistic Inquiry and Word Count (LIWC) (Pennebaker et al., 2007), to detect and forecast emotional trends in Twitter in an unbiased way.

LIWC uses internal "dictionaries" of words which correspond to various domains of linguistic processes, psychological processes, personal concerns, and spoken categories. For instance, one dictionary under psychological processes is filled with *positive emotion* words (e.g., "love," "nice," and "sweet"). Another dictionary under personal concerns includes *death* words (e.g., "bury," "coffin," "kill"). When a researcher runs a text file through LIWC, the program compares the words in the file to the dictionaries and outputs a ratio of dictionary words to total words (e.g., 1% of all words are positive emotion words). Researchers have used LIWC to analyze a variety of texts, most notably newspaper coverage of a bonfire tragedy at Texas A&M (Gortner and Pennebaker, 2003), one of the earliest examples of using LIWC to understand emotions around disaster management.

First created in English, LIWC has also been translated into other languages. This project is developing a set of LIWC dictionaries in Tagalog in order to understand social media usage in the Philippines, particularly usage during the typhoon. Tagalog was chosen and distinguished from Filipino for three main reasons: namely, that more information about and translations in Tagalog are readily available, to highlight the fact that there are more Philippine languages beyond "Filipino" that could be translated as well, and because most tweets originated from Manila, where Tagalog is the main Philippine language spoken.

2 Process

On November 8, 2013, super typhoon Yolanda made landfall in the central Philippines. Over 11 million people were affected, with 2.5 million people in need of food aid and over 2,000 people dead (BBC News Asia, 2013).

As the Philippines is linguistically diverse, there remained a need to also explore the tweets that were posted in mixed languages, primarily Tagalog since it is one of the major languages in the nation. A LIWC dictionary of disaster-related words in Tagalog was developed in order to gauge how many tweets during the period of the typhoon related to the disaster. To explore the impact of the typhoon from the publics perspective in social media, mixed language Twitter posts geographically restricted to the Philippines were analyzed.

Using a commercially available social search and analytics too which filters Twitter content based on variables such as location, time and date, tweet type (original, retweet, reply), language (although Tagalog is not included) and others, a volume of approximately 1.5 million tweets from the Philippines were identified within a two-week date range around the typhoon. This set was isolated based on restricting the tweets to those originating from the Philippines between the dates of November 3-18, 2013 and included any of the following terms: *typhoon*, *yolanda*, *haiyan*, *supertyphoon*, as well as corresponding hashtags.

A wide range of words and concepts relating to typhoons and disasters, such as *baha* (storm), *donasyon* (donation), *nagugutom* (starving), *patay* (dead), and *sagip* (save) were identified. Related terms were also identified and included in the search, such as *#bangon* (rise up), a nationalistic call of inspiration; *#walangpasok* (no entry), colloquially a school closing alert; *Libreng Tawag* (free calls), used to alert users which telecommunication companies were allowing no charge phone calls; and *PAGASA* (hope), which is also an acronym for the Philippine weather alert service.

In order to develop a clean data set, these terms were then narrowed down based on what would make appropriate inclusions for a LIWC dictionary, resulting in the discarding of hash tags, multi-word phrases, and proper nouns. Certain words were also found to be too broad (i.e., false positives), such as donasyon, which was used in non-disaster contexts just as frequently as in typhoon-related tweets within the date range analyzed. Words like nagugutom and patay were actually used more frequently in non-disaster contexts (e.g., "I am starving, I want a sandwich").

The dictionary was designed to include different grammatical forms of words. For example, for nouns, both *baha* (flood) and *bahang* (flood), where ng is a linking suffix, were included. For verbs, different tenses were included, e.g., *tulong* (help), *tumulong* (helped), and *tumutulong* (helps). In the case of the verbs, other forms of the words were searched, but not included in the dictionary if they were not frequently used in tweets. The complete dictionary is included in the Appendix.

3 Remarks and Future Work

The Tagalog LIWC disaster dictionary was developed to quickly explore and understand perceptions expressed on social media about the typhoon. While the terms were included for the 2013 typhoon, additional research and validation is required for generalization for understanding future natural disasters. While social media can contain a wealth of information, the processes of filtering and searching for terms would benefit from a more rigorous standard of including words in the dictionary. For instance, researchers may want to consider what counts as high frequency for a word, e.g., if it appears over a certain absolute number of times or if it appears in high proportion compared to other words. Overall, a move from qualitative analysis to more quantitative analysis would clarify the connection between the dictionary and the source corpus.

The process of creating a conceptual LIWC dictionary should also be vetted against other use cases and concepts. For instance, the word *lindol* (earthquake) was included in the dictionary since earthquakes are common in the Philippines, although earthquake activity was not recorded during the typhoon. The dictionary could be evaluated or validated against other social media responses to other recent disasters, such as the October 2013 earthquake in Bohol, an island near the typhoon-struck areas, in order to see how users tweet about disasters.

Geography also plays an important role in how the disaster dictionary can be used. For the purposes of creating this dictionary, tweets were restricted to the Philippines. It would be worthwhile to examine if the same words in the dictionary occur if tweets were collected from different origins, such as Leyte (the island which sustained most of the damage) versus Manila (the capital city of the Philippines) versus a location with a large concentration of Filipino immigrants (such as California, USA).

Additionally, other concepts related to disaster management should be explored and considered for inclusion in the dictionary, such as words relating to property, family, and emotions. As the original (English-language) LIWC application already has categories for such concepts, future work would include translating the complete set of LIWC dictionaries into Tagalog while also including culturally specific words without exact translations. This work is currently in progress.

Furthermore, the areas hit by the typhoon speak and use social media in other Philippines languages in addition to Tagalog (primarily Cebuano and Waray). It may also be helpful to have dictionaries in other languages predominant in the area where a disaster occurs. This may be a difficult task to undertake, as translations for other Philippine languages are not as readily available as translations for Tagalog.

This paper details the process for creating the dictionary; how the dictionary was used in actual social media datasets concerning the typhoon is still in progress. Upon reviewing how the disaster dictionary was used, this process of creating concept LIWC dictionaries and its utility will be better assessed and validated. Since this tool and the additional LIWC dictionaries are still in their preliminary formats, there are no current plans to make the tools commercially available until they are reviewed and vetted by native Tagalog speakers. As the work progresses, the disaster dictionary will be maintained and kept up-to-date in order to include additional terms which may apply to future disasters.

References

Mohammad-Ali Abbasi, Shamanth Kumar, Jose Augusto Andrade Filho, and Huan Liu. 2012. Lessons learned in using social media for disaster relief - ASU crisis response game. *Social Computing, Behavioral-Cultural Modeling and Prediction*, 7227, 282-289.

Abiel Abuy. 2012. "Twitter crosses 500 million mark, Philippines in the top 10 in terms of Twitter accounts." 2 Aug 2012. *KabayanTech.* http://kabayantech.com/2012/08/twitter-crosses-500-million-mark-philippines-in-the-top-10-in-terms-of-twitter-accounts/

Gertrudes R. Ang. 1978. The Filipino as a bilingual or multilingual: Some implications. *Philippine Quarterly of Culture and Society*, 187-189.

Gregory Bankoff. 2002. *Cultures of disaster: Society and natural hazard in the philippines.* Routledge-Curzon, New York, NY.

Joseph Baumgartner. 1989. The controversy about the national language: Some observations. *Philippine Quarterly of Culture and Society*, 168-172.

BBC News Asia. 2013. "Typhoon Haiyan: Aid in numbers." 14 Nov 2013. *BBC News.* http://www.bbc.co.uk/news/world-asia-pacific-24899006

CDRC Admin. 2013. "Philippines is most disaster-affected country in 2012." 8 Apr 2013. *Citizens' Disaster Response Center.* http://www.cdrc-phil.com/philippines-is-most-disaster-affected-country-in-2012/

Adam Crowe. 2012. *Disasters 2.0: The application of social media systems for modern emergency management.* CRC Press: Boca Raton, FL.

Juiji Gao, Geoffrey Barbier, and Rebecca Goolsby. 2011. Harnessing the crowdsourcing power of social media for disaster relief. *Intelligent Systems, IEEE*, 26(3), pp.10,14, May-June 2011.

Global WebIndex. 2011. "Global Map of Social Networking 2011." *GlobalWebIndex.Net.* https://globalwebindex.net/wp-content/uploads/downloads/2011/06/Global-Map-of-Social-Networking-GlobalWebIndex-June-20112.pdf

Andrew Gonzalez. 1998. The language planning situation in the Philippines. *Journal of Multilingual and Multicultural Development.* 19(5), 487-525.

Eva-Maria Gortner and James W. Pennebaker. 2003. The archival anatomy of a disaster: Media coverage and community-wide health effects of the Texas A&M bonfire tragedy. *Journal of Social and Clinical Psychology.* 22, 580-603.

Mark Maybury. 2010. "Social Radar for Smart Power." *The MITRE Corporation.* http://www.mitre.org/sites/default/files/pdf/10_0745.pdf

Seema Nagar, Aaditeshwar Seth, and Anupam Joshi. 2012. Characterization of social media response to natural disasters. *Proceedings of the 21st international conference companion on World Wide Web (WWW '12 Companion)*, ACM, 671-674.

Iluminado Nical, Jerzy J. Smolicz, and Margaret J. Secombe. 2004. Rural students and the Philippine bilingual education program on the island of Leyte. *Medium of instruction policies - Which agenda? Whose agenda?*, 153-176. Lawrence Erlbaum Associates, Mahwah, NJ.

James W. Pennebaker, Roger J. Booth, and Martha E. Francis. 2007. Linguistic Inquiry and Word Count: LIWC2007 Operators manual. *LIWC.net.*

Andy Pilkington. 2011 "Axe shows consistency is key to a successful multi-lingual page in the Philippines." 26 Oct 2011. *WaveMetrix.* http://wave.wavemetrix.com/content/axe-shows-consistency-key-successful-multi-lingual-page-philippines-00844

Les Servi and Sara Beth Elson. 2012. A mathematical approach to identifying and forecasting shifts in the mood of social media users. *The MITRE Corporation.* Bedford, MA.

Paul Schachter, and Fe T. Otanes. 1972. *Tagalog Reference Grammar.* University of California Press, Berkeley, CA.

A Appendix

The completed dictionary is included in the following table. consists of the Tagalog and English columns. In some cases, multiple dictionary entries correspond to the same Tagalog lexeme. For example:

bagyong
bagyo-ng
storm-LIGATURE

For more on Tagalog grammar, see Schachter and Otanes 1972.

Tagalog	**English**
bagyo	storm
bagyong	storm
baha	flood
bahang	flood
biktima	victims
hangin	wind
lindol	earthquake
lumikas	evacuate
nagsilikas	refugees
nasawi	casualty
sagip	rescue
sagipin	rescue
sinalanta	devastated
sugatan	wounded
tulong	help
tumulong	help
tumutulong	help
ulan	rain

Text Analysis of Aberdeen Burgh Records 1530-1531

Adam Wyner[1], Jackson Armstrong[2], Andrew Mackillop[2], and Philip Astley[3]
[1]University of Aberdeen, Department of Computing Science, Aberdeen, Scotland
azwyner@abdn.ac.uk
[2]University of Aberdeen, Department of History, Aberdeen, Scotland
{j.armstrong,a.mackillop}@abdn.ac.uk
[3]Aberdeen City and Aberdeenshire Archives, Aberdeen, Scotland
PAstley@aberdeencity.gov.uk

Abstract

The paper outlines a text analytic project in progress on a corpus of entries in the historical burgh and council registers from Aberdeen, Scotland. Some preliminary output of the analysis is described. The registers run in a near-unbroken sequence form 1398 to the present day; the early volumes are a UNESCO UK listed cultural artefact. The study focusses on a set of transcribed pages from 1530-1531 originally hand written in a mixture of Latin and Middle Scots. We apply a text analytic tool to the corpus, providing deep semantic annotation and making the text amenable to linking to web-resources.

1 Introduction

The council registers of Aberdeen, Scotland are the earliest and most complete body of town (or burgh) council records in Scotland, running nearly continuously from 1398 to the present; they are hand written in Latin and (largely) Middle Scots. Few cities in the United Kingdom or in Western Europe rival Aberdeen's burgh registers in historical depth and completeness. In July 2013, UNESCO UK recognised the register volumes from 1398 to 1509 as being of outstanding historical importance to the UK. The registers offer a detailed *legal* view into one of Scotland's principal burghs , casting light on administrative, legal, and commercial activities as well as daily life. The registers include the elections of office bearers, property transfers, regulations of trade and prices, references to crimes and subsequent punishment, matters of public health, credit and debt, cargoes of foreign vessels, tax and rental of burgh lands, and woods and fishings. Thus the entries present the burgh's relationships with the countryside and countries around the North Sea.

To make this historical resource available to a wider audience, the National Records of Scotland and Aberdeen City and Aberdeenshire Archives collaborated to image the volumes digitally up to 1511 and made them (temporarily) available on the internet.[1] However, the images of scribal records are inaccessible to all but a few scholars. To address this, a pilot project at the University of Aberdeens Research Institute of Irish and Scottish Studies (RIISS) has transcribed 100 pages of the records from the period 1530-1531, translated the Latin and Middle Scots, and provided a web-accessible database application; the application allows users to query the database for locations and names of individuals, returning the textual portions that contain the names and locations.[2] However, the pilot project does not make use of text analytic or Semantic Web technologies to facilitate understanding of and access to the records.

In this paper, we outline a funded text analytic project in progress on this corpus of 100 pages and provide some preliminary output. The project *A Text Analytic Approach to Rural and Urban Legal Histories* has been funded by the dot.rural Resource Partnership at the University of Aberdeen.[3] We outline the project objectives, present the text analytic tool, provide some sample results, relate our work to other projects, and sketch future work. The paper and project contribute to the application of language technologies for cultural heritage and the humanities. We discuss deep semantic annotation of the documents as well as plans to address linguistic variation and linking of the annotated material to other digital, web-based resources.

[1]http://www.scotlandsplaces.gov.uk/digital-volumes/burgh-records/aberdeen-burgh-registers/

[2]http://www.abdn.ac.uk/riiss/Aberdeen-Burgh-Records-Project/connecting-projecting.shtml

[3]http://www.dotrural.ac.uk

2 Objectives

The project engages legal historians, council archivists, and computational linguists. For legal historians, the burgh registries are an opportunity to study source materials concerned with the law and community concerning questions as:

- What legal roles in jurisdictions do individuals perform?
- What are the social and legal networks?
- How do social and legal concepts evolve?
- What does the historical record say about resource management and conflict?

While traditional historical methodology applied to archival material has served well enough, it is costly, slow, and does not allow analysis of the volume and complexity of information. In particular, some of the questions above are *relational*, e.g. relations of individuals in legal roles, which are difficult to track across a large corpus. With text analytic support, legal historians can query a corpus and receive data either in context or extracted.

For council archivists, the agenda is to increase public access to archival materials for tourism, curriculum development, business, and research. This can be done, we believe, by making the rich content of the archives accessible by translation, semantic search, or link to the content of the archival materials or other web-accessible resources such as dictionaries, maps, DBPedia entries, other council archival material, and so on.

For computational linguists, the objective is to annotate, enrich, and link the burgh records in order to support semantic querying, extraction, and reuse. One challenge is to find or develop the range of necessary text analytic components to do so. For non-standardised historical languages, e.g. Middle Scots, the issues are orthographical variation, lack of electronic lexicons, and so on. A more substantive challenge is to develop the appropriate set of semantic annotations, tailored to the historical, legal context and the goals of historical legal analysis.

3 Text Analysis

To identify, query, and extract the textual elements from the source material with respect to semantic annotations, we use the GATE framework (Cunningham et al., 2002), which we briefly describe. We then discuss our approach to analysis, the representation of textual elements using GATE, the annotations we introduce to the text, and then provide the results of sample queries.

3.1 Components of a Tool

GATE is a framework for language engineering applications, which supports efficient and robust text processing (Cunningham et al., 2002); it is highly scalable and has been applied in many large text processing projects; it is an open source desktop application written in Java that provides a user interface for professional linguists and text engineers to bring together a wide variety of natural language processing tools and apply them to a set of documents. The tools are formed into a pipeline of natural language processors. Our approach to GATE tool development follows (Wyner and Peters, 2011), which is: bottom-up, rule-based, unweighted, modular, iterative, incremental, among others. Once a GATE pipeline has been applied, we can view the annotations either *in situ* or queried using GATE's ANNIC (ANNotations In Context) corpus indexing and querying tool.

For our purposes, we emphasise the role of *gazetteers* and *JAPE rules*, which form the *bottom level* of the analysis. A gazetteer is a list of words that are associated with a central concept as provided by an analyst. In the lookup phase of processing the text, textual passages in the corpus are matched with terms on the lists, then assigned an annotation, e.g. a token term *burgi* is annotated with *LegalBody*, for it is one of the legal bodies reported in the text. Similarly, tokens such as *common council*, *curia*, *guild court*, and others are all annotated *LegalBody*. The gazetteer thus annotates related terms (e.g. *burgi* and *guild court*) with the same annotation; in this way, annotations serve as *conceptual covers* for tokens. We have gazetteers that provide a range of semantic concepts for named entities as well as:

- LegalBody - burgi, common council, ...
- LegalConcept - gude faith, ...
- LegalRole - Archbishop, Bailie, ...
- Offence - barganyng, tulyheing, etc
- Office - alderman, burgess, preposito, ...
- RegisterEntry - Bailie Court, Ordinance, ...
- MiddleScot - The, said, day, bailyeis, ...

Alternative spellings of a word would be represented as different tokens in the gazetteer. The selection and content of the gazetteer lists is preliminary and will be the object of significant research over the course of the project. However, they are sufficient to facilitate exercise of the tool.

JAPE rules are transductions that take annotations and regular expressions as input (based on the gazetteers) and produce annotations as output. The annotations produced by JAPE rules are visible as highlighted text and are easily searchable in ANNIC. Querying for an annotation, we retrieve all the terms with the annotation. The annotations can also be used in JAPE rules to create higher level annotations, though we have not developed these at this point.

3.2 Output and Queries

Once the corpus is annotated, we can view the annotations *in situ*. In Figure 1, we have a passage that has been highlighted with the indicated (checked) annotation types (differentiated by colour in the orginal). In this figure, we see where the annotations appear and in relation to other annotations within a particular textual passage. Observations at this point can be used to analyse the text further.

Alternatively, we can use the ANNIC tool to index and query a database of annotated text. Searching in the corpus for single annotations returns all those strings that are annotated with the search annotation along with their context and source document. Complex queries can also be formed. A query and a sample result appear in Figure 2, where the query finds all sequences of annotated text where the first string is annotated with *Name*, followed by zero to five other *Tokens*, followed by a string with an *Office* annotation. The search returned four candidate structures. The extract identifies a *relation* between an individual and their office. Similar relational queries can be made about other aspects of the text. With the query language, we can search for any number of the annotations in the corpus in any order; the tool allows incremental refinement of searches, allowing for a highly interactive way to examine the semantic content of the texts. Thus, a range of semantic patterns can be identified that would otherwise be very hard to detect or extract. Such an approach can ground multi-disciplinary investigations of historical societies in large-scale textual sources of information, providing interpretable material on topics such as elites and social practice, relations between social classes and land, urban and rural development, and natural resource management. The text analysis also makes applicable a range of social web-mining approaches on historical text.

4 Related Work

Our work is closely related to other projects that have applied text analytic methods to *mine* information from the cultural heritage objects, broadly Digital Humanties. Most recently, there has been an extensive n-gram study of Scottish legal records. This takes a very different, though nonetheless relevant approach to the study of these records ngrams (Kopaczyk, 2013). Several recent projects in the UK and Ireland have applied such tools in limited ways to historical legal documents, e.g. *1641 Depositions* (Sweetnam and Fennell, 2012), which analysed verbal patterns in the text [4]; *The Old Bailey*, which was largely manually annotated though some elements were automatically annotated [5]; and Trading Consequences, a text an-

[4] http://1641.tcd.ie

[5] http://www.oldbaileyonline.org

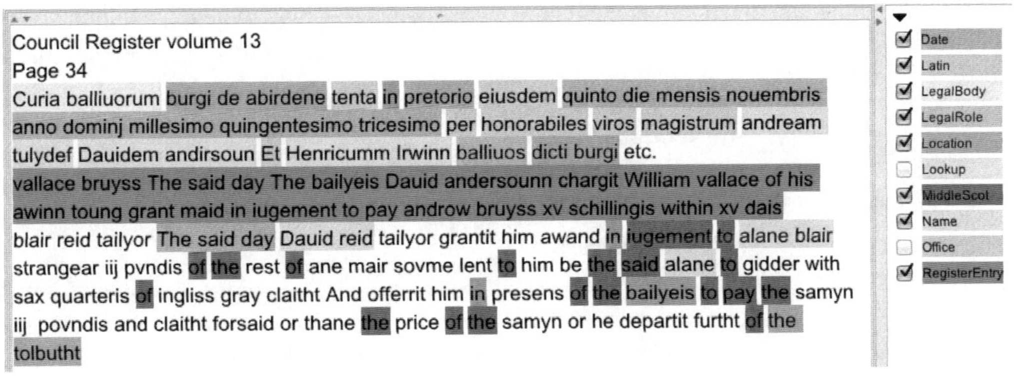

Figure 1: Highlighting Annotations in the Text

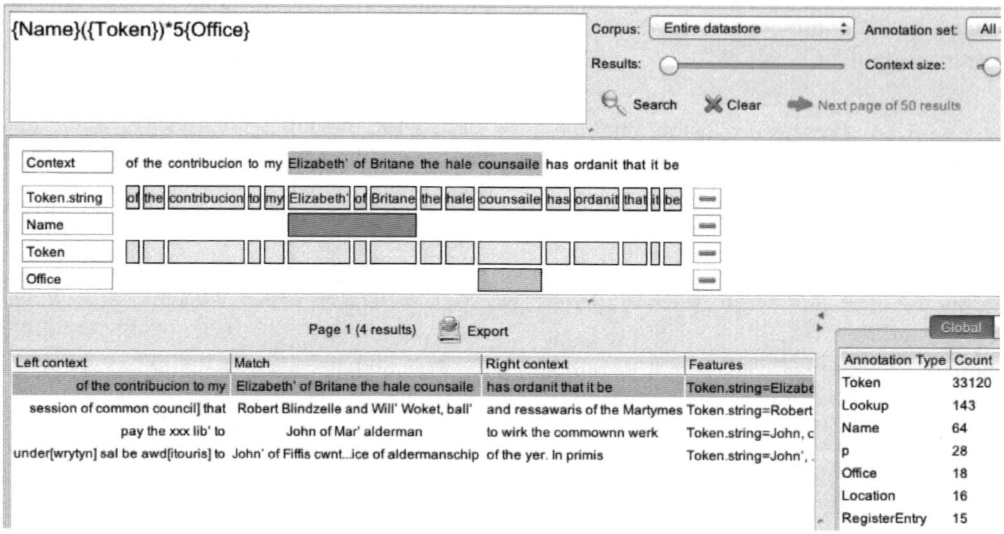

Figure 2: Searching for Relations in the Corpus

alytic study of British Empire records [6]. There are ongoing Semantic Web projects in the Humanities, e.g. the Curios Project [7], the CULTURA Project [8], projects at King's College London Centre for Digital Humanities [9].

5 Future Plans

Over the course of the project, we will develop and refine a useful set of annotations that reveal important information this is distributed over this corpus. Asides from the main categories previously discussed, there will be annotations to indicate orthographic variants, translations, and links to external material amongst other annotations to be developed. Legal historical questions will be posed with respect to the contents of the text, then the text will be queried using the annotations in complex patterns. In this way, the questions of legal historians are grounded in and tested against the textual substance. Another objective is to link the annotated material to other relevant material that is external to the corpus. For instance, locations could be associated with maps, names could be associated with DBPedia entries, words could be linked to Scottish and Latin dictionaries, and so on. This would not only further enrich the contents of the corpus, but also enrich these other materials by linking to the corpus. Similarly, these texts can be tied to other legal historical projects, focussing on the period c.1400 c.1800, that will inter-relate the council register source material with cognate collections held in Aberdeen (at the Aberdeen City and Aberdeenshire Archives, and at the University of Aberdeens Special Collections Centre, and elsewhere), in Scotland (in other local archives and in the National Records of Scotland), in the United Kingdom, or the European Union. This will foster both a comparative understanding of the city and its regions position regionally, nationally, and internationally, and over time.

Beyond the project, we look forward to enlarge the council register corpus and extend the text analysis. It would then be very attractive to create a web-based, interactive interface with which to interrogate the council register in complex and novel ways, not just by querying the text with semantic annotations, but also by following links to maps, recordings, images, related words, and so on. For example, the content could be linked to time series maps, showing development of social, legal, and political relationships over time and space.

Acknowledgments

The authors are grateful for support from RIISS, dot.rural, and the Aberdeen Council. We particularly thank Dr. Edda Frankot for her work on the pilot project at RIISS that produced the transcribed materials for this project.

[6] `http://tradingconsequences.blogs.edina.ac.uk/`

[7] `http://www.dotrural.ac.uk/curios/`

[8] `www.cultura-strep.eu`

[9] `http://www.kcl.ac.uk/artshums/depts/ddh/index.aspx`

References

Hamish Cunningham, Diana Maynard, Kalina Bontcheva, and Valentin Tablan. 2002. GATE: A framework and graphical development environment for robust NLP tools and applications. In *Proceedings of the 40th Anniversary Meeting of the Association for Computational Linguistics (ACL'02)*, pages 168–175.

Joanna Kopaczyk. 2013. *The Legal Language of Scottish Burghs*. Oxford University Press.

Mark S. Sweetnam and Barbara A. Fennell. 2012. Natural language processing and early-modern dirty data: applying IBM *languageware* to the 1641 depositions. *Literary and Linguistic Computing*, 27(1):39–54.

Adam Wyner and Wim Peters. 2011. On rule extraction from regulations. In Katie Atkinson, editor, *Legal Knowledge and Information Systems - JURIX 2011: The Twenty-Fourth Annual Conference*, pages 113–122. IOS Press.

From Syntax to Semantics. First Steps Towards Tectogrammatical Annotation of Latin

Marco Passarotti
CIRCSE Research Centre
Università Cattolica del Sacro Cuore
Largo Gemelli, 1 – 20123 Milan, Italy
marco.passarotti@unicatt.it

Abstract

Assuming that collaboration between theoretical and computational linguistics is essential in projects aimed at developing language resources like annotated corpora, this paper presents the first steps of the semantic annotation of the *Index Thomisticus* Treebank, a dependency-based treebank of Medieval Latin. The semantic layer of annotation of the treebank is detailed and the theoretical framework supporting the annotation style is explained and motivated.

1 Introduction

Started in 1949 by father Roberto Busa SJ, the *Index Thomisticus* (IT; Busa, 1974-1980) has represented a groundbreaking project that laid the foundations of computational linguistics and literary computing. The IT is a morphologically tagged and lemmatized corpus of Medieval Latin containing the *opera omnia* of Thomas Aquinas (118 texts), as well as 61 texts by other authors related to Thomas, for a total of around 11 million tokens.

The *Index Thomisticus* Treebank (IT-TB: http://itreebank.marginalia.it) is the syntactically annotated portion of the IT. Presently, the IT-TB includes around 220,000 nodes (approximately, 12,000 sentences).

The project of the IT-TB is now entering a new phase aimed at enhancing the available syntactic annotation with semantic metadata. Starting such a task needs to choose a theoretical approach and framework that supports the annotation style. Indeed, performing linguistic annotation of a textual corpus should be strictly connected to fundamental issues in theoretical linguistics in a kind of virtuous circle. On its side, theoretical linguistics serves as the necessary backbone for solid annotation guidelines; no theory-neutral representation of a sentence is possible, since every representation style needs a theory to extract its meaning. On the other hand, applying a theoretical framework to real data makes it possible to empirically test and possibly refine it. According to Eva Hajičová, "corpus annotation serves, among other things, as an invaluable test for the linguistic theories standing behind the annotation schemes, and as such represents an irreplaceable resource of linguistic information for the construction and enrichment of grammars, both formal and theoretical" (Hajičová, 2006: 466).

Further, the task of developing language resources like annotated corpora supports interaction between intuition-based and corpus-based/-driven approaches in theoretical linguistics (Tognini-Bonelli, 2001). No intuition-based grammar is able to manage all the possible variations in real data, and no induction-based grammar can reflect all the possible well-formed constructions of a language (Aarts, 2002; Sinclair, 2004a).

This paper describes the first steps towards the semantic annotation of the IT-TB, by first presenting and motivating its theoretical background (section 2) and then sampling a number of specific aspects of annotation (section 3). Finally, section 4 reports a discussion and sketches the future work.

2 The Theoretical Background of the *Index Thomisticus* Treebank

Hosted at the CIRCSE research centre of the Università Cattolica del Sacro Cuore in Milan, Italy (http://centridiricerca.unicatt.it/circse), the IT-TB is a dependency-based treebank (McGillivray et al., 2009). The choice of a representation framework alone does not determine the representation for a given sentence, as there can be many (correct) dependency-based (as well as constituency-based) trees for even simple sentences. Thus, a fine-grained linguistic theory must be selected to support the specific aspects raised by a large-scale annotation of real data. In this respect, the annotation style of the IT-TB is based on Functional Generative Description (FGD; Sgall et al., 1986), a dependency-based theoretical framework developed in Prague and intensively applied and tested while building the Prague Dependency Treebank of Czech (PDT).

FGD is rooted in Praguian structuralism-functionalism dating back to the 30s, one assumption of which is the stratificational approach to sentence analysis pursued by Functional Sentence Perspective (FSP), a linguistic theory developed by Jan Firbas in the mid-1950s on the basis of Vilém Mathesius' work (Firbas, 1992). According to FSP, the sentence is conceived as: (a) a singular and individual speech event [utterance-event]; (b) one of the possible different minimal communicative units (means) of the given language [form]; (c) an abstract structure (a pattern) [meaning].

Considering language as a form-meaning composite is a basic assumption also of FGD, which is particularly focused on the last point above, aiming at the description of the so-called 'underlying syntax' of the sentence. Underlying syntax (the meaning) is separated from (but still connected with) surface syntax (the form) and represents the linguistic (literal) meaning of the sentence, which is described through dependency tree-graphs.

This approach is consistent with the functional and pragmatic analysis of language pursued by the Prague Linguistic Circle since its very beginning, along the so-called 'first period' of the Circle (Raynaud, 2008). Language is conceived as "un système de moyens d'expression appropriés à un but" ("a system of purposive means"; Cercle linguistique de Prague, 1929: 7). The "moyens d'expression" correspond to the 'form' (surface syntax), while the fact that they are "appropriés à un but" corresponds to the 'meaning' (underlying syntax).

The description of surface and underlying syntax in FGD is dependency-based mostly because dependency grammars are predicate-focused grammars. This enables FGD to face one of the basic statements of the Prague Linguistic Circle: "l'acte syntagmatique fondamental [...] est la prédication" ("the basic syntagmatic act is predication"; Cercle linguistique de Prague, 1929: 13). Further, during the second period of the theory of predication pursued by the Circle, while accounting for the three-level approach to sentence in FSP, Daneš claims that "[t]he kernel syntactic relation is that of dependance" (Daneš, 1964: 227) and stresses the strict connection holding between form and meaning: "we are convinced that the interrelations of both levels, semantic and grammatical must necessarily be stated in order to give a full account of an overall linguistic system" (Daneš, 1964: 226).

Consistently with such a theoretical background, the PDT (as well as the IT-TB) is a dependency-based treebank with a three-layer structure, in which each layer corresponds to one of the three views of sentence mentioned above (Hajič et al., 2000). The layers are ordered as follows:

- a morphological layer: morphological tagging and lemmatization;
- an 'analytical' layer (i.e. the presently available layer of annotation of the IT-TB): annotation of surface syntax;
- a 'tectogrammatical' layer: annotation of underlying syntax.

The development of each layer requires the availability of the previous one(s). Both the analytical and the tectogrammatical layers describe the sentence structure with dependency tree-graphs, respectively named analytical tree structures (ATSs) and tectogrammatical tree structures (TGTSs).

In ATSs every word and punctuation mark of the sentence is represented by a node of a rooted dependency tree. The edges of the tree correspond to dependency relations that are labelled with (surface) syntactic functions called 'analytical functions' (like Subject, Object etc.).

TGTSs describe the underlying structure of the sentence, conceived as the semantically relevant counterpart of the grammatical means of expression (described by ATSs). The nodes of TGTSs represent autosemantic words only, while function words and punctuation marks are left out. The nodes are labeled with semantic role tags called 'functors'. These are divided into two classes according to valency: (a) arguments, called 'inner participants', i.e. obligatory complementations of verbs, nouns, adjectives and adverbs: Actor, Patient, Addressee, Effect and Origin; (b) adjuncts, called 'free modifications': different kinds of adverbials, like Place, Time, Manner etc.. The 'dialogue test' by Panevová (1974-1975) is used as the guiding criterion for obligatoriness. TGTSs feature two dimensions that represent respectively the syntactic structure of the sentence (the vertical dimension) and its information structure ('topic-focus articulation', TFA), based on the underlying word order (the horizontal dimension). In FGD, TFA deals with the opposition between contextual boundness (the 'given' information, on the left) and contextual unboundness (the 'new' information, on the right). Also ellipsis resolution and coreferential analysis are performed at the tectogrammatical layer and are represented in TGTSs through newly added nodes (ellipsis) and arrows (coreference).

Since its beginning, the IT-TB has been following the PDT annotation style for both typological and structural reasons. As far as the former are concerned, Latin and Czech share certain relevant properties, such as being richly inflected, showing discontinuous phrases, and having a moderately free word-order and a high degree of synonymity and ambiguity of the endings. Both languages have three genders (masculine, feminine, neuter), cases with roughly the same meaning and no articles. As for the latter, the tight connection between the three-layer structure of the PDT and a sound background theory like FGD integrates each layer of annotation into a more general framework driven by a functional perspective aimed at understanding the underlying meaning of sentences through its relation with the surface form. Moreover, tectogrammatical annotation includes several pragmatic aspects that, although much present in Latin linguistics research, are still missing from the available treebanks of Latin[1].

The organization of functors into inner participants and free modifications is further exploited by linking textual tectogrammatical annotation with fundamental lexical information

[1] Some semantic-pragmatic annotation of Latin texts is available only in the PROIEL corpus (Haug & Jøndal, 2008). The Latin subset of PROIEL includes Classical texts from the 1st century BC (Caesar, Cicero), the *Peregrinatio Aetheriae* and the *New Testament* by Jerome (both from the 5th century AD).

provided by a valency lexicon that features the valency frame(s) for all those verbs, nouns, adjectives and adverbs capable of valency that occur in the treebank. The valency lexicon of the IT-TB is being built in a corpus-driven fashion, by adding to the lexicon all the valency-capable words that annotators progressively get through[2].

3 Moving From Analytical to Tectogrammatical Tree Structures

As the tectogrammatical annotation of the IT-TB has just started and no Latin texts annotated at the tectogrammatical layer are available yet, we cannot train and use probabilistic NLP tools to build TGTSs. Thus, the annotation workflow is based on TGTSs automatically converted from ATSs. The TGTSs that result from conversion are then checked and refined manually by two independent annotators. Conversion is performed by adapting to Latin a number of ATS-to-TGTS scripts provided by the NLP framework Treex developed in Prague (Popel and Žabokrtský, 2010). Relying on ATSs, the basic functions of these scripts are: (a) to collapse ATSs nodes of function words and punctuation marks, as they no longer receive a node for themselves in TGTSs, but are included into the autosemantic nodes; (b) to assign basic functors (such as Actor and Patient); (c) to assign 'grammatemes', i.e. semantic counterparts of morphological categories (for instance, pluralia tantum are tagged with the number grammateme 'singular').

The annotation guidelines are those for the tectogrammatical layer of the PDT (Mikulová et al., 2006).

In the following, three examples of tectogrammatical annotation of sentences taken from the IT-TB are reported and discussed in detail.

[2] A syntactic-based valency lexicon of the IT-TB (named IT-VaLex) was induced automatically from the analytical layer of the treebank and made available on-line (http://itreebank.marginalia.it/itvalex) (McGillivray and Passarotti, 2009).

3.1 Example A

Figure 1 reports the ATS of the following sentence of the IT-TB: "tunc enim unaquaeque res optime disponitur cum ad finem suum convenienter ordinatur;" ("So, each thing is excellently arranged when it is properly directed to its purpose;", *Summa contra Gentiles* 1.1).

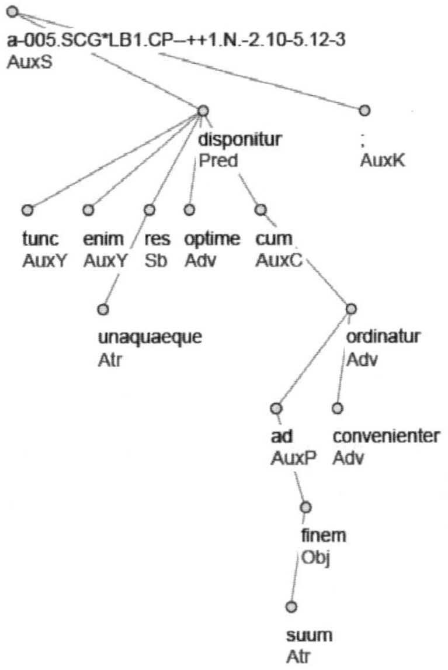

Figure 1. Analytical Tree Structure A

Except for the technical root of the tree (holding the textual reference of the sentence), each node in the ATS corresponds to one word or punctuation mark in the sentence. Nodes are arranged from left to right according to surface word-order. They are connected in governor-dependent fashion and each relation is labelled with an analytical function. For instance, the relation between the word *res* and its governor *disponitur* is labelled with the analytical function Sb (Subject), i.e. *res* is the subject of *disponitur*.

Four kinds of analytical functions that occur in the tree are assigned to auxiliary sentence members, namely AuxC (subordinating conjunctions: *cum*), AuxK (terminal punctuation marks), AuxP (prepositions: *ad*) and AuxY (sentence adverbs: *enim*, *tunc*). The other analytical functions occurring in this sentences are the following: Atr (attributes), Adv (adverbs and adverbial modifications, i.e. adjuncts), AuxS (root of the tree), Obj (direct and indirect objects), Pred (main predicate of the sentence).

Figure 2 shows the TGTS corresponding to the ATS of this sentence.

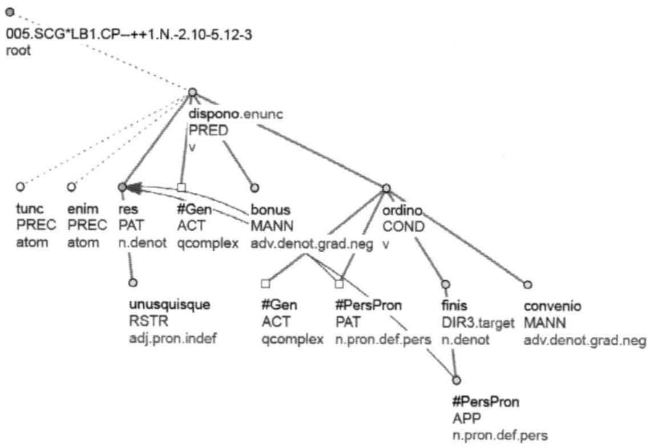

Figure 2. Tectogrammatical Tree Structure A[3]

As only autosemantic nodes can occur in TGTSs, auxiliary sentence members labelled with AuxC, AuxK, or AuxP are collapsed.

Analytical functions are replaced with functors. The nodes of the lemmas *tunc* and *enim* are both assigned the functor PREC, since they represent expressions linking the clause to the preceding context; further, *tunc* and *enim* are given nodetype 'atom' (atomic nodes), which is used for adverbs of attitude, intensifying or modal expressions, rhematizers and text connectives (which is the case of *tunc* and *enim*) (Mikulová et al., 2006: 17). *Res* is the Patient (PAT) of *dispono*, as it is the syntactic subject of a passive verbal form (*disponitur*)[4]. Both the adverbial forms of *bonus* (*optime*) and *convenio* (*convenienter*) are labelled with functor MANN, which expresses manner by specifying an evaluating characteristic of the event, or a property. *Unusquisque* is a pronominal restrictive adnominal modification (RSTR) that further specifies the governing noun *res*. The clause headed by *ordinatur* (lemma: *ordino*; analytical function: Adv) is assigned the functor COND, as it reports the condition on which the event expressed by the governing verb (*disponitur*; lemma: *dispono*) can happen. The lemma *finis* is assigned the functor DIR3 (Directional: to), which expresses the target point of the event. *Finis* is then specified by an adnominal modification of appurtenance (APP).

Three newly added nodes occur in the tree (square nodes), to provide ellipsis resolution of those arguments of the verbs *dispono* and *ordino* that are missing in the surface structure. *Dispono* is a two-argument verb (the two arguments being respectively the Actor and the Patient), but only the Patient is explicitly expressed in the sentence, i.e. the syntactic subject *res*. The missing argument, i.e. the Actor (ACT), is thus replaced with a 'general argument' (#Gen), because the coreferred element of the omitted modification cannot be clearly identified, even with the help of the context. The same holds also for the Actor of the verb *ordino* (#Gen), whose Patient (#PersPron, PAT) is coreferential with the noun *res*, as well as the possessive adjective *suus* (#PersPron, APP). In the TGTS, these coreferential relations are shown by the blue arrows that link the two #PersPron nodes with the node of *res*. #PersPron is a 't-lemma' (tectogrammatical lemma) assigned to nodes representing possessive and personal pronouns (including reflexives).

The nodes in the TGTS are arranged from left to right according to TFA, which is signalled by the colour of the nodes (white nodes: topic; yellow nodes: focus) A so-called 'semantic part of speech' is assigned to each node: for instance, 'denotational noun' is assigned to *finis*. Finally, the illocutionary force class informing about the sentential modality is assigned to the main predicate of the sentence *dispono* ('enunciative').

---

[3] In the default visualization of TGTSs, wordforms are replaced with lemmas.

[4] Conversely, syntactic subjects of active verbal forms are usually labelled with the functor ACT (Actor). However, this does not always hold true, since the functor of the subject depends on the semantic features of the verb.

3.2 Example B

Figure 3 shows the ATS of this sentence: "unde et earum artifices, qui architectores vocantur, nomen sibi vindicant sapientum." ("Thus, also the makers of them, who are called architects, claim the title of wise men for themselves", *Summa contra Gentiles* 1.1).

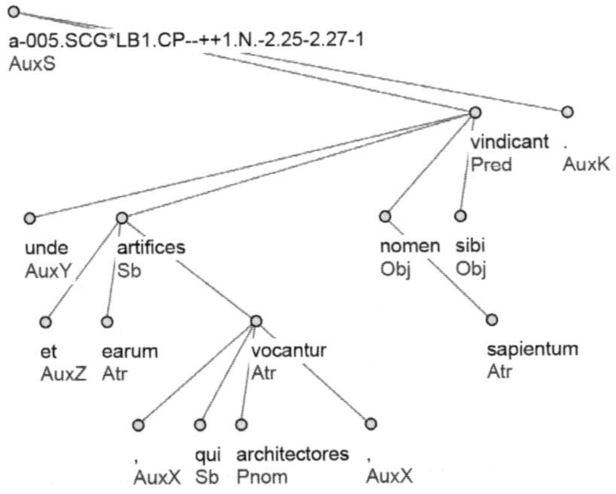

Figure 3. Analytical Tree Structure B

In addition to the analytical functions assigned to auxiliary sentence members in the tree of figure 1, this tree features one occurrence of AuxZ (particles that emphasize a specific sentence member) and two of AuxX (commas).

Figure 4 presents the TGTS of the sentence in question.

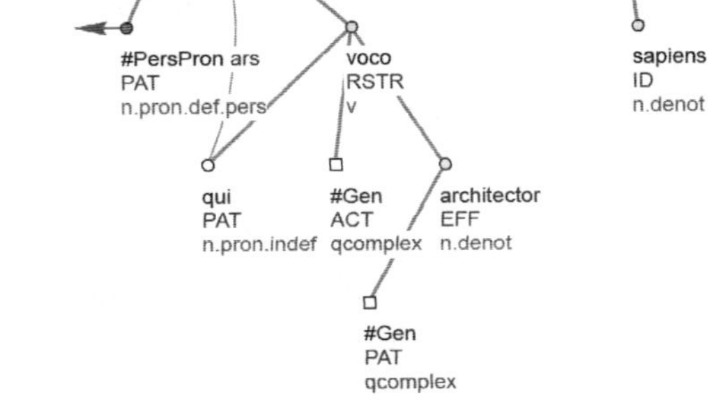

Figure 4. Tectogrammatical Tree Structure B

Sentence members labelled with AuxK, or AuxX are collapsed.

The tree reported in figure 4 features arrows of different colour. The red arrows that link both the relative pronoun *qui* and the reflexive pronoun *sibi* (assigned t-lemma #PersPron) with the noun *artifex* stand for so-called 'grammatical coreferences', i.e. coreferences in which it is possible to pinpoint the coreferred expression on the basis of grammatical rules. Instead, the blue arrow represents a 'textual coreference', i.e. a coreference realized not only by grammatical means, but also via context (mostly with pronouns) (Mikulová et al., 2006: 998 and 1,100). In figure 4, a blue arrow links *earum* (#PersPron) with the word *ars*, which occurs in the previous sentence in the text.

Sibi (#PersPron) is assigned the functor BEN, because it is the beneficiary of the action carried out by the Actor (*artifex*) of the verb *vindico*. *Sapiens* has functor ID (Identity), which labels explicative genitives. *Earum* (#PersPron) is the Patient (PAT) of the noun *artifex*, because agent nouns are valency-capable nouns; for this reason, a newly added node with functor PAT is made dependent on the agent noun *architector*. This is assigned functor EFF (Effect), which is used for arguments referring to the result of the event, among which are obligatory predicative complements (i.e. the role played by *architector* with respect to *voco*). *Voco* is a RSTR, which is the functor assigned to the main predicates of attributive relative clauses. *Et* is a rhematizer, which has the noun *artifex* in its scope. According to Mikulová et al. (2006: 1,170), in a TGTS the node representing the rhematizer is placed as the closest left sister of the first node of the expression that is in its scope. This is why the node of *et* in the TGTS reported in figure 4 depends on *vindico* instead of *artifex*, while in the ATS of figure 3 it depends on the node of *artifices*. Despite its left position in the TGTS, the node of *et* is marked as focus in TFA and thus the colour of its node is yellow.

3.3 Example C

Figure 5 presents the ATS of the following sentence: "ego in hoc natus sum, et ad hoc veni in mundum, ut testimonium perhibeam veritati." ("For this I was born and for this I came to the world, to provide the truth with evidence", *Summa contra Gentiles* 1.1, quoting the Gospel of John 18:37).

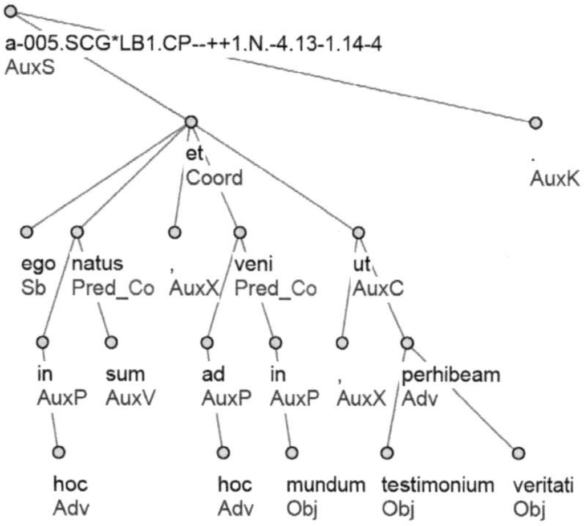

Figure 5. Analytical Tree Structure C

This sentence features two main predicates coordinated by the conjunction *et*: *veni* and *natus sum*, the latter being a complex verb, formed by the perfect participle *natus* and by the auxiliary verb *sum*, which is assigned the analytical function AuxV (collapsed in the corresponding TGTS). The fact that the two predicates are coordinated is signalled by the suffix _Co appendend to their analytical function (Pred). Those nodes that depend on the coordinating conjunction *et* and are not labelled with an analytical function suffixed with _Co are meant to depend on every member of the coordination. Thus, *ego* is the subject of both *natus sum* and *veni*, as well as the subordinate clause headed by *perhibeam* (via the subordinative conjunction *ut*) represents an adverbial modification of both the verbs.

Figure 6 presents the TGTS corresponding to the ATS of figure 5.

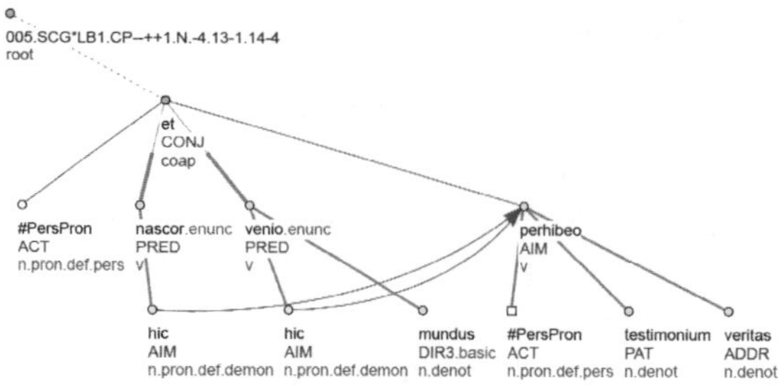

Figure 6. Tectogrammatical Tree Structure C

The conjunction *et* is assigned nodetype 'coap' (coordinations and appositions) and functor CONJ (Conjunction), used for the root nodes of paratactic structures.

Veritas is the Addressee (ADDR) of the verb *perhibeo*[5]. *Mundus* is assigned functor DIR3 and subfunctor 'basic', the latter specifying that here the meaning of DIR3 is the basic one, i.e. "where to"[6]. The two occurrences of *hic* are respectively the Aim (AIM) of the verb *nascor* and of the verb *venio*, as well as the subordinate clause headed by *perhibeo* represents the Aim of both the coordinated predicates.

The TGTS in figure 6 presents two textual coreferences, linking both the occurrences of *hic* with *perhibeo*. Indeed, the subordinate clause "[...] ut testimonium perhibeam veritati" is coreferent with the two occurrences of *hic* and makes their meaning explicit in a cataphoric manner; this is signalled by the direction of the arrows, which go from left to right (cataphora) instead of from right to left (anaphora), like in figures 2 and 4.

4 Discussion and Future Work

Recently funded by the Italian Ministry of Education, Universities and Research (MIUR), the project aimed at both providing semantic annotation of Latin texts and building a semantic-based valency lexicon of Latin has just

[5] On the bordeline between Beneficiary and Addresse, see Mikulová et al. (2006: 123-126).

[6] Instead, the DIR3 node occurring in the tree of figure 2 is specified by subfunctor 'target'.

started. So far, only the first 200 sentences of *Summa contra Gentiles* of Thomas Aquinas have been fully annotated at tectogrammatical level (corresponding to 3,112 words and 451 punctuation marks). Such a limited experience on data does not make it possible to provide an evaluation neither of the ATS-to-TGTS conversion scripts nor of the inter-annotator agreement. Presently, the valency lexicon contains 221 verbs; the task of building the lexical entries for nouns, adjectives and adverbs is going to start in the very near future.

Analytical annotation is available not only for Medieval Latin texts, but also for Classical Latin, as the guidelines for the analytical layer of annotation of the IT-TB are shared with the Latin Dependency Treebank (LDT; http://nlp.perseus.tufts.edu/syntax/treebank/), a dependency-based treebank including around 55,000 words from texts of different authors of the Classical era (Bamman et al., 2007). By exploiting the common annotation style of the IT-TB and the LDT, our project will also perform tectogrammatical annotation of the Classical Latin texts available in the LDT and will build the corresponding valency lexicon.

While enhancing a corpus with a new layer of annotation from scratch still remains a labor-intensive and time-consuming task, today this is simplified by the possibility of exploiting the results provided by previous similar experiences in language resources development. Such results can be used for porting background theories, methods and tools from one language to another in a rapid and low-cost fashion. This is the approach pursued by our project, which wants to apply to Latin a treebank scenario originally created for Czech and now used also for other languages (including Arabic and English). Such an application meets and raises a number of issues specifically related to corpora of ancient languages, which make tectogrammatical annotation of such data a particularly difficult task. For instance, while treebanks of modern languages mostly include texts taken from newspapers, this does not hold true for both the IT-TB and the LDT, which contain respectively philosophical (IT-TB) and literary texts (LDT). These textual genres present several specific linguistic features in terms of syntax (quite complex in poetry), semantics (some words undergo a kind of technical shift of meaning in philosophical texts) and lexicon (high register words are pretty frequent). Further, the absence of native speakers often makes different interpretations of texts possible and increases the difficulty of tasks like TFA.

As mentioned above, a large-scale application of a linguistic theory to real data helps to empirically test how much sound the theory is. In our case, the evaluation of the degree of applicability of FGD to Latin is at its very beginning. However, analytical annotation has shown a strong compatibility between the ATS-based description of surface syntax and its application to Latin. As a matter of fact, the PDT manual for analytical annotation was adapted in just a few details for the treatment of specific constructions of Latin (such as the ablative absolute or the passive periphrastic) that could be syntactically annotated in several different ways (Bamman et al., 2008). This experience represents a positive background for a project that wants to build a set of theoretically-motivated advanced language resources for Latin that will provide users with information about morphology, surface syntax and semantics at both textual and lexical level.

Such advanced language resources for Latin will both improve the understanding of Latin language and question the usual research methods pursued by scholars in Classics.

As for the former, research in Latin linguistics dealing with issues like semantic role labelling, valency, ellipsis resolution, coreferential analysis and information structure will finally be able to ground on a relevant amount of empirical evidence not created for the aims of one specific research, thus preventing the vicious circle of building a corpus just for studying a single linguistic phenomenon (Sinclair, 2004b). Also, making available language resources that both feature Latin texts of differents eras and share the same annotation style with language resources of modern languages will impact diachronic research and support studies in comparative linguistics.

As for the latter, building advanced language resources for Latin by connecting a large-scale empirical analysis of Latin data with a modern and broadly evaluated linguistic theory represents a challenging and unconventional approach, which is expected to strongly impact the usual research methods in the field of Classics. Indeed, due to an age-old split holding between linguistic and literary studies, the study of Latin (and of Ancient Greek, as well) has been primarily pursued by focusing on literary, philological and glottological aspects. Further, a large number of classicists is, still today, unwilling both to apply computational methods to textual analysis and to use language resources like annotated corpora and computational lexica. Computational linguists, in turn, are more prone to develop language resources and NLP tools for living languages, which have stronger commercial, media and social impact. Considering collaboration between Classics and computational linguistics to be essential, this project provides an opportunity for innovation of both fields.

Both the treebanks and the valency lexicon will be publicly available datasets with explicit annotation guidelines. This will make the results achieved by using these language resources replicable, which is a not yet consolidated practice in Classics.

Acknowledgments

This research is part of the project "Developing and Integrating Advanced Language Resources for Latin", supported by the Italian Ministry of Education, Universities and Research (MIUR) as part of the grant FIR-2013.

References

Jan Aarts. 2002. Does corpus linguistics exist? Some old and new issues. Leiv Breivik and Angela Hasselgren (eds.), *From the COLT's mouth...and others*. Rodopi, Amsterdam, 1-17.

David Bamman, Marco Passarotti, Gregory Crane and Savina Raynaud. 2007. *Guidelines for the Syntactic Annotation of Latin Treebanks*. «Tufts University Digital Library». Available online from http://hdl.handle.net/10427/42683.

David Bamman, Marco Passarotti, Roberto Busa and Gregory Crane. 2008. The annotation guidelines of the Latin Dependency Treebank and *Index Thomisticus* Treebank. The treatment of some specific syntactic constructions in Latin. *Proceedings of the Sixth International Conference on Language Resources and Evaluation (LREC 2008)*. ELRA, Marrakech, 71-76.

Roberto Busa. 1974-1980. *Index Thomisticus*. Frommann-Holzboog, Stuttgart-Bad Cannstatt.

Cercle linguistique de Prague. 1929. Thèses présentées au Premier Congrès des philologues slaves. *Travaux du Cercle linguistique de Prague 1: Mélanges linguistiques dédiés au Premier Congrès des philologues slaves*. Jednota Československých matematiků a fysiků, Prague, 5-29.

František Daneš. 1964. A three-level approach to syntax. Josef Vachek (ed.), *Travaux linguistiques de Prague 1: L'École de Prague d'aujourd'hui*. Éditions de l'Académie Tchécoslovaque des Sciences, Prague, 225-240.

Jan Firbas. 1992. *Functional Sentence Perspective in Written and Spoken Communication*. Cambridge University Press, Cambridge, UK.

Jan Hajič, Alena Böhmová, Eva Hajičová and Barbora Vidová Hladká. 2000. The Prague Dependency Treebank: A Three-Level Annotation Scenario. Anne Abeillé (ed.), *Treebanks: Building and Using Parsed Corpora*. Kluwer, Amsterdam, 103-127.

Eva Hajičová. 2006. Old Linguists Never Die, They Only Get Obligatorily Deleted. *Computational Linguistics*, 32(4): 457-469.

Dag Haug and Marius Jøhndal. 2008. Creating a Parallel Treebank of the Old Indo-European Bible Translations. *Proceedings of the Language Technology for Cultural Heritage Data Workshop (LaTeCH 2008)*. ELRA, Marrakech, 27-34.

Barbara McGillivray and Marco Passarotti. 2009. The Development of the *Index Thomisticus* Treebank

Valency Lexicon. *Proceedings of LaTeCH-SHELT&R Workshop 2009, Athens, March 30, 2009*. 43-50.

Barbara McGillivray, Marco Passarotti and Paolo Ruffolo. 2009. The *Index Thomisticus* Treebank Project: Annotation, Parsing and Valency Lexicon. *Traitement Automatique des Langues*, 50(2): 103-127.

Marie Mikulová, et alii. 2006. *Annotation on the Tectogrammatical Layer in the Prague Dependency Treebank*. Institute of Formal and Applied Linguistics, Prague. Available online from http://ufal.mff.cuni. cz/pdt2.0/doc/manuals/en/t-layer/html/index.html.

Jarmila Panevová. 1974-1975. On verbal Frames in Functional Generative Description. *Prague Bulletin of Mathematical Linguistics*, 22: 3-40. Part II published in PBML, 23: 17-52.

Martin Popel and Zdeněk Žabokrtský. 2010. TectoMT: Modular NLP Framework. *Proceedings of IceTAL, 7th International Conference on Natural Language Processing, Reykjavík, Iceland, August 17, 2010*. 293-304.

Savina Raynaud. 2008. The basic syntagmatic act is predication. *Slovo a slovesnost*, 69(1-2): 49-67.

Petr Sgall, Eva Hajičová, and Jarmila Panevová. 1986. *The Meaning of the Sentence in its Semantic and Pragmatic Aspects*. D. Reidel, Dordrecht, NL.

John Sinclair. 2004a. Intuition and Annotation – the Discussion Continues. Karin Aijmer & Bengt Altenberg (eds.), *Advances in Corpus Linguistics. Papers from the 23rd International Conference on English Language Research on Computerized Corpora (ICAME 23)*. Rodopi, Amsterdam, 39-59.

John Sinclair. 2004b. Corpus and Text: Basic Principles. Martin Wynne (ed.), *Developing Linguistic Corpora: a Guide to Good Practice*. Oxbow Books, Oxford, 1-16. Available online from http://ahds.ac.uk/linguistic-corpora/

Elena Tognini-Bonelli. 2001. *Corpus Linguistics at Work*. J. Benjamins, Amsterdam Philadelphia.

On the syllabic structures of Aromanian

Sergiu Nisioi
Faculty of Mathematics and Computer Science
Center for Computational Linguistics
University of Bucharest
Bucharest, Romania
sergiu.nisioi@gmail.com

Abstract

In this paper we have investigated the syllabic structures found in Aromanian a Romance language spoken in the Balkans across multiple countries with important communities which spread from Greece to Romania. We have created a dictionary of syllabified words and analyzed a few general quantitative and phonological aspects of the dictionary. Furthermore, we have approached the syllabic complexities, the sonority patterns present in the syllable's constituents and the degree in which the Sonority Sequencing Principle (SSP) holds for this language. Based on all the information gathered we have devised an automatic syllabification algorithm which has a 99% accuracy on the words in the dictionary. In this way we hope to extend the existing phonological studies on Eastern Romance and to spread and preserve meta-linguistic information on this endangered language.

1 Introduction

Aromanian, according to linguists (Papahagi, 1974) or (Saramandu, 1984) is part of a larger family of Eastern Romance languages consisting from Daco-Romanian (standard Romanian), Aromanian, Megleno-Romanian and Istro-Romanian. We underline this characteristic because some of the linguistic properties that are present in Aromanian are also present, more or less, in the other three languages largely due to the common historical and linguistic context in which they formed and evolved. Unfortunately, Istro-Romanian and Megleno-Romanian are labeled by the UNESCO Red Book (2010) as "severely endangered" languages with approximately 300 (Filipi, 2002) and respectively 5000 speakers (Atanasov, 2002). Aromanian is not in a better situation carrying the label of "definitely endangered" with approximately 500,000 speakers (Atanasov, 2002). Currently, the language has no accepted standard, being written in various forms depending on social and political factors of the regions in which it is spoken (Kahl, 2006). This is why we believe that a study on Aromanian can only be done empirically, on corpus data or dictionaries or by adopting a multi-valued dialectal approach justified by field work.

2 Previous work

Although Capidan (1932) offers an exhaustive study on Aromanian with valuable comments on previous research, very few modern linguistic studies target this language and there are no computational linguistic studies as far as we are aware at this point. Caragiu-Marioţean (1968) offered one of the first modern studies with respect to the phonology and structural morphology of the language; her work represents our linguistic baseline. Since Aromanian is spoken in various regions, there are expected geographical particularities. Caragiu-Marioţeanu (1997) classifies the Aromanian sub-dialects into two types: *type F* - the variants that resemble the Farsherot, predominant in Albania and some parts of Greece and *type A* - all the other variants. She argues that type F sub-dialects are spoken by smaller communities which have been influenced by type A. Type F sub-dialects have certain phonetic features: the closed-central vowel [ɨ] does not exist, the groups of consonants [rl], [rn] are transformed into a sound that could be classified as a velar [r] (Capidan, 1932) and the diphthongs [e̯a] and [o̯a] are transformed into [e] and [o].

Place →	Labial		Coronal			Dorsal	
Manner ↓	**Bilabial**	**Labio-dental**	**Dental**	**Alveolar**	**Postalveolar**	**Palatal**	**Velar**
Trill				∼r			
Lateral approximant				∼l		ʎ	
Nasal	∼m			∼n		∼ɲ	
Sibilant fricative				s∼z	ʃ∼ʒ		
Non-sibilant fricative		f∼v	θ∼ð			ç∼ʝ	x∼ɣ
Stop	p∼b		t̪∼d̪			c∼ɟ	k∼g
Affricates			t̪s∼d̪z		tʃ∼tʒ		

Table 1: The consonant inventory of Aromanian as it is described by Caragiu-Marioţeanu (1975). Our dictionary uses the same alphabet to store the syllabified words.

3 Dictionary of syllables

The dictionary used in our study is compiled by Cunia (2010) from the dictionaries of Papahagi (1974) and the one of Dalametra (1906). The main advantage of this resource is its lexical richness, including specific variants of words known by the author. Moreover, for most of the words, the syllabification is reproduced from a different dictionary compiled by Papahagi (1974). The later is considered a valuable and reliable linguistic resource for this language. The final size of the dictionary has approximately 69.000 syllabified words. Among the disadvantages, we could count a significant amount of misspelled words (that we have manually corrected), and words syllabified incorrectly. Also, the dictionary is written with the orthography proposed by Cunia (1997) using an alphabet that has only one diacritic. The purpose of the alphabet is to be more practical in the digital era, departing from other related phonemically spelled languages like Italian or Spanish. One of the main drawbacks of this alphabet is the compression of two different sounds (the mid-central vowel [ə] and the closed-central vowel [ɨ]) into the letter "ã", leaving the reader to decide which phoneme is actually used. The motivation behind the compression comes from the two vowels being geographical allophones for Aromanian (depending on type F or type A sub-dialect). In this case we should be cautious when analyzing vowels as phonological units. This is not the only case where orthography can influence our study.

Aromanian, together with Romanian (Chitoran, 2001), contrasts diphthongs [e̯a], [o̯a] from semivowel (glide) to vowel sequences [ja] and [wa] (written here as [i̯a] and [u̯a]). This means that the phonological representation of diphthongs is the one proposed by Chitoran (2002): *both elements of the diphthong are represented as sharing a syllable nucleus. According to this representation, diphthongs are predicted to function as a single unit and a single segment.*

The orthography of our dictionary restricts us to partially operate with these distinctions. Similar to Romanian (Chitoran, 2001), the glide-vowel sequence [u̯a] is less frequent - in our dictionary with less than 100 occurrences - compared to the larger number of occurrences for the diphthong [o̯a]. However, other dictionaries like the one of Caragiu-Marioţeanu (1997), which is complete only to the letter 'D', uses a different orthography and the actual contrasts might differ from resource to resource. Since this doesn't guarantee consistent results we represent internally all the above pairs as single units in the nucleus.

In the current state, the exact phonetic value of the letter "ã" is ambiguous and the disambiguation is a non-trivial task unless parallel resources are available.

To overcome the difficulty of using a specific alphabet, we have decided to convert the entire set of consonants from Latin script into IPA (International Phonetic Alphabet). The consonant inventory of Aromanian is detailed in Table 1, the same alphabet is used internally to store the syllabified words. Our representation does not have the same amount of detail as a phonetic transcription would, instead, it offers a general unified format which could be used by linguists in future studies. Our dictionary also contains the accented vowels and a distinction between [u, e, o, i] and the semivowels [u̯, e̯, o̯, i̯].

The palatalized pairs of consonants [c]∼[ɟ] and [ç]∼[ʝ] are to be found only before [i, i̯, e, e̯] according to Caragiu-Marioţeanu (1968). In all the other places the velar ones will be encountered. In practice, native speakers do not always use the palatalized before [i, i̯, e, e̯] but we will keep this rule to be consistent across the dictionary.

Romanian		Aromanian	
CV structures	Percentage	CV structures	Percentage
cv	55.04%	cv	24.84%
cvc	15.06%	cvc	6.28%
v	6.91%	cvcv	5.07%
ccv	5.82%	cvv	2.76%
cvv	5.43%	ccv	2.54%
vc	3.40%	v	2.36%
cvcv	2.86%	vc	1.47%
ccvc	1.33%	ccvc	1.29%
vv	0.83%	cvvcv	0.91%
cvcc	0.73%	cvvc	0.37%
cvvc	0.43%	cccv	0.36%
ccvv	0.24%	vv	0.26%
cvccv	0.23%	ccvcv	0.25%
vcv	0.23%	vcv	0.22%
cvvv	0.22%	ccvv	0.20%
cccv	0.22%	cvcvv	0.13%
vvc	0.16%	cvvv	0.12%
ccvcc	0.12%	cccvc	0.12%
cvvcv	0.11%	vvcv	0.09%
cccvc	0.11%	vvc	0.09%

Table 2: The first most common CV structures in Romanian and Aromanian. Semivowels are also denoted with "v". The syllables in both languages allow complex CV structures. Both languages share similar structures the difference is made in the distribution of each. The most frequent structure is, in both cases, "cv" (consonant vowel).

4 Syllabic structures

4.1 CV structures

Both Aromanian and Romanian share a large degree of common features, but no comparative studies have been made on the CV (here: consonant-vowel) structures available in the two languages. For Romanian, a database of syllables was already provided by (Barbu, 2008) under the title "RoSyllabiDict". This database contains almost all the morphological forms of Romanian words. Among the existing studies with respect to the CV structures in Romanian we count the one of Dinu and Dinu (2006). Comparing two grammatically similar languages in terms of the distribution of CV units can bring a new perspective on the similarities at the phonological level. In CV-theory (Clements and Keyser, 1983) a syllable σ is represented in a three-tier form.

For example the word "rat":

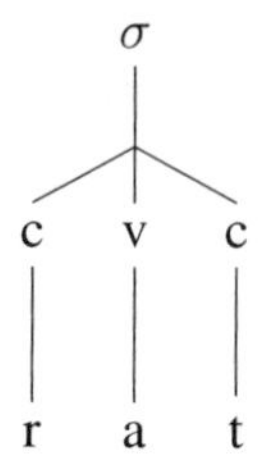

The CV structures are a part of the phonological layer in the universal grammar and the most common one, encountered in all the natural languages is the "cv" structure . In Table 2, both Romanian and Aromanian have this structure as the most frequent one. Theoretically, the four primary types of CV-structures are "cv", "v", "cvc" and "vc". The CV-theory (Clements and Keyser, 1983) predicts that if a language has "vc" syllables then all the other three primary structures will be encountered in that language.

In Table 2, it's not unusual to see CV structures of the form [ccvcv], this is because the standard Romanian orthography, as opposed to English in most of the cases, makes no distinction between the grapheme of a semivowel and the one of a vowel. If the CV structure has the following form [ccvcv] then the second "v" is a glide. In our internal representation of our dictionary two glides can be encountered at the end of syllables: [i̯] the mark for plural in all the Romanian dialects and [u̯] - frequently emphasized in the texts since the first Aromanian writers of the eighteen century (Papahagi, 1909).

4.2 Menzerath-Altmann law

Menzerath-Altmann law (Altman, 1980) states that the size of a linguistic construct is inversely correlated with the size of its constituents. Which means, in this particular case, that the average size of a word in syllables increases as the average size of the syllable (in phonemes) decreases. Previous studies proved that this law has applicability for more general linguistic constructs, in syntax (Buk, 2007) and even beyond linguistics in genome structures (Baixeries et al., 2013). In the syllable-phoneme context, extensive studies have been made. Fenk et al. (2006) investigated this law on 33 different languages and found an active correlation between the CV complexity of the syllables and the decay of the ratio between number of syllable and number of phonemes per syllable. In this sense, we have investigated the relation between Romanian and Aromanian with re-

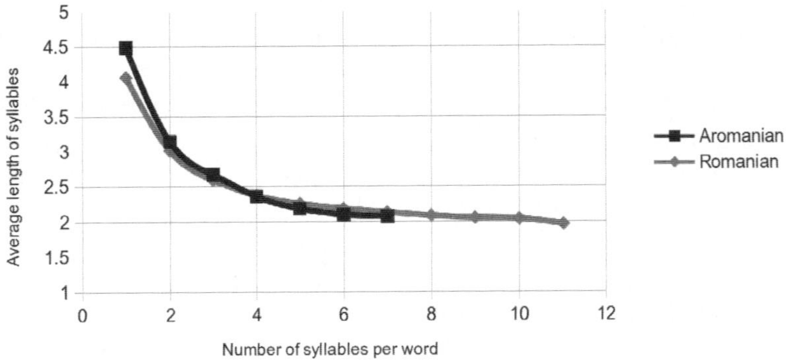

Figure 1: Menzerath-Altmann law. The word/syllable ratio in Romanian and Aromanian

spect to the Menzerath-Altmann law. We used the "RoSyllabiDict" dictionary of Romanian syllables compiled by Barbu (2008). This dictionary is constructed from almost all the morphological word-forms in Romanian, having a considerable size of about 520.000 entries.

The results can be visualized in Figure 1 - Romanian has a smaller average length of syllables, somewhere close to 4 but a significantly larger average length of words - close to 11. While Aromanian has a slightly larger length of syllables, close to 4.5 but the length of the words does not exceed 7 syllables in average. Moreover, Romanian is a highly developed language containing a vast set of neologisms and loans that can affect the word length. While Aromanian is more an archaic language spoken in small communities usually used between family members lacking the lexical richness of a general-use language. On one hand, Aromanian has a smaller average length of words than its developed relative, on the other hand, at the phonological level, even though the decay is similar (overlapping most of the times), Aromanian presents a slightly larger length of syllables (in phonemes). This suggests that Aromanian is slightly more complex in terms of syllable phonotactics than Romanian.

4.3 The structure of the syllable

In order to investigate the complexity and diversity of the syllables in Aromanian, we have chosen to examine the constituents of the syllables in terms of sonority sequences. Phonetically, the spoken chain consists in waves of sonority or sound intensity (Lehmann, 2005). The Sequence Sonority Principle (SSP) (Clements, 1990) regards the syllable as the phonological unit behind the waves of sonority. A representation of this concept can be visualized in Figure 2.

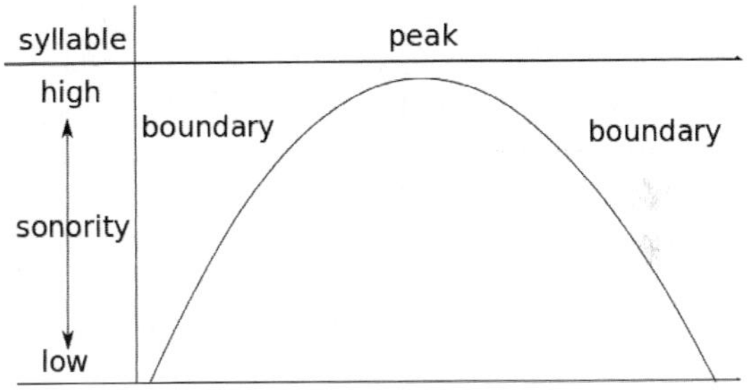

Figure 2: The sonority wave

The sonority of a phoneme can be regarded as "its loudness relative to that of other sounds with the same length, stress, and pitch" (Ladefoged, 1975). The sonority is given by a concept called strength (Escure, 1977), on one side strength can be represented by the sonorance in which the phonemes are ordered by their acoustic energy: Stops → Fricatives → Nasals → Liquids → Glides → Vowels. On the other side, the scale can be represented by the articulatory resistance (Anderson and Ewen, 1987) of the phonemes as in Figure 3.

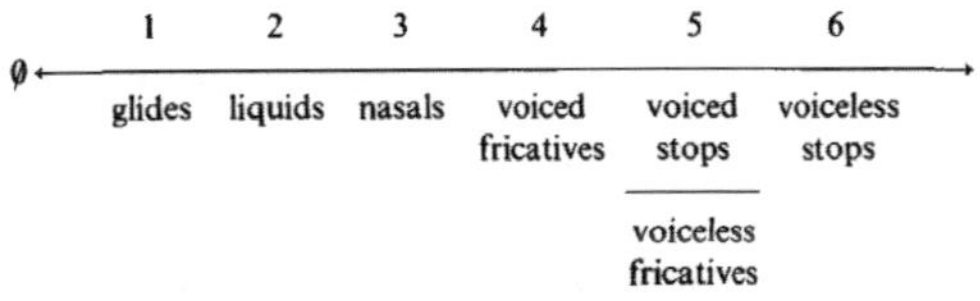

Figure 3: Scale of articulatory resistance

The Sonority Sequence Principle states that the syllable's peak is a group of segments of high sonority while the syllable's boundaries consists of phonemes of low sonority. In almost every natural language there are exceptions to this principle and investigating it can be valuable in speech recognition and in automatic syllabification based on phonotactic rules (Frampton, 2011). If the exceptions are accounted then the number of sonority peaks in a word is correlated with the number of syllables. In the same manner, the number of syllable boundaries is correlated with the number of low sonority phonemes.

As previously mentioned, the "cv" structure is universal in every language, thus the syllable may have two basic constituents (Fudge 1969, 1987): an onset (governed by the consonant) and a rhyme (governed by the vowel). The rhyme is further divided into a nucleus (forming the syllable's sonority peak) and a coda (consonants of descending sonority), the following schema exemplifying the word "tram" is relevant to the definition:

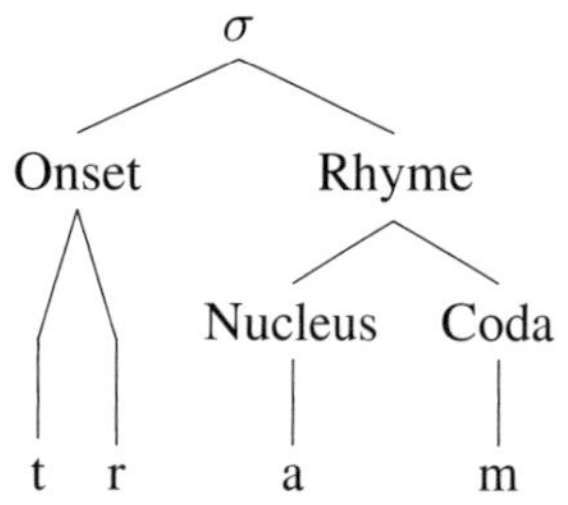

A constituent (onset, nucleus, coda) is branching if multiple phonemes are to be found in its structure and non branching if it is constructed from a single unit. Onsets and codas in Aromanian can be empty (syllable made of nucleus only - "v"), branching (two or more consonants "ccv" for onsets and "vcc" rarely for coda) or non-branching ("cvc" - the most frequent construct, single consonant only). In Table 2 the CV structures already suggested this fact. Compared to codas, the onsets in these languages tend to be more complex branching in up to three consonants.

4.4 Sonority and the coda

The first observation arises with respect to the Aromanian coda and the fact that it can end in glides [i̯] and [u̯]. This creates a peak of sonority inside the structure of the coda, thus a sonority reversal right at the end of the syllable. In this situation the SSP is broken since the sonority is not decreasing towards the end boundary of the syllable. These types of codas appear in final syllables, the semivowel [i̯] being morphologically determined while the semivowel [u̯] is a particular feature of Aromanian. Table 3 contains the percentages regarding the sonority of the codas. Because of the final glides, a large number of codas (41%) will break the SSP by having a sonority reversal (a sequence of phonemes in ascending sonority inside the coda). Mixed codas have a sequence of phonemes that is neither ascending neither descending.

Coda sonority	**Percentage**
Ascending	41.21%
Descending	58.72%
Mixed	0.06%

Table 3: Percentages of the syllable coda. The majority labeled with 'Ascending' are sonority reversals constructed from Cons + Glide.

Given that the presence of these glides in word-final syllables is frequent in all the Romanian dialects, we decided to adopt the following structure of the coda for word-final syllables:

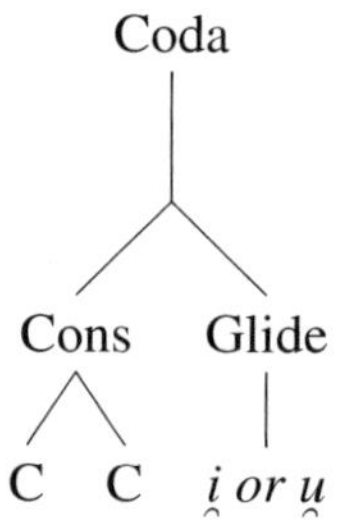

Using this design we have also investigated the sonority of the coda in its "Cons" structure which is limited in Aromanian to not having more than two consonants.

It was noticeable to observed that the SSP is always obeyed by the "Cons" substructure of the coda.

4.5 Sonority and the onset

All the results so far, indicate that the coda is not a very complex structure in this language. In fact, Caragiu-Marioţeanu (1968) stated that Aromanian previously had open syllables. A fact attested in the early works of the eighteenth century writers (Papahagi, 1909) describing the syllables as being opened. The linguistic study of Davis and Baertsch (2011) offers a model in which the structure of the onset is related to that of the coda through a shared component called margin. The model predicts that a complex onset in a language requires the presence of a coda (Kaye and Lowenstamm, 1981). For Aromanian, in particular, the formation of the coda could be a result of the increased complexity of the onsets.

We have investigated the different patterns of sonorities found in onsets, Table 4 contains the percentages of each of these patterns. Aromanian has four types of sonority sequences in the onset:

- "Constant" ⟶ - one or more consonants (sonority plateau) with equal sonorities
- "Ascending" ↗ - a sequence of phonemes with ascending sonorities
- "Descending" ↘ - a sequence of phonemes with descending sonorities
- "Nadir" ↘↗ - a sequence in which the sonority descends and then rises towards the nucleus (e.g. the onset "mbr" or other Nasal+Stop+Liquid)

Onset sonority	**Percentage**
Constant	89.10%
Ascending	5.63%
Descending	4.11%
Nadir	1.13%

Table 4: Sonority patterns found in syllable onsets.

The "Constant" and "Ascending" sequences of sonorities in onsets obviously obey the SSP and they count as the majority in the language. The ascending onsets can take the following forms: *[bl], [br], [dr], [ðr], [fl], [fʎ], [fr], [gl], [gʎ], [gn], [gr], [ɣl], [ɣn], [ɣr], [kl], [kʎ], [kr], [ks], [kʃ], [pç], [pl], [pʎ], [pr], [ps], [sl], [sm], [tl], [tr], [tsr], [vl], [vr], [xl], [xʎ], [xr], [zl], [zm], [zn], [zn], [θr]* from which the onsets ending in nasal consonants (i.e. [n], [m] or [ɲ]) are found only in word initial syllables.

About 5% of the onsets can be classified as exceptions from the SSP and the majority of them are to be found in word-initial syllables. In word-medial syllables we could count only rare examples of fricative + stop clusters. The descending consonant clusters in the onsets can be constructed by the patterns in Table 5.

The most interesting phonotactic constraint to mention is related to "Nadir" onsets - all of them appear only in word initial syllables. Intuitively, we may consider these onsets as being constructed from two types of clusters: on one hand "Descending" + "Constant" onset clusters and on the other hand "Constant" + "Ascending" onset clusters.

[f] ∼ [v]	+ [t] ∼ [d̪z]
[m]	+ bilabial, fricative
[n]	+ most of the less sonorous consonants
[s] ∼ [z]	+ [p] ∼ [b], [t] ∼ [d], [k] ∼ [g], [t̪ʃ] ∼ [ɟ]
[ʃ]	+ [k], [p], [t], [t̪s]

Table 5: Descending consonant clusters in the onset. The marker ∼ underlines the voiceless/voiced feature of the sounds. The phonemes tend to cluster together depending on the voice (e.g. [z] being a voiced consonant is more likely to be encountered near other voiced consonants - [b], [d], [g] or [ɟ]).

Quantitatively, the two approaches are equivalent and have the following form:

1. "Descending" onset cluster + liquid ([l], [ʎ] or [r])
2. [m], [n], [s], [ʃ], [z] + "Ascending" onset cluster

From a linguistic perspective the onsets that do not respect the SSP can be analyzed using the concept of semysillable. Cho and King (2008) proposed this model of a syllable by imposing certain restrictions:

- no nucleus
- no codas
- no stress/accent/tone
- prosodically invisible
- well-formed onset clusters (observing SSP)
- restricted to morpheme peripheral positions

The concept has been applied on Georgian, Polish and Bella Coola - languages with highly complex clusters of consonants (Cho and King, 2008) and even on French (Féry, 2003) to split complex codas. In Aromanian, for both "Nadir" and the "Descending" sequences, the semisyllable are word-initial. These semisyllables contain only the onset from one of the following phonemes: f, v, m, n, s, ʃ or z.

5 Phonetic syllabification algorithm

Studying the phonotactics of a language can be valuable for rule based automatic syllabification (Clements, 1990). Previous studies on phonologically complex languages like Imdlawn Tashlhiyt Berber (Frampton, 2011) validated the universality of this approach. The work of Iacoponi and Savy (2011) addresses the same problem on Italian, their rule-based phonetic algorithm reaching a precision of over 98%. Not any phonetic algorithm can be generalized or applied to different languages but in all the cases the same pattern is preserved: the syllable boundary is defined by a point of low sonority in a sequence of phonemes, see Figure 2.

In our particular case, based on the previous analysis of the sonority patterns, we have devised the following seven rules for establishing a syllable boundary:

1. diphthongs [e̯a] and [o̯a] are treated as single units (Chitoran, 2001)

2. maximal onset principle: $\searrow |c+ \nearrow$ - if the phoneme c is a sonority minimum then the syllable boundary is placed before the minimum and c is added to the next onset (Kahn, 1976)

3. word-medial c+nasal split: $\searrow +c| \nearrow$ - if the consonant c is a sonority minimum and it is followed by a nasal consonant (i.e. [n], [m] or [ɲ]) then the syllable boundary is placed after the minimum and c is added to the current syllable's coda - based on the results in Section 4.5

4. special [s] + stop cluster - the fricative consonant [s] will be treated as having the same sonority as any other stop consonants ([p], [b] etc.)

5. split plateau: $\longrightarrow | \longrightarrow$ - if a sonority plateau is found then put a syllable boundary in between

6. initial semisyllables consisting from consonants will be glued to the immediately next syllable

7. word-final coda can end in one or two glides - as described in Section 4.4

The second and the third rules are the ones referring to the actual minimum points of sonority within a word. The key is whether we want to cut the syllable before or after the minimum point and this fact is determined by phonotactic constraints. The initial semisyllables, although they respect the SSP, are merged within the next syllable and the word final codas may end in glides.

We have compared the output of this algorithm with the actual data already in our dictionary. Almost one percent of the words were incorrectly syllabified because they were exceptions to the above rules and the overall precision was 99%. This algorithm can easily be extended to other Eastern Romance languages by verifying the seven rules provided.

6 Conclusions and future work

In this paper we have offered a quantitative approach to the syllable structures and substructures found in Aromanian. In addition, we propose a dictionary resource to inspire future studies and to help preserve a "definitely endangered" Romance language. It is not an easy task to execute a study on a language that lacks an institutionalized standard. Our approach is empirical, corpus based and the quality of the results is strictly dependent on the quality of the corpus. This is why we have focused on investigating general phonological properties of the language in the limits afforded by the corpus at our disposal. Comparisons with existing studies on Romanian reaffirm the tight relation between the two languages and offer confidence that the results obtained are in accordance with existing facts about them. Moreover, based on phonotactic investigations, we have constructed an algorithm for automatic syllabification in Aromanian that has a 99% accuracy.

Future studies involve developing this resource to disambiguate the letter "ã" and adding more detail in the phonetic representation by recording native speakers. The current phonological study will help us to further develop rule-based resources on morphology considering existing theoretical studies (Caragiu-Marioţeanu, 1968) and may help us to better understand the evolution of the Eastern Romance languages and the relations between them. Last but not least, we hope that developing these linguistic and computational resources will encourage a widespread use of Aromanian.

References

Altmann, G. 1980 *Prolegomena to Menzerath's law* In Glottometrika 2, pp. 1-10

Anderson, John M. and Colin J. Ewen 1987 *Principles of Dependency Phonology* In Cambridge University Press

Atanasov, Petar 2002 *Meglenorumänisch. Lexikon der Sprachen des europäischen Ostens*, Wieser Enzyklopädie des europäischen Ostens 10

Baixeries, Jaume, Hernandez-Fernandez, Antoni, Forns, Nuria, Ferrer-i-Cancho, Ramon 2013 *The parameters of Menzerath-Altmann law in genomes* In Journal of Quantitative Linguistics 20 (2), pp. 94-104.

Barbu, Ana-Maria 2008 *Romanian Lexical Data Bases: Inflected and Syllabic Forms Dictionaries* In Proceedings of the Sixth International Conference on Language Resources and Evaluation, pp. 28-30

Buk, Solomiya and Rovenchak, Andrij 2007 *Menzerath-Altmann Law for Syntactic Structures in Ukrainian* In CoRR Journal 2, pp. 1-10

Boiagi, M. C. 1813. *Grammatiki Romaniki itoi Makedones Vlachikiki,* Wien

Capidan, Theodor 1932. *Aromânii. Dialectul aromân. Studiu lingvistic* Monitorul Oficial şi Imprimeriile Statului, Imprimeria Naţională, Bucureşti

Caragiu-Marioţeanu, Matilda 1968 Alterntion. *Fonomorfologie aromână. Studiu de dialectologie structurală* Editura Academiei Române, Bucharest

Caragiu-Marioţeanu, Matilda 1975 *Compendiu de dialectologie română* Bucureşti, Editura ştiinifică şi enciclopedică

Caragiu-Marioţeanu, Matilda 1997 *Dicţionar aromân (macedo-vlah) DIARO. A-D. Comparativ (român literar-aromân)* Editura Enciclopedică, Bucharest

Chitoran, Ioana 2001 *The Phonology of Romanian: A Constraint-Based Approach*, Mouton de Gruyter, Berlin, New York

Chitoran, Ioana 2002 *A perception-production study of Romanian diphthongs and glide-vowel sequences* Journal of the International Phonetic Association, 32, pp. 203-222

Cho, Young-mee Yu and King, Tracy Holloway 2008 *Semisyllables and Universal Syllabification* In The Syllable in Optimality Theory, Cambridge University Press, pp. 183-212

Clements, George N. and Keyser, Samuel Jay 1983 *CV Phonology: A Generative Theory of the syllable* MIT Press. Cambridge

Clements, George N. 1990 *The role of the sonority cycle in core syllabification* In J. Kingston and M. E. Beckman (eds.) Papers in Laboratory Phonology I, pp. 283-333

Cunia, Tiberius 1997. *On the Standardization of the Aromanian System of Writing*, The Bituli-Macedonia Symposium of August 1997

Cunia, Tiberius 2010 *Dictsiunar a limbăljei armãneascã*, Editura Cartea Aromãnã

Dalametra, I. 1906 *Dicţionar macedo-român*, Editura Academiei Române, Bucharest

Davis, Stuart and Baertsch, Karen 2011 *On the relationship between codas and onset clusters* In Handbook of the syllable, Leiden, pp. 71-98 Netherlands: Brill.

Dinu, Anca and Dinu, Liviu P. 2006 *On the data base of Romanian syllables and some of its quantitative and cryptographic aspects* In Proceedings of the Fifth International Conference on Language Resources and Evaluation, pp. 1795-1798

Escure, G. J. 1977 *Hierarchies and phonological weakening* Lingua 43 (1), pp. 55-64

Fenk, A., Fenk-Oczlon, G. and Fenk, L 2006 *Syllable complexity as a function of word complexity*, In The VIII-th International Conference "Cognitive Modeling in Linguistics" Vol. 1, pp. 324-333

Féry, Caroline 2003 Markedness, Faithfulness, Vowel Quality and Syllable Structure in French *Syllable complexity as a function of word complexity*, Journal of French Language Studies, Volume 13, Issue 2, pp. 247 - 280

Filipi, Goran 2002 *Istrorumänisch. Lexikon der Sprachen des europäischen Ostens*, Wieser Enzyklopädie des europäischen Ostens 10

Fudge, E.C. 1969 *Syllables* In Journal of Linguistics 5, pp. 253-286.

Fudge, E.C. 1987 *Branching Structures within the Syllable* In Journal of Linguistics 23:359-377

Frampton, John 2011 *GDE syllabification A generalization of Dell and Elmedlaoui's syllabification algorithm* The Linguistic Review, 28, (3), pp. 241-279

Iacoponi, L. and Savy, R. 2011 *Sylli: Automatic Phonological Syllabication for Italian* In proceeding of: INTERSPEECH 2011, 12th Annual Conference of the International Speech Communication Association, pp. 27-31

Kahl, Thede 2006. *Istoria aromânilor*, Editura Tritonic, Bucureşti

Kahn, Daniel 1976. *Syllable-based generalizations in English phonology*, Doctoral dissertation, MIT

Kaye, Jonathan and Lowenstamm, Jean 1981 *Theory of markedness in generative grammar* Pisa, Italy: Scuola normale superiore di Pisa.

Lehmann, Christian 2005 *Latin syllable structure in typological perspective* Journal of Latin Linguistics, 9 (1), pp. 127-148

Ladefoged, Peter 1975. *A course in phonetics* Harcourt Brace Jovanovich : New York

Moseley, Christopher (ed.) 2010. *UNESCO Atlas of the Worlds Languages in Danger* 3rd edn. Paris, UNESCO Publishing

Papahagi, Pericle (ed.) 1909. *Scriitori aromâni in secolul al XVIII-lea (CAVALIOTI, UCUTA, DANIIL)* Editura Academiei Române, Bucureşti

Papahagi, Tache 1974. *Dicionarul dialectului aromân. General şi etimologic* Editura Academiei Române, Bucureşti

Saramandu, Nicolae 1984. *Româna, in Tratat de dialectologie românească* Scrisul românesc, Craiova

A Gazetteer and Georeferencing for Historical English Documents

Claire Grover
School of Informatics
University of Edinburgh
grover@inf.ed.ac.uk

Richard Tobin
School of Informatics
University of Edinburgh
richard@inf.ed.ac.uk

Abstract

We report on a newly available gazetteer of historical English place-names and describe how it was created from a recent digitisation of the Survey of English Place-Names, published by the English Place-Name Society (EPNS). The gazetteer resource is accessible via a number of routes, not currently as linked data but in formats that do provide connections between a number of different datasets. In particular, connections between the historical gazetteer and the Unlock[1] and GeoNames[2] gazetteer services have been established along with links to the Key to English Place-Names database[3]. The gazetteer is available via the Unlock API and in the final part of the paper we describe how the Edinburgh Geoparser, which forms the basis of Unlock Text, has been adapted to allow users to georeference historical texts.

1 Introduction

Place and time are important concepts for historical scholarship and it has frequently been observed that an ability to examine document sets through spatial and temporal filters is one that is highly useful to historians. Georeferencing (or geoparsing) is therefore a technology that has been applied to historical data in numerous projects (for example Hitchcock et al. (2011), Crane (2004), Rupp et al. (2013), Isaksen et al. (2011), Hinrichs et al. (to appear 2014), Grover et al. (2010)). A significant problem, however, is that available georeferencing tools are mostly only able to access modern gazetteer information, meaning that place-names that have changed over time are less likely to be recognised and are highly unlikely to be properly grounded to correct coordinates. The problems can be illustrated with two examples, first the name *Jorvik* which is a well-known historical name for the English city of York and second the name *Bearla*, a historical name attested in a document from 1685 for the modern settlement Barlow in the West Riding of Yorkshire (now North Yorkshire). A first observation is that a named entity recognition (NER) component of a georeferencing system may or may not recognise these as place-names: recognition will depend on the lexical resources or training data used as well as the document context in which the name occurs. Assuming both the names can be recognised, they must then be disambiguated with reference to a gazetteer so that coordinates can be assigned to them. A search for the names using Unlock Places, which provides access to Ordnance Survey records, returns no results for either. A search in GeoNames returns York for *Jorvik* but nothing for *Bearla*. Another historical form for Barlow is *Borley*: both GeoNames and Unlock have records for a modern Borley in Essex but this is clearly not the correct interpretation of the historical *Borley*. These examples illustrate some of the problems and indicate that a historian wanting to georeference a particular document will get patchy output at best from current technology.

The Digital Exposure of English Place-names (DEEP) project[4] has addressed these issues by digitising and processing the Survey of English Place-Names to create the DEEP Historical Gazetteer (DHG). Below we first describe the Survey of English Place-Names and then explain how we have used XML-based language processing tools to convert the digitised volumes into the DHG and other structured resources. We outline the ways in which the resources are made available to users and we discuss the modifications we have made to the Edinburgh Geoparser to allow users to

[1] http://edina.ac.uk/unlock/
[2] http://www.geonames.org
[3] http://kepn.nottingham.ac.uk/
[4] http://englishplacenames.cerch.kcl.ac.uk/

1. Barlow (97–6428) [ˈba:lə]

Bernlege c. 1030 YCh 7

Berlai(a), *-ley(e)*, *-lay(e)* 1086 DB, 1130–9 YCh vi, Hy 1 Dugd vi, 1154–81, e. 13 YCh vi, 13 Selby, 1204 FF, 1214 Abbr, 1250 YI, 1251 FF *et passim* to 1498 Ipm, *-legh* 13, c. 1246 Selby, *-le* 1218 FF

Barlow(e) 1458 YD iii, 1641 Rates, 1665 PRClt

Barley 1469, 1472 Pat, 1519 FF *et freq* to 1641 Rates, *Barle* 1520 BM

Borley 1605 FF   *Bearla* 1685 SelbyW

The OE form suggests that the first el. is OE *bern* 'barn' (*v.* **bere-ærn**) or possibly OE **beren**[2] 'growing with barley', later reduced simply to **bere** 'barley'. In any event, loss of *-n-* in such a combination is common (cf. Farnley Tyas ii, 267 *supra*, Fairburn 48 *infra*). *v.* **lēah**.

Figure 1: Survey entry for Barlow in the West Riding of Yorkshire

georeference their historical documents. We conclude by discussing some outstanding issues and consider the steps that will be needed to turn our resources into linked data.

2 The Survey of English Place-Names

The Survey of English Place-Names is a scholarly body of work aimed primarily at readers interested in the origins and development of the place-names of England. The Survey is arranged by historic counties, with the first volume, from 1925, covering Buckinghamshire, and the most recent volume, published in 2012, dealing with part of Shropshire. In the early volumes the Survey was largely limited to major place-names, i.e. the names of towns and villages, but from the 1950s onwards the volumes have become more complex and include many minor names as well as field-names and street-names. More recently treated counties are described across multiple volumes and the growing scale of coverage has meant that there are still some counties which are only partly covered or not covered at all. Nevertheless, the vast majority of the English counties have been surveyed and the resulting body of work is a valuable resource for scholars of many kinds.

Figure 1 shows an excerpt from p. 23 of Vol. 33 of the Survey (1961) which covers the Wapentakes of Barkston Ash, Skyrack and Ainsty in the West Riding of Yorkshire. The excerpt shows the start of the entry for Barlow, the first settlement described in the parish of Brayton. In brackets after the name is an Ordnance Survey (OS) map reference followed by an indication of the pronunciation of the name. Next comes a block of historical forms of the name with information about their attestations. For example, *Bernlega* is attested in a document dated around 1030 referred to by the abbreviation YCh 7, standing for volume 7 of Early Yorkshire Charters (ed. W. Farrer, C. T. Clay, 1914-55). A set of related forms, *Berlai*, *Berlaia*, *Berley*, *Berleye*, *Berlay*, and *Berlaye*, have been attested in several documents ranging from the Domesday Book (DB) in 1086 through to Inquisitions post mortem (Ipm) in 1498. Other forms, including *Borley* and *Bearla* discussed above, follow. The final paragraph deals with the etymology of the name, relating it to the Old English words for 'barn' or 'barley' (and for the second part to the element lēah meaning 'clearing').

3 Conversion to structured format

It can be seen from Figure 1 that the Survey provides a wealth of information with the potential to be useful for many purposes and, in particular, it contains precisely the kind of information that is needed to make a historical gazetteer. In the DEEP project we have digitised all 86 volumes of the Survey and have processed the output of OCR to convert it into a structured format.

As the example illustrates, the format of the volumes is semi-structured with a fairly consistent use of style and font to indicate various kinds of information (e.g. bold font for etymological elements, italics for historical forms). The layout is extremely important with every comma and tab contributing to the interpretation of the information. For this reason, OCR quality needs to be exceptionally high and we have been fortunate that our digitisation partner was able to ensure this high quality. As the survey was created over a period of decades under the supervision of several editors, there is some variability in format across the volumes. The most pertinent variation concerns grid references: early volumes either do not have any or use grid references that cannot be converted to

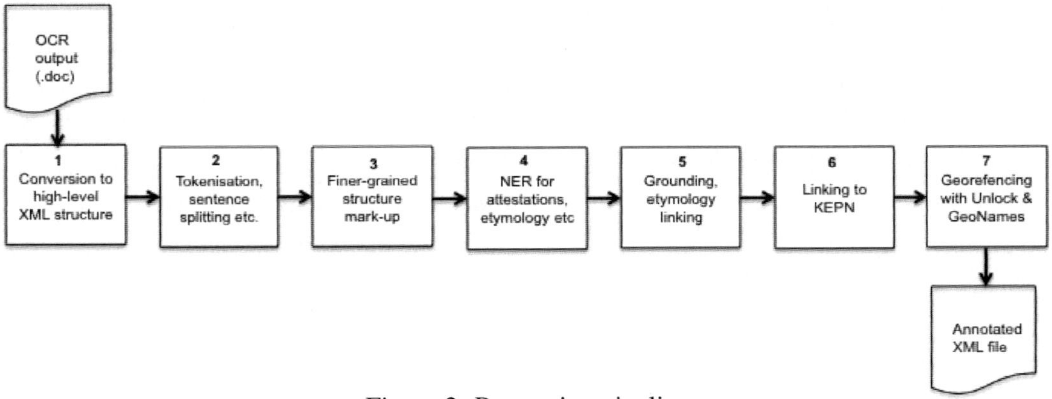

Figure 2: Processing pipeline

latitude/longitude. In many of the later volumes modern OS grid references or older OS sheet-number grid references are provided for main settlements within parishes and sometimes for more minor settlements. However, many of the later volumes do not contain any grid references at all and a significant part of the processing deals with these problems (see Section 3.2).

3.1 Processing pipeline

Figure 2 shows the XML-based processing pipeline that we have created for converting from the OCR output of a Survey volume into a heavily annotated XML version of the volume's text. The input is not raw OCR output but a version in which human OCR correctors have also added pseudo-XML tags to indicate very high level structure corresponding to the nesting of blocks of text. Thus the block of text for a parish contains subordinate blocks for settlements within that parish and they in turn contain subordinate blocks for minor places and street- and field-names located within them. The parish text blocks are themselves contained within blocks for larger historical administrative units such as hundreds, wapentakes, wards, boroughs, chapelries etc. and the block that encompasses all the places within it is the county itself.

In step 1 in Figure 2 the input file is converted from Word (.doc file) to OpenOffice's XML (.odt) format. From this we extract the textual content, the manually added structural tags and all relevant font and style information. The manual structural mark-up is converted to XML elements so that containment relations between places are encoded in the tree-structure of the XML document. From this point all further processing incrementally adds mark-up within the XML structure.

We use the LT-XML2 and LT-TTT2 tools which form the basis of the Edinburgh Geoparser and which have been developed specifically for rule-based processing of text in NLP systems (Grover and Tobin (2006), Tobin et al. (2010)). Along with shell scripting these tools allow us to build up the components that comprise the pipeline. The output of step 2 contains XML elements for paragraphs, sentences and word/punctuation tokens. Font and style information is encoded as attributes on the tokens and line break hyphenation is repaired. Part-of-speech tagging is unnecessary: the named entity classes we recognise are primarily identified by position in the document or on the page in combination with font and style information.

Once the tokens are marked up, finer-grained structural mark-up can be computed inside the wider structure (step 3). Blocks of attestations and etymology descriptions are identified and the title lines of the sections are segmented into elements—e.g. in Figure 1 BARLOW is marked up as the modern name of the place, 97-6428 is recognised as a grid reference and ˈbaːlə is recognised as a pronunciation. Also at this stage, lists of smaller place-, field- and street-names are segmented into individual items.

The NER processing in step 4 uses specially developed rule sets to add detailed mark-up inside sets of attestations. The first line of the attestations in Figure 1 is given the following structure (tokenisation, font and style information suppressed):

```
<altset>
 <alt>
  <histform>Bernlege</histform>
  <attested>
   <date>c. 1030</date>
   <source id="wr796">YCh <item>7</item></source>
  </attested>
 </alt>
</altset>
```

Here YCh is the source of the attestation for the historical form *Bernlege* and the interpretation of the YCh abbreviation is referenced by the id attribute on the source element. Step 4 also uses rule sets to recognise parts of etymological descriptions adding within-sentence mark-up like this:

```
<s> ...
 <etympart>
  <lang>OE</lang>
  <form>bern</form>
  </etympart>
  '<gloss>barn</gloss>' (v.
  <etympart>
   <pn-element>bere-aern</pn-element>
  </etympart>) ...
</s>
```

Step 5 applies rules for non-geographic grounding. For dates, begin and end attributes are computed with obvious values for simple dates and date ranges, a twenty-year window for *circa* dates, other sized windows for century parts (e.g. the first twenty-five years for the early part of a century) and specific periods for regnal dates (Hy 1 denotes Henry I who reigned from 1100 to 1135):

```
<date begin="1086" end="1086">1086</date>
<date begin="1130" end="1139">1130-9</date>
<date begin="1020" end="1040">c. 1030</date>
<date begin="1200" end="1225">e. 13</date>
<date begin="1100" end="1135">Hy 1</date>
```

Place-name elements (<pn-element>) are dealt with at the same stage. These are etymological parts, indicated with bold font in the Survey texts, which belong to a finite set of vocabulary items used in place-names. Place-name elements are catalogued in the Key To English Place-Names (KEPN) database. We look the elements up in KEPN and record their database ID when a match is successful. The final two steps in the processing relate to geographic grounding and are described in more detail in the next section.

We have not been able to perform a formal evaluation of the NER component in the pipeline because we do not have a manually annotated test set. However, we did implement cycles of quality assurance by place-name experts to feed into rule set improvements, so we are confident that the information extracted is of high quality. Our main priority was to capture the historical name attestations for the parishes and main settlements in the Survey. For the blocks that these occur in (e.g. the attestation block in Figure 1) we can get an informal indication of performance by counting the number of non-punctuation tokens that fail to be recognised as part of a historical name or attestation entity. For example, for the three volumes for Derbyshire (published in 1959), there are 342 blocks of main settlement attestations in which our system found 4,052 historical forms associated with 5,817 attestations. There were nine lines of text in these blocks where the processing failed to assign all the words to an entity, resulting in around 20 histform-attestation pairs being missed. Performance is slightly more variable for smaller settlements and lists of streets and field-names, but it is harder to estimate an error rate for these.

3.2 Georeferencing the Survey

To create a historical gazetteer, we need to associate coordinates with every place-name and we do this by aggregating information from several sources and by allowing un-georeferenced place-names to inherit coordinates from a place higher in the XML structure. As described above, some of the Survey volumes associate grid references with some of the places but the coverage is too sporadic to rely on. We therefore use the geographic information in the KEPN database to acquire reliable geo-references as far as possible. KEPN supplies latitude/longitude point coordinates for major settlements (the larger units inside parishes) and we automatically query KEPN for these references, adding the coordinates into the XML in special <geo> elements. For our example of Barlow the <geo> is this:

```
<geo source="kepn" kepnref="14600" long="-1.02337"
     lat="53.7489" placename="Barlow"/>
```

This information is the most authoritative geographic information that we can access but we do not want to discard the other authoritative source of information contained in the grid references in some of the volumes, especially since these may be attached to smaller places not covered by KEPN. We therefore recognise them during the processing, convert them to latitude/longitude and store their coordinates in <geo source="epns"> elements:

```
<geo source="epns" lat="53.7489" long="-1.02337"/>
```

(In this case the coordinates from the two sources are identical but there are cases where they differ slightly.)

Once we have stored KEPN/EPNS geographic information, we implement strategies to achieve high-quality georeferencing of some of the places which do not yet have a georeference. A first step is to utilise the containment relations between places and propagate known georeferences up and down between certain nodes. For example, we do this when a parish with no georeference has the same name as a settlement within it—since they are different administrative levels of the same place, we propagate the <geo> from the settlement to the parish. We aim to provide an authoritative georeference for every parish and larger settlement in the output, and we have manually built a separate additional resource to supply missing coordinates for 560 parishes/settlements in the entire collection that couldn't be georeferenced using either the volume itself or the KEPN database. While some of these are missing from the database, many are present but couldn't be unambiguously matched because of differences in spelling and punctuation.

At this point there are still many smaller places which do not have a georeference, so we turn to external resources, namely OS data provided through Unlock and the GeoNames gazetteer. We use the geoparser in a non-standard set-up to look up place-names in the external gazetteers and to select the most probable records. To get the results, we feed the geoparser algorithm with the information that we already know from the previous look-up in KEPN/EPNS and we set parameters to choose records which are as close as possible to the known coordinates either of the place-name itself or of its immediate parent or child node. We also apply the geoparser not to whole documents but to individual parishes. This is because the georesolver maximises geographical coherence in its input by choosing coordinates for all the places that will minimize the distance between them—if it is set to work on a single parish, it will automatically tend to select records which are as close to each other as possible. In our running example, Barlow is the first settlement described in the parish of Brayton and the other major settlements within the parish are Brayton, Burn, Gateforth, Hambleton and Thorpe Willoughby. The georesolution algorithm looks at the parish and considers possible groundings of these places together, ensuring as far as possible that the chosen gazetteer records cluster tightly together. If either Unlock or GeoNames does not have a correct entry for one of the places but it does have an entry for somewhere else with the same name, that other entry would be incorrectly chosen. To remedy this situation, we filter the georesolution output and discard any choices which are further than a certain distance (3km) away from coordinates assigned by the earlier KEPN/EPNS step which are known to be correct. This conservative strategy sometimes results in correct groundings being thrown away but it ensures that the Unlock and GeoNames information that we add is highly likely to be correct. The output at this stage for Barlow contains two more <geo> elements in addition to the two already created:

```
<geo source="geonames" gazref="geonames:2656317"
     lat="53.7499300" long="-1.0216400"/>
<geo source="unlock" gazref="unlock:4580690"
     lat="53.74993" long="-1.02164"/>
```

The georeferencing with Unlock and GeoNames considers smaller places as well. In our example there are three minor settlements in the parish, Brayton Barff, Burton Hall and Hambleton Hough, which get assigned coordinates from the OS information in Unlock.

4 User access to the processed data

The XML annotated files that are output from the processing pipeline are an intermediate representation of the information in the Survey which is then converted to other formats in order to make it available to users. Figure 3 summarises how the data is handled after this point. Since the XML output preserves the textual content of the input volumes along with layout, font and style information, it can be used to provide HTML renderings of the text that are visually very similar to the original printed text. The website at EPNS[5] builds on this aspect of the XML output by providing a browse and search interface to all the text associated with a place-name, including both the historical attestation information and the etymological descriptions. Access to this website is restricted to academic users but it provides an invaluable resource for place-name scholars since the information can be searched using the mark-up that we have added (e.g. by map coordinates; by date or source of attestation; by presence of etymological elements or languages, etc.).

On the geographic side, the XML annotated files are converted to a structured format which stores just the historical gazetteer information from the Survey (the DHG). The textual content is discarded while the relevant annotations are transformed into a data structure conforming to the Library of Congress Metadata Authority Description Schema (MADS)[6]. Figure 4 shows parts of the MADS record for Barlow. The modern name is encoded in the mads/authority/geographic element, while the historical variants appear in mads/variant/geographic elements. Geographical coordinates appear in mads/extension/geo elements and attestations, linked to particular variants, are also put in the extension element. The historical forms may be unexpanded shorthands from the original volumes, e.g. *Berlai(a)* meaning either *Berlai* or *Berlaia*, so these are expanded

[5]http://epns.nottingham.ac.uk

[6]http://www.loc.gov/standards/mads/

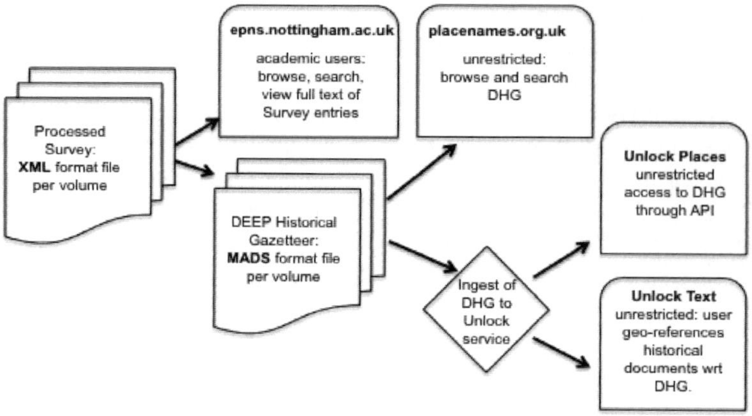

Figure 3: Accessing the DEEP Historical Gazetteer

out in mads/extension/searchterm elements to assist indexing for search. The MADS format feeds all the access mechanisms to the DHG—the data is ingested into the DEEP gazetteer website[7] which allows unrestricted search and browsing access. It is also converted into Unlock's gazetteer format in order that it can be used programmatically via the Unlock API, adding a new resource for users of Unlock Places. The Unlock Text service is one to which users submit documents for geoparsing, and this has been extended to allow them to do this using the DHG. The following section briefly describes how we have adapted the Edinburgh Geoparser for this purpose.

5 Geoparser adaptations

The Edinburgh Geoparser in Unlock standardly georeferences users' documents with reference to the Ordnance Survey and/or GeoNames gazetteers in Unlock. We have reported on this system in Tobin et al. (2010) and evaluated its performance on both modern newspaper text and a variety of historical texts. Other researchers have adapted it for use on different collections of historical text (Isaksen et al., 2011). The two main components of the geoparser are a rule-based NER system for recognising place-names in text and a heuristics-based georesolver to ground the place-names to coordinates (i.e. to choose between competing gazetteer records). In order to update the geoparser to use the historical gazetteer effectively, both of these components need to be extended. We have made the necessary adaptations so that Unlock Text can be used on historical English documents, however it is hard to create a one-size-fits-all version of the system which will perform optimally for all users on all documents—we return to this issue in the final section.

Like many other rule-based NER systems, the NER component in the Edinburgh Geoparser relies in part on lexicons of known entities of relevant types and in part on descriptions of possible contexts for entities encoded as rules. For modern names the geoparser NER system uses extensive place-name lexicons both for Great Britain and globally. To deal with historical names, we converted the MADS-format data into a lexicon of over 500,000 unique entries derived from the searchterms and the modern names and we filtered it to exclude certain lower case forms corresponding to common words. The NER system was given a parameter to specify 'historical mode' and this causes the DHG-derived lexicon to be applied instead of the modern place-name lexicons. Rules for place-name contexts apply as usual, as do rules and lexical look-up for other entity types.

For the georesolution component, the DHG was added to the list of available gazetteers. Using it results in a set of records with associated coordinates that need to be disambiguated in order to ground the place-names. This is sufficient for use of the DHG in georeferencing but there are some extra functionalities that suggest themselves in this context. The first concerns the users' knowledge about the geographic focus of their documents: assuming they know that the document is about a particular county or sub-area of England, it is useful to constrain the georeferencing results to exclude out-of-area interpretations. To achieve this we allow the user to specify one or more of the DHG counties as a constraint. A second extension follows from the fact that Unlock returns DHG records that include date of attestation. We have

[7] http://placenames.org.uk

```
<mads ID="epns-deep-33-b-subparish-000011">
  <authority ID="33-b-name-subparish-000011">
   <geographic valueURI="http://placenames.org.uk/id/placename/33/001099">Barlow</geographic>
  </authority>
  <related type="broader" xlink:href="#33-a-parish-000004">
   <geographic>Brayton</geographic>
  </related>
  <variant ID="33-b-name-w52628">
   <geographic valueURI="http://placenames.org.uk/id/placename/33/001100">Bernlege</geographic>
  </variant>
  <variant ID="33-b-name-w52652">
   <geographic valueURI="http://placenames.org.uk/id/placename/33/001101">
     Berlai(a), Berley(e), Berlay(e)</geographic>
  </variant>
......
  <recordInfo>
   <recordCreationDate>2013-10-10</recordCreationDate>
   <recordContentSource valueURI=
"http://epns.nottingham.ac.uk/England/West%20Riding%20of%20Yorkshire/Barkston%20Ash%20Wapentake/Brayton/Barlow"/>
  </recordInfo>
  <extension>
   <geo source="geonames" gazref="geonames:2656317" lat="53.7499300" long="-1.0216400"/>
   <geo source="epns" lat="53.74422247" long="-1.029470762"/>
   <geo source="unlock" gazref="unlock:11070229" lat="53.74865601989839" long="-1.021785033055991"/>
   <geo source="kepn" kepnref="14600" lat="53.7489" long="-1.02337"/>
   <attestation variantID="33-b-name-w52628">
    <date subtype="circa" begin="1020" end="1040">c. 1030</date>
    <source id="wr796" style="">YCh</source>
    <item>7</item>
   </attestation>
   <attestation variantID="33-b-name-w52652">
    <date subtype="simple" begin="1086" end="1086">1086</date>
    <source id="wr123" style="">DB</source>
   </attestation>
......
   <searchterm variantID="33-b-name-w52628">Bernlege</searchterm>
   <searchterm variantID="33-b-name-w52652">Berlaia</searchterm>
   <searchterm variantID="33-b-name-w52652">Berlai</searchterm>
......
  </extension>
 </mads>
```


Figure 4: MADS Sample (redacted)

adapted the geoparser to allow the user to specify a date range as a constraint.

Figure 5 shows a screenshot of our development visualisation tool where we have used the adapted geoparser to georeference a Dorset Feet of Fines document from the Internet Archive[8]. The geoparser was run with the county constraint set to 'Dorset' in order to exclude any possible matches from outwith that county. The display shows a map with purple (darker) pins for the preferred groundings of the places that were recognised and could be grounded, and green (lighter) pins for alternative possible groundings. The scrollable text pane shows the text with place-name entities highlighted (ones which are links are those that have been successfully grounded). The third pane shows the coordinates for the gazetteer entries that have been returned. The first (purple) coordinates are the preferred ones and the remaining (green) ones are lower ranked alternatives. Note that because we use only the historical gazetteer and a Dorset constraint, several of the modern names are not grounded (e.g. *Westminster*, *Taunton*). The correct *Westminster* is in the Survey under Middlesex and therefore not accessed. In the case of *Taunton*, there are two instances in the DHG: a modern name for a minor settlement in Surrey and a historical form of modern *Taynton* in Gloucestershire. The actual interpretation is likely to be modern Taunton in Somerset, which is one of the counties not yet in the Survey. Several of the historical place-names recognised in the text have not been grounded to a place in Dorset. There are entries in the DHG for some of these, e.g. a *Bundebi* in Lincolnshire and a *Rading* in Berkshire.

[8]This is the full text, i.e. OCR-ed version, of the document at `https://archive.org/details/fullabstractsfe00frygoog`.

6 Discussion

The example in Figure 5 is intended to illustrate some of the issues that are involved in using the geoparser on a particular historical text. The user who wants this particular text georeferenced has a number of options. Without using any constraint on the area to be considered, many of the place-names would be wrongly grounded. The Dorset-only constraint is probably too conservative and the user might instead prefer to use a different option available as standard with the geoparser which is to specify a bounding box or circle to weight the entries within them more highly. This option differs from the Dorset-only constraint, which only considers DHG entries known to be in Dorset, in

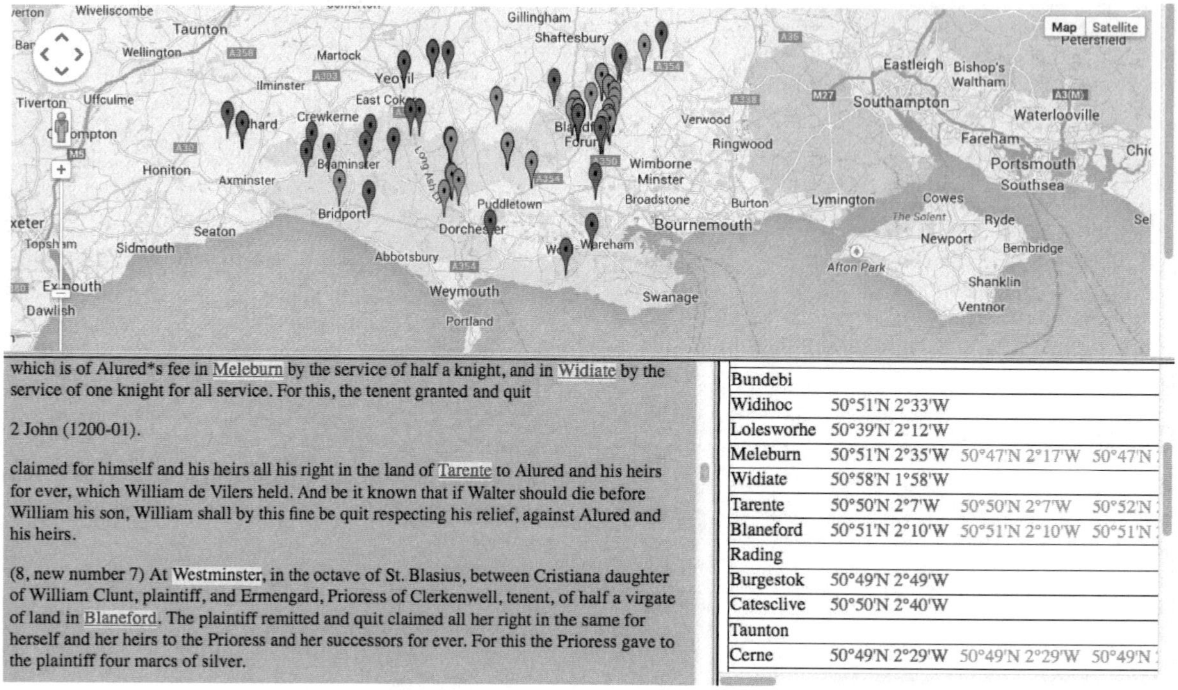

Figure 5: Visualisation of geoparser output on Dorset Feet of Fines

that it considers entries from all of the counties and influences the rankings of the possible entries. The user can follow it with a clean-up stage to remove groundings which fall outside the bounding box or circle. To get interpretations for place-names like *Westminster* and *Taunton*, the user could submit the document to a second run of the geoparser using the modern OS gazetteer and then combine the results of the two runs. Alternatively, the user might opt to manually post-edit the output of the geoparser: a tool would be useful for this so we are planning to add a map-based georeference annotation capability to the geoparser.

The Edinburgh Geoparser is available as a service from Unlock Text but there are so many types of historical document and so many user needs, that it is unlikely to provide all the possible options and flexibility that might be required. For this reason we anticipate that many users will prefer to access the DHG via Unlock Places for integration with their own systems; other users will want access to the source of the geoparser in order to tailor it for their specific needs. An open source version will shortly be available from `http://www.ltg.ed.ac.uk`.

The data described here is not linked data in the usual sense of the term (i.e. it is not RDF). However, we have been careful to add as many linkages as we can. The core data structure is the MADS data collection (Figure 4) and this contains two kinds of URI: in the valueURI attribute on mads/authority/geographic there is a link to the relevant page on the EPNS website, while in the valueURI attribute on mads/recordInfo/recordContentSource there is a link to the placenames.org.uk site. Three of the mads/extension/geo elements contain references to external data sources: the kepnref id points to the KEPN database and gazref ids point to the relevant records in Unlock and GeoNames. Because the MADS data collection conforms to a recognised standard, it would be relatively easy to convert it to RDF and publish it as linked data. Moreover, the Unlock version of the DHG retains all the information in the MADS collection and this means that the output of the geoparser can be made to retain the links out from the entries, enabling the user to link their historical texts to the DHG and to KEPN, Unlock and GeoNames.

Acknowledgements

DEEP was funded by JISC's Digitisation and Content Programme. We are indebted to our partners from the Institute for Name-Studies at the University of Nottingham, the Centre for Data Digitization and Analysis at Queen's University Belfast, the Centre for eResearch at King's College London and EDINA at the University of Edinburgh.

References

Gregory Crane. 2004. Georeferencing in historical collections. *D-Lib Magazine*, 10(5).

Claire Grover and Richard Tobin. 2006. Rule-based chunking and reusability. In *Proceedings of the Fifth International Conference on Language Resources and Evaluation (LREC 2006)*.

Claire Grover, Richard Tobin, Kate Byrne, Matthew Woollard, James Reid, Stuart Dunn, and Julian Ball. 2010. Use of the Edinburgh geoparser for georeferencing digitised historical collections. *Philosophical Transactions of the Royal Society A*.

Uta Hinrichs, Beatrice Alex, Jim Clifford, and Aaron Quigley. to appear 2014. Trading consequences: A case study of combining text mining and visualisation to facilitate document exploration. In *Digital Humanities 2014*.

Tim Hitchcock, Robert Shoemaker, and Jane Winters. 2011. Connected Histories: A new web search tool for British historians. *History*, 96(323):354–356.

Leif Isaksen, Elton Barker, Eric C. Kansa, and Kate Byrne. 2011. GAP: A NeoGeo Approach to Classical Resources. *Leonardo Transactions*, 45(1).

C.J. Rupp, Paul Rayson, Alistair Baron, Christopher Donaldson, Ian Gregory, Andrew Hardie, and Patricia Murrieta-Flores. 2013. Customising geoparsing and georeferencing for historical texts. In *2013 IEEE International Conference on Big Data*, pages 59–62.

Richard Tobin, Claire Grover, Kate Byrne, James Reid, and Jo Walsh. 2010. Evaluation of georeferencing. In *Proceedings of Workshop on Geographic Information Retrieval (GIR'10)*.

Towards Automatic Wayang Ontology Construction using Relation Extraction from Free Text

Hadaiq Rolis Sanabila
Faculty of Computer Science
Universitas Indonesia
hadaiq@cs.ui.ac.id

Ruli Manurung
Faculty of Computer Science
Universitas Indonesia
maruli@cs.ui.ac.id

Abstract

This paper reports on our work to automatically construct and populate an ontology of *wayang* (Indonesian shadow puppet) mythology from free text using relation extraction and relation clustering. A reference ontology is used to evaluate the generated ontology. The reference ontology contains concepts and properties within the *wayang* character domain. We examined the influence of corpus data variations, threshold value variations in the relation clustering process, and the usage of entity pairs or entity pair types during the feature extraction stages. The constructed ontology is examined using three evaluation methods, i.e. cluster purity (CP), instance knowledge (IK), and relation concept (RC). Based on the evaluation results, the proposed method generates the best ontology when using a consolidated corpus, the threshold value in relation clustering is 1, and entity pairs are used during feature extraction.

1 Introduction

As a country rich in cultural diversity, Indonesia certainly has an outstanding wealth of national culture. *Wayang* (shadow puppets performance art) is one instance of Indonesian culture that has cultural values and noble character. Although the stories are generally taken from the Mahabharata and Ramayana books, they involve the wisdom and greatness of the Indonesian culture. *Wayang* shows rely heavily on the knowledge and creativity of the puppeteer (*dalang*). Often, the story and knowledge about the shadow puppets is known only to the puppeteer and not set forth in writing. Such a lack of knowledge transfer process results in a lot of knowledge that is known only by the puppeteer cannot be shared to others, which leads to the loss of cultural richness. The knowledge held by the puppeteer ought to be propagated to future generations in order to be learned and developed.

Information about the shadow puppets can be represented as textual data describing hundreds of characters. Constructing an ontology manually from such a large data source is time consuming and labor intensive.

Work on relation extraction has already been conducted in the past. Initially, supervised learning approaches were used, for example feature-based supervised learning (Kambhatla, 2004; Zhao and Grishman, 2005). Some features that are generally used are words that lie among the entities, the entity type, the number of words between two entities, and the number of entities between two entities. In addition, there are several studies that use kernel-based approach. The kernel $K(x, y)$ defines the similarity between objects x and y in the high-dimensional objects. There are various elements used to construct kernels such as word subsequence (Bunescu and Mooney, 2005) and parse trees (Zelenko et al., 2003; Culotta et al., 2004).

In addition, several studies use semi-supervised learning. DIPRE (Brin, 1998) tries to find the relationship between the author interest and the book he/she had written. Snowball (Agichtein and Gravano, 2000) uses an architecture that is not very different from DIPRE to determine the relationship between an organization and its location. Meanwhile, Knowitall (Etzioni at al., 2005) examines relation extraction in heterogeneous domains of text data from the web automatically. Finally TextRunner (Banko at al., 2007) is a system that automatically searches the relationships between entities that exist in a corpus. This method produces a binary relation *(e_1, r, e_2)* where e_1 and e_2 are entities and *r* is a relation between them.

Work on automatic ontology construction has been done by several researchers. Celjuska et al. (2004) developed a semi-automatic ontology construction system named Ontosophie. The system generates an ontology with the instances derived from unstructured text. Shamsfard et al. (2004) developed an automatic ontology construction approach which utilizes a kernel based method. Alani et al. (2003) tries to construct an ontology using data from the web. The system, named Artefakt, performs information summarization about the artist. Furthermore, the constructed ontology is used to generate personalized narrative biographies. The system consists of three components, namely knowledge extraction, information management, and biography construction component.

The majority of the information extraction methods mentioned above require reliable NLP tools and resources. Unfortunately these are not readily available for Indonesian, the language our wayang data is in. To overcome this challenge, we employ information extraction methods that only require simple resources such as gazetteers **and stopword** lists, which are potentially used in a variety of problem domains. In this study, we explore methods to automatically construct an ontology using a corpus of wayang character descriptions using relation extraction and clustering. This method requires a gazetteer which contains a list of entities from the text. The entity types that are contained in the gazetteer are the name of the puppet characters, their kingdoms of origin, and their various artefacts such as weapons or spells. We realize our method does not yet fully **constitute** the **develop**ment of a complete **ontology**, but provides an important step towards that direction, namely the identification of relations to be found within the ontology.

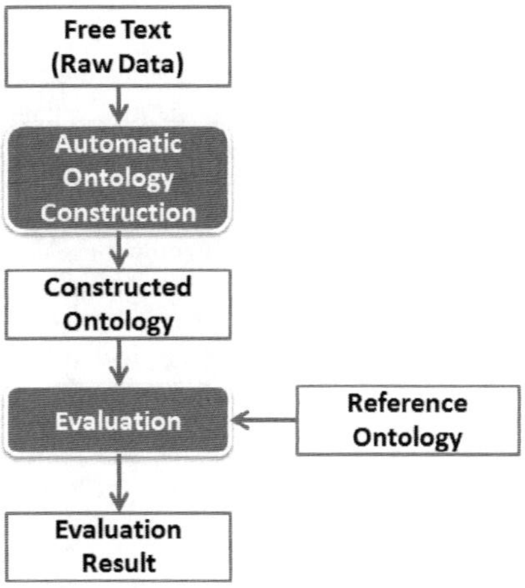

Figure 1. Automatic ontology construction and evaluation stages

2 Automatic Ontology Construction

We aim to automatically build a *wayang* ontology from free text. The information or knowledge that is contained within the text is extracted by employing relation extraction. This method will extract instance candidates that are subsequently clustered using relation clustering. Furthermore, the ontology will be evaluated using a reference ontology to examine the quality of the constructed ontology. The stages of automatic ontology construction and evaluation are depicted in Figure 1.

2.1 Automatic Ontology Construction

During this stage, the system attempts to find all possible relationships that occur between any two entities. These relationships are further analysed to obtain a set of valid relationships between entities. The valid relations will be used to construct the ontology. The ontology construction stage is depicted in Figure 2.

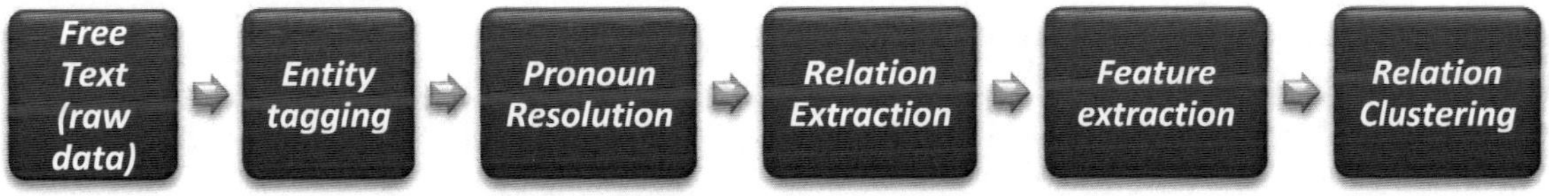

Figure 2. The ontology construction stages

<Person> *Anoman* **</Person>** *kera berbulu putih seperti kapas. Ia adalah anak* **<Person>** *Betara Guru* **</Person>** *dengan* **<Person>** *Dewi Anjani* **</Person>**, *seorang putri bermuka dan bertangan kera.* **<Person>** *Anoman* **</Person>** *juga bernama* **<Person>** *Maruti* **</Person>**, *karena mempunyai angin, seperti juga Raden* **<Person>** *Werkudara* **</Person>** *dan oleh karenanya* **<Person>** *Anoman* **</Person>** *disebut juga saudara* **<Person>** *Werkudara* **</Person>** *yang berkesaktian angin;* **<Person>** *Anoman* **</Person>** *juga bernama* **<Person>** *Ramadayapati* **</Person>**, *berarti yang diaku anak oleh Sri* **<Person>** *Rama* **</Person>**;. **<Person>** *Anoman* **</Person>** *juga bernama* **<Person>** *Bayutanaya* **</Person>**, *berarti yang diaku anak* **<Person>** *Betara Bayu* **</Person>**;. **<Person>** *Anoman* **</Person>** *juga bernama* **<Person>** *Kapiwara* **</Person>**,. *Bermula* **<Person>** *Anoman* **</Person>** *hidup pada jaman Sri* **<Person>** *Rama* **</Person>**, *membela Sri Ramapada waktu kehilangan permaisurinya, Dewi* **<Person>** *Sinta* **</Person>**,*yang dicuri oleh raja raksasa Prabu* **<Person>** *Dasamuka* **</Person>** *dari negara* **<Kingdom>** *Alengka* **</ Kingdom >**

Figure 3. Tagging result using non-detailed entities

The raw data is free text that consists of several paragraphs describing short biographies of *wayang* characters. Firstly, the free text is tagged using gazetteer data, i.e. a list of entities contained in the text. Every word contained in the gazetteer will be tagged in accordance to its entity type. The number of entities in the gazetteer is still general. Thus, the entities are subdivided into more specific groups. The entity group is based on Pitoyo Amrih (Amrih, 2011) which consists of 29 groups. In this study we used two tagging methods, i.e. by using a *wayang* entity that has not been detailed and by using detailed entities (based on the type of *wayang* entity). Different tagging treatment was conducted to examine whether this affects the ontology result or not. The example of tagged text using wayang entity that has not been detailed and detailed entities can be seen in Figures 3 and 4.

Subsequently, pronoun resolution is employed to resolve the entity reference of a pronoun. The system will then perform relation extraction by analyzing the words occurring between tagged entities. This process will generate candidate relationship patterns between entities *(X, r, Y)*, where *X* and *Y* are entities and *r* is the textual pattern that defines the relationship between the two entities.

The patterns that are obtained from the previous process are passed on to the next step

<BangsaKera> *Anoman* **</BangsaKera>** *kera berbulu putih seperti kapas. Ia adalah anak* **<DewaDewi>** *Betara Guru* **</DewaDewi>** *dengan* **<BangsaKera>** *Dewi Anjani* **</BangsaKera>**, *seorang putri bermuka dan bertangan kera.* **<BangsaKera>** *Anoman* **</BangsaKera>** *juga bernama* **<BangsaKera>** *Maruti* **</BangsaKera>**, *karena mempunyai angin, seperti juga Raden* **<Pandawa>** *Werkudara* **</Pandawa>** *dan oleh karenanya* **<BangsaKera>** *Anoman* **</BangsaKera>** *disebut juga saudara* **<Pendawa>** *Werkudara* **</Pendawa>** *yang berkesaktian angin.* **<BangsaKera>** *Anoman* **</BangsaKera>** *juga bernama* **<BangsaKera>** *Ramadayapati* **</BangsaKera>**, *berarti yang diaku anak oleh Sri* **<KerabatAyodya>** *Rama* **</KerabatAyodya>**;. **<BangsaKera>** *Anoman* **</BangsaKera>** *juga bernama* **<BangsaKera>** *Bayutanaya* **</BangsaKera>**, *berarti yang diaku anak* **<DewaDewi>** *Betara Bayu* **</DewaDewi>**;. **<BangsaKera>** *Anoman* **</BangsaKera>** *juga bernama* **<BangsaKera>** *Kapiwara* **</BangsaKera>***Bermula* **<BangsaKera>** *Anoman* **</BangsaKera>** *hidup pada jaman Sri* **<KerabatAyodya>** *Rama* **</KerabatAyodya>**, *membela Sri Ramapada waktu kehilangan permaisurinya, Dewi* **<KerabatAyodya>** *Sinta* **</KerabatAyodya>**,*yang dicuri oleh raja raksasa Prabu* **<KerabatAlengka>** *Dasamuka* **</KerabatAlengka>** *dari negara* **<Kingdom>** *Alengka* **</Kingdom>.**

Figure 4. Tagging result using detailed entities

that is the process of eliminating irrelevant information, so that only valid are used in the next process. It runs as follows:

1. Discard stopwords and honorifics.
2. If there is a comma and punctuation located at the beginning of a pattern then the relation

a) <Person> *Anoman* </Person> anak <Person> Guru </Person>
b) <Person> Anoman </Person> bernama <Person> Maruti </Person>
c) <Person> Anoman </Person> disebut saudara <Person> Werkudara </Person>
d) <Person> Anoman </Person> bernama <Person> Ramadayapati </Person>
e) <Person> Anoman </Person> bernama <Person> Bayutanaya </Person>
f) <Person> Bayutanaya </Person> berarti diaku anak <Person> Bayu </Person>
g) <Person> Anoman </Person> bernama <Person> Kapiwara </Person>
h) <Person> Anoman </Person> hidup jaman <Person> Rama </Person>
i) <Person> Rama </Person>membela Ramapada waktu kehilangan permaisurinya <Person> Sinta </Person>
j) <Person> Sinta </Person> dicuri raja raksasa <Person> Dasamuka </Person>
k) <Person> Dasamuka </Person> negara <Kingdom> Alengka </Kingdom>

Figure 5 The list of patterns as a result of eliminating irrelevant information

is considered valid.

3. Discard punctuation and do the trimming.
4. If there is a pattern that is empty or exceeds 5 words, the pattern is considered invalid.
5. Change the pattern to lowercase.

The result of the data in Figure 3 after this process can be seen in Figure 5.

Subsequently, we perform feature extraction by converting the textual data into matrix form. This matrix contains the occurrence of candidate patterns between all possible pairs of entities. There are two types of feature extraction tried out in this study, i.e. based on entity pairs and entity type pairs. The cell in row i and column k of this feature matrix is the occurrence frequency of the ith pattern and the kth entity pair. The matrix form of Figure 5 when using feature extraction based on entity pairs is depicted in Figure 6. The next step is to perform relation clustering using semantic relational similarity as a similarity measure in a feature domain. The text patterns contained in each cluster are deemed to represent the same relationship. The clustering process will ignore candidate patterns that occur less than twice in the corpus. The result of this process is a set of clusters that each contains textual patterns that have a greater or equal similarity degree to a given threshold. The pseudocode of this algorithm is depicted in Figure 7.

The generated clusters in this process comprise the relations found in the constructed ontology. The representative pattern, i.e. the candidate pattern that has the highest occurrence frequency within a cluster, will be used as a property that describes the relationship represented by a cluster. Suppose there is a cluster that contains three candidate patterns, e.g. "*anak*" (child of) with an occurrence frequency of 40, "*putera*" (son of) with an occurrence frequency of 30, and "*mendekati*" (come near to), with an occurrence frequency of 3. By using the representative pattern "*anak*" as a property, it is assigned as the relation between pairs of entities found within this cluster. The illustration of the constructed ontology after clustering is depicted in Figure 8.

Pattern \ Entity Pair	A,G	A,M	A,W	A,Ra	A,B	B,Ba	A,K	A,R	R,S	S,D	D,Al
anak	1	0	0	0	0	0	0	0	0	0	0
bernama	0	1	0	1	1	1	1	0	0	0	0
disebut saudara	0	0	1	0	0	0	0	0	0	0	0
hidup jaman	0	0	0	0	0	0	0	1	0	0	0
Membela ramapada waktu kehilangan permaisurinya	0	0	0	0	0	0	0	0	1	0	0
Dicuri raja raksasa	0	0	0	0	0	0	0	0	0	1	0
negara	0	0	0	0	0	0	0	0	0	0	1

A= Anoman, Al = Alengka B = Bayutanaya, Ba = Bayu, D = Dasamuka, G = Guru, K = Kapiwara

M = Maruti, R = Rama, Ra = Ramadayapati, S = Sinta, W = Werkudara,

Figure 6. The matrix form of Figure 5

```
Relation Clustering Algorithm
Input  : pattern P = {p1, p2, .., pn}, threshold θ
Output: cluster C
    SORT (P)
    C ← {}
    for pattern pi ∈ P do
        max ← -∞
        c* ← null
        for cluster cj ∈ C do
            sim ← cosine (pi,cj)
            if sim > max then
                max ← sim
                c* ← c* ⊕ cj
            end if
        end for
      if max ≥ θ then
          c* ← c* pi
      else
          C ← C ∪ ⊕
      end if
    end for
    return C
```

Figure 7. Relation Clustering Pseudocode

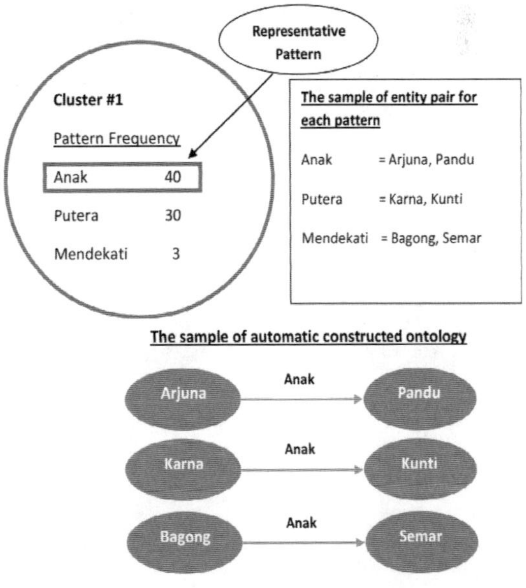

Figure 8. The illustration of constructed ontology subsequent to relation clustering

2.2 Evaluation

2.2.1 Reference Ontology

To measure and ensure that the quality of the constructed ontology is in accordance with what is desired, we evaluate the constructed ontology against a reference ontology. The reference ontology acts like a "label" on the testing data in machine learning. The testing data label used in the evaluation process is used to determine how accurate and reliable the model established by machine learning is in recognizing unseen data. The evaluation process is performed by comparing the relations in the constructed ontology with the labeled testing data. As well as the data labels in machine learning, the reference ontology will be used to test how accurate the system is able to generate ontology from free text.

We define several ontology components that can be obtained from the knowledge of a particular topic. This knowledge is obtained by looking at the types of entities and relations among them. It can also be obtained by looking at the group/category of any entity in the text. Each group/category defines the entity relationship that will occur between one entity to another one.

The ontology components which are defined in the reference ontology are concept and property. An illustration of the relationship between concept and property can be seen in Figures 9 and 10. A concept is something that is described in the ontology and it can be one of: objects, category or class. Concepts in the reference ontology are entities that are incorporated within the gazetteer categories i.e. puppet character, spell, weapons, and nations.

The ontology property describes the relationship between one concept to another. By observing the entity and relationship between them we can obtain the potential properties. For example, there are several entity groups, e.g. puppet character, kingdoms, weapons, and spell. Between each group there is the relationship that may occur. This relationship may occur between entities within the group/category or among entities contained in different group/categories.

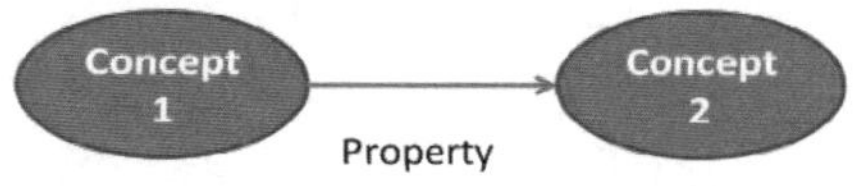

Figure 9. The relation between concept and property in ontology

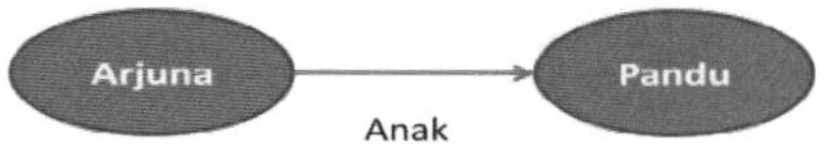

Figure 10. The example of concept and property relation

In this reference ontology, the authors define certain properties that potentially appear in the text. There are 14 properties which consist of 11 properties describing the relationship between person and person, 1 property describing the relationship between person and country, 1 property describing the relationship between person and weapon, and 1 property describing the relationship between person and spell. The relationship between concepts in the reference ontology is depicted in Figure 11.

2.2.2 Evaluation method

After relation clustering, each cluster is grouped based on the reference ontology property. This grouping is performed based on the synonym of the representative pattern on particular cluster and the property of reference ontology. If the representative pattern does not match (i.e. does not contain a synonym) with the ontology reference property then it is ignored.

In this research we use three evaluation methods i.e. cluster purity, instances of knowledge, and relations concept.

1. **Cluster Purity (CP)**

Cluster purity (CP) is the ratio between the

Figure 11. The relationship amongst concept in a reference ontology

number of representative patterns and the number of all patterns in a cluster. Cluster Purity (CP) calculation ignores singleton clusters, i.e. when there is only one pattern in a cluster. It can be formulated as seen below:

$$\text{CP} = \frac{1}{N}\sum_{1}^{j}\Omega_j$$

where Ω (Ω_1, Ω_2, ..., Ω_j) is the set of representative patterns for each cluster and N is the number of patterns in a set of clusters.

Each cluster contains textual patterns and its occurrence frequency. For example, the result of relation clustering can be seen below.

***Cluster* 1**	*anak 32* *putra 12*
***Cluster* 2**	*raja 3*
***Cluster* 3**	*negara 24* *menangis 3*

The CP value of that relation clustering is $\frac{(32+24)}{(32+12+24+3)} = 78.87\%$

2. Instances Knowledge (IK)

Instances Knowledge (IK) evaluation is intended to measure the information degree on each property. There is the possibility that the relationship among two entities is valid but the knowledge therein is not as expected. This evaluation is performed by conducting queries of multiple instance samples. The queries are instance samples that have valid knowledge and are taken randomly from the corpus for each property. It can be formulated as seen below:

$$\text{IK}\ (Prop_i) = Avg\left(\frac{1}{N}\sum_{1}^{j}Q_{j\text{Prop}_i}\right)$$

where $Prop_i$ is the ith property, j is a query for the ith property, and N is the number of queries for the ith property.

For example, there are 6 instances for property *anak* (child of). The instances are *Kakrasana putra* Basudewa , *Werkudara putra Pandu., Kakrasana anak Baladewa, Rupakenca putra Palasara, Basukesti negara Wirata*, and *Dandunwacana negara Jodipati.*

Then there are 5 queries for this property i.e. *Kakrasana putra Basudewa, Werkudara anak Pandu, Arjuna putra Pandu, Rupakenca putra Palasara*, and *Aswatama anak Durna.*

Based on that query, 3 instances are valid (1st, 2nd, 4th) and the rest is invalid. Thus, the IK value is $\frac{3}{5} = 60\%$

3. Relation Concept (RC)

Relation Concept is a measure to examine the valid relations in each property. A valid relation is an instance that has an appropriate relationship with the defined property in the reference ontology. This evaluation can be formulated below:

$$(\text{RC}\ (Prop_i) = \frac{1}{N}\sum_{1}^{j}valid(I_{j\text{Prop}_i})$$

where $Prop_i$ is the ith property , $valid(I_{j\text{Prop}_i})$ is the valid instances of the ith property, and N is the number of pattern.

For example, there are 6 instances for property *anak* (child of). The instances are *Kakrasana putra Basudewa ,Werkudara putra Pandu, Kakrasana anak Baladewa, Rupakenca putra Palasara, Basukesti negara Wirata* and *Dandunwacana negara Jodipati.*

There are 4 instances (1st-4th) that are appropriate and 2 instance (5th-6th) that are not appropriate to property *anak* (child of). So that, the RC value is $\frac{4}{6} = 66.66\%$

3 Experimental Data and Setup

In this research we obtain our raw web data from two separate sources: ki-demang.com and Wikipedia. Ki-demang.com is a website that contains various Javanese culture such as *wayang*, *gamelan* (Javanese orchestra), Javanese songs, Javanese calendar and Javanese literature. Meanwhile Wikipedia is the largest online encyclopedia, it provides a summary of Ramayana and Mahabharata characters.

In this study, we will only use corpora in the Indonesian language, and use 3 types of corpora, namely ki-demang corpus (derived from ki-demang.com), Wikipedia corpus (derived from id.wikipedia.org) and consolidated corpus (combination of ki-demang and Wikipedia corpus).

Ki-demang corpus is containing *wayang* character annotations according to Javanese cultural community. The ki-demang corpus writing and spelling is not as good as the Wikipedia corpus. Punctuation and spelling errors frequently occur, as well as fairly complex sentence structures. This corpus consists of 363 *wayang* characters; where there are 187 puppet characters that have annotations and 176 puppet characters that do not have annotations.

The Wikipedia corpus has substances of *wayang* character annotation from the Mahabaratha and the Ramayana book and it also contains the description of particular characters in Indonesian culture. The Wikipedia corpus consists of 180 puppet characters, which all have their respective annotations.

The last corpus is a combination of ki-demang and Wikipedia corpus. Merging data from both corpora is expected to enrich the annotation of *wayang* characters. Combining these data led to two perspectives in *wayang* character annotation, which is based on Mahabaratha/Ramayana book and based on the Javanese culture community.

In this study, we will perform some experiments to examine the influence of various parameters. The parameters include the corpus data variety, the threshold value in the clustering process, and the usage of entity pair or entity type pair during feature extraction.

4 Result and Analysis

We conduct experiments for various parameters. The constructed ontology is evaluated using cluster purity (CP), instances knowledge (IK), and relation concept (RC). The experiment results and details of various parameters can be seen in Figures 12 and 13.

For the first experiment we want to evaluate the corpus variation. The objective of this experiment is to find the most representative corpus used in ontology construction. Based on the experiment, when the system is employing entity type pairs in feature extraction, ki-demang corpus has a high CP (76.54%) rate and a lower IK (11.49%) and RC (44.8%) rate. When the CP rate is high, it means that the pattern variation in particular cluster is modest and tends to be a singleton (only one pattern in a cluster). It is the impact of the information homogeneity of ki-demang corpus compared to the other corpora. The IK and RC rate of Wikipedia corpus and consolidated corpus is better than ki-demang corpus. The Wikipedia corpus has better information content compared to the ki-demang corpus, thus the consolidated corpus has a better RC and IK rate compared to individual corpora.

Meanwhile, when the system employs entity pairs during feature extraction stage, the the consolidated corpus has a fairly better result compare to single corpus. It means that the consolidated corpus has richer information than ki-demang or Wikipedia corpus.

The second experiment was conducted to evaluate the threshold value in clustering process. The objective of this experiment is to find the best threshold value for relation clustering. For further analysis in a corpus variation, we used the average value of cluster purity (CP), instances knowledge (IK) and relation concept (RC) for all corpora. When the system employs entity type pairs during feature extraction, the CP rate is 97.15%, IK rate is 49.43%, and RC rate is

Threshold / *Corpus*	1			0.75			0.5			0.25		
	CP	IK	RC	CP	IK	RC	CP	IK	RC	CP	IK	RC
Ki-demang	96.53	19.54	63.95	96.52	19.54	63.95	95.88	19.54	62.02	94.27	12.64	58.83
Wikipedia	99.38	79.31	75.60	98.66	79.31	76.24	88.71	75.86	67.14	65.31	75.86	61.10
Consolidated	98.50	93.10	80.08	62.29	91.95	79.82	53.95	91.95	75.61	46.94	88.51	71.41

Figure 12. The evaluation result of entity pair usage in feature extraction

Threshold / *Corpus*	1			0.75			0.5			0.25		
	CP	IK	RC	CP	IK	RC	CP	IK	RC	CP	IK	RC
Ki-demang	96.30	14.94	60.02	95.80	14.94	58.45	58.74	13.79	50.05	55.34	2.30	10.70
Wikipedia	97.57	55.17	61.62	83.02	17.24	42.43	27.92	10.34	16.61	12.29	5.75	10.86
Consolidated	97.58	78.16	71.60	42.74	57.47	63.49	59.01	12.64	8.97	44.24	14.94	21.05

Figure 3. The evaluation result of entity pair type usage in feature extraction

64.41% for threshold value is 1. This result is always higher than using other threshold value.

Hereafter, when the system employs entity pairs during feature extraction, the CP rate is 98.14%, the IK rate is 49.43%, and RC rate is 64.41% for threshold value is 1. Given the experiment result, it is clear that a threshold value of 1 always gives a better result than the other threshold values. The higher pattern similarity in a cluster will yield a better constructed ontology result.

The last experiment was conducted to evaluate the consequence of using entity pairs or entity type pairs during feature extraction to the constructed ontology. For further analysis in a feature extraction variation, we used the average value of cluster purity (CP), instances knowledge (IK) and relation concept (RC) for all threshold value in a clustering process.. Based on the experiment result above, the usage of entity pairs in feature extraction always brings a better result than the entity type pairs. When using entity type pairs in feature extraction, it will reduce some detail of extracted feature. The feature only describes the relationship of entity type, not the entity itself. This leads to suboptimally constructed ontologies.

5 Conclusion

This paper presented a model for automatic ontology construction from free text. Firstly, relation extraction is used to retrieve the candidate patterns. Furthermore, relation clustering is used to group relations that have the same semantic tendency. An experiment has been carried out on various parameters such as on the corpus variety, the threshold value in relation clustering process, the usage of simple process for eliminating irrelevant information and the usage of entity pairs or entity type pairs during feature extraction.

Based on the experimental result, the consolidated corpus (combination of ki-demang and Wikipedia corpus) is most beneficial in ontology construction. By integrating the corpus, it will increase the information quality which yields a better result. Meanwhile for the other parameters, the most beneficial result is obtained when using 1 as a threshold value in clustering process, and using entity pairs during feature extraction. The higher pattern similarity in a cluster will yield a better resulting ontology. Furthermore, simple processing is employed to remove some punctuation, stopwords and honorifics which are a source of noise in the extracted patterns. The usage of entity type pairs during feature extraction will result in reduced or lost detail of pattern features and bring a detrimental consequence to the ontology result.

References

Agichtein, Eugene, & Gravano, Luis. 2000. Snowball: Extracting relations from large plain-text collections. Proceedings of the Fifth ACM International Conference on Digital Libraries,

Alani, Harith, Kim, Sanghee, Millard, David. E., Weal, Mark J., Hall, Wendy, Lewis, Paul. H. and Shadbolt, Nigel. R. 2003. Automatic Ontology-Based Knowledge Extraction from Web Documents. IEEE Intelligent Systems, 18 (1). pp. 14-21,.

Amrih, Pitoyo. Galeri Wayang Pitoyo.com. http://www.pitoyo.com/duniawayang/galery/index.php (accessed at November 4th, 2011)

Banko, Michele, Michael J. Cafarella, Stephen Soderland,Matt Broadhead, and Oren Etzioni. 2007. Open information extraction from the web. InIJCAI'07: Proceedings of the 20th international joint conference on Artifical intelligence, pages 2670–2676.

Brin, Sergey. 1998 . Extracting patterns and relations from the world wide web. WebDB Workshop at 6th International Conference on Extending Database Technology, EDBT

Bunescu, Razvan. C., & Mooney, Raymond. J. 2005. A shortest path dependency kernel for relation extraction. HLT '05: Proceedings of the conference on Human LanguageTechnology and Empirical Methods in Natural Language Processing (pp. 724–731). Vancouver, British Columbia, Canada: Association for Computational Linguistics

Celjuska, David and Vargas-Vera, Maria. 2004. Ontosophie: A Semi-Automatic System for Ontology Population from Text. In Proceedings International Conference on Natural Language Processing ICON., Hyderabad, India

Culotta, Aron, McCallum, Andrew, & Betz, Jonathan. 2006. Integrating probabilistic extraction models and data mining to discover relations and patterns in text. Proceedings of the main conference on Human Language Technology Conference of the

North American Chapter of the Association of Computational Linguistics (pp. 296–303). New York, New York: Association for Computational Linguistics.

Etzioni, Oren, Cafarella, Michael, Downey, Doug, Popescu, Anna-Mariana, Shaked, Tal, Soderland, Stephen, Weld, Daniel S., & Yates, Alexander. 2005. Unsupervised Named-Entity Extraction from the Web: An Experimental Study. Artificial Intelligence (pp. 191–134).

Kambhatla, Nanda. 2004. Combining lexical, syntactic, and semantic features with maximum entropy models for extracting relations. Proceedings of the ACL

Shamsfard Mehrnoush , Barforoush Ahmad Abdollahzadeh. 2004. Learning Ontologies from Natural Language Texts, International Journal of Human- Computer Studies, No. 60, pp. 17-63,

Zelenko, Dmitry, Aone, Chinatsu, & Richardella, Anthony. Kernel methods for relation extraction. Journal of Machine Learning Research, 2003 .

Zhao, Shubin, & Grishman, Ralph. Extracting relations with integrated information using kernel methods. Proceedings of the 43rd Annual Meeting on Association for Computational Linguistics (pp. 419–426, 2005

Author Index